Giuseppe Riva, Brenda K. Wiederhold, Pietro Cipresso (Eds.)

The Psychology of Social Networking

Personal Experience in Online Communities

Giuseppe Riva, Brenda K. Wiederhold,
Pietro Cipresso (Eds.)

The Psychology of Social Networking:

Personal Experience in Online Communities

Managing Editor: Aneta Przepiórka

Language Editor: Matthew Coleshill

DE GRUYTER
OPEN

ISBN: 978-3-11-047377-3
e-ISBN: 978-3-11-047378-0

Published by De Gruyter Open Ltd, Warsaw/Berlin
Part of Walter de Gruyter GmbH, Berlin/Boston
The book is published with open access at www.degruyter.com.

Library of Congress Cataloging-in-Publication Data
A CIP catalog record for this book has been applied for at the Library of Congress.

Managing Editor: Aneta Przepiórka
Language Editor: Matthew Coleshill

www.degruyteropen.com

Cover illustration: iStock/ Daniel Rodr├iguez Quintana

Contents

List of Contributing Authors

Giuseppe Riva, Ph.D.
IRCCS Istituto Auxologico Italiano and Catholic University of Milan
giuseppe.riva@unicatt.it

Brenda K. Wiederhold, Ph.D., MBA, BCB, BCN
CEO, Interactive Media Institute, a 501c3 non-profit
President, Virtual Reality Medical Center
b@imi-europe.eu

Pietro Cipresso, Ph.D.
IRCCS Istituto Auxologico Italiano
p.cipresso@auxologico.it

Nicholas David Bowman, Ph.D.
West Virginia University
Nicholas.Bowman@mail.wvu.edu

Jaime Banks, Ph.D.
West Virginia University
jabanks@mail.wvu.edu

Edward Paul Downs, Ph.D.
University of Minnesota-Duluth
epdowns@d.umn.edu

Sean Young, PhD
Executive Director of the University of California Institute for Prediction Technology (UCIPT) and the UCLA Center for Digital Behavior (CDB), as well as Assistant Professor of Family Medicine, UCLA.
youngsean@ucla.edu

Jamie Guillory, PhD
Center for Health Policy Science & Tobacco Research
RTI International
jamieguillory@gmail.com

Jeffrey T. Hancock, PhD
Department of Communication
Stanford University
jeffreyhancock@gmail.com

Jesse Fox, Ph.D.
The Ohio State University
fox.775@osu.edu

Elizabeth Sillence, Ph.D.
Department of Psychology, Faculty of Health and Life Sciences, Northumbria University
elizabeth.sillence@northumbria.ac.uk

Hui-Tzu Grace Chou, Ph.D.
Utah Valley University
chougr@uvu.edu

Ron Hammond, Ph.D.
Utah Valley University
ronh@uvu.edu

Ryan C. Martin, Ph.D.
University of Wisconsin-Green Bay
martinr@uwgb.edu

Lauren E. Vieaux
University of Wisconsin-Green Bay

Megan Moreno, MD, MSEd, MPH
University of Washington and Seattle Children's Research Institute
mamoreno@uw.edu

Natalie Goniu, BSN
University of Wisconsin Madison
goniu@wisc.edu

Peter Moreno, MS, JD
University of Washington
psmoreno@uw.edu

Doug Diekema, MD, MPH
University of Washington and Seattle Children's Research Institute
Doug.diekema@seattlechildrens.org

Shengli Deng, Ph.D.
School of Information Management, Wuhan University
victorydc@sina.com

Noella Edelmann, BA(Hons), MSc, MAS
Centre for E-Governance, Danube University Krems
noella.edelmann@donau-uni.ac.at

Ma. Regina M. Hechanova, Ph.D.
Ateneo de Manila University
rhechanova@ateneo.edu

Antover P. Tuliao, M.A.
University of Nebraska - Lincoln
antover.tuliao@gmail.com

Arsenio S. Alianan, Ph.D.
Ateneo de Manila University
aalianan@ateneo.edu

Lota A. Teh, Ph.D.
Ateneo de Manila University
lateh@ateneo.edu

Jen-Wei Chang, Ph.D.
Department of Electrical Engineering, Graduate Institute of Communication Engineering, National Taiwan University
jenweichang@ntu.edu.tw

Chun-Chia Lee, Ph.D.
Department of Information Management, Fooyin University
ft031@fy.edu.tw

Silvia Casale,
Department of Health Sciences, Psychology and Psychiatry Unit, University of Florence, Italy
silvia.casale@unifi.it

Caterina Primi,
Department of NEUROFARBA, Section of Psychology, University of Florence, Italy
primi@unifi.it

Giulia Fioravanti,
Department of Health Sciences, Psychology and Psychiatry Unit, University of Florence, Italy
giulia.fioravanti@unifi.it

Selim Gunuc, Ph.D.
Computer Education and Instructional Technology Department
Educational Faculty
Yuzuncu Yil University
selimgunuc@hotmall.com

Ozge Karakus, Ph.D.
Computer Education and Instructional Technology Department
Educational Faculty
Eskisehir Osmangazi Univeristy
ozgeekarakus@gmail.com

Hatice Ferhan Odabasi, Ph.D.
Computer Education and Instructional Technology Department
Educational Faculty
Anadolu University
fodabasi@anadolu.edu.tr

Mike Yao, Ph.D.
City University of Hong Kong
mike.yao@cityu.edu.hk

Olatz Lopez-Fernandez, Ph.D.
University of Barcelona
olatzlopez@ub.edu

José A. Carmona-Torres, Ph.D.
University of Almería (Spain)
jacarmona@ual.es

Adolfo J. Cangas, Ph.D.
University of Almería (Spain)
ajcangas@ual.es

Roberto Zárate, Ph.D.
University of California at Los Angeles (UCLA) (USA)
rzarate@ucla.edu

Ari Ucar
University of California at Los Angeles (UCLA) (USA)
ariaucar2692@gmail.com

Alvaro I. Langer, Ph.D
RedGesam Clinical Center and Pontifical Catholic University of Chile
alvaro.langer@gmail.com

Meagan Ramsey, Ph.D.
University of Utah
meagan.ramsey@psych.utah.edu

Ann M. Oberhauser, Ph.D.
Iowa State University
annober@iastate.edu

D'Arcy J. Reynolds Jr.
University of Southern Indiana
dreynolds1@usi.edu

Gregor Petrič, Ph.D.
Faculty of Social Sciences, University of Ljubljana
gregor.petric@fdv.uni-lj.si

Amy L. Gentzler, Ph.D.
West Virginia University
amy.gentzler@mail.wvu.edu

Lise Haddouk, Lecturer in Psychology,
Rouen University
lise.haddouk@gmail.com

Christa Nieuwboer, Ph.D.
Fontys University of Applied Sciences
c.nieuwboer@fontys.nl

Ruben Fukkink, Ph.D.
University of Amsterdam
r.fukkink@uva.nl

Danilo Garcia, Ph.D. Assistant Professor
Blekinge Centre of Competence, Blekinge County Council, Karlskrona, Sweden

Department of Psychology, University of Gothenburg, Gothenburg, Sweden

Department of Psychology, Lund University, Lund, Sweden

Network for Empowerment and Well-Being, Sweden

Anthropedia Foundation, Washington, Missouri, USA

Institute of Neuroscience and Physiology, Centre for Ethics, Law and Mental Health (CELAM), University of Gothenburg, Gothenburg, Sweden

danilo.garcia@icloud.com

Oscar N. E. Kjell, M. Sc.
Department of Psychology, Lund University, Lund, Sweden

Network for Empowerment and Well-Being, Sweden

oscar.kjell@psy.lu.se

Sverker Sikström, Ph. D. Professor
Department of Psychology, Lund University, Lund, Sweden

Network for Empowerment and Well-Being, Sweden

sverker.sikstrom@psy.lu.se

Lina Gega, PhD
Northumbria University at Newcastle
lina.gega@northumbria.ac.uk

David Fowler, DClinPsych
University of Sussex
D.Fowler@sussex.ac.uk

Richard White, Ph.D.
University of Exeter, UK
rw440@exeter.ac.uk

Andrew O'Neill, BSc(Hons)
University of South Africa
andrew.uk.oneill@gmail.com

Leanne M. Casey, PhD.
Griffith University and Menzies Health Institute - Queensland
l.casey@griffith.edu.au

Bonnie A.Clough, BPsySc (Hons.)
Institute for Resilient Regions, University of Southern Queensland BPsySc (Hons.)
Bonnie.Clough@usq.edu.au

Nicole Muscanell, Ph.D.
Pennsylvania State university, York
nlm19@psu.edu

Rosanna Guadagno, Ph.D
University of Texas, Dallas
Rosanna.Guadagno@utdallas.edu

Giuseppe Riva, Brenda K. Wiederhold, Pietro Cipresso

Introduction

The proposal of this book in the scientific panorama was to produce an edited collection of original chapters to provide a core and supplementary text with a number of well-recognized co-authors. There was a need for such a book as currently no all-encompassing compilation of diverse online behaviors from a social media perspective exists. Therefore, this collection makes a unique contribution to the rapidly growing area of cyberpsychology, and has the additional advantage of being written in a sufficiently accessible way to appeal to cross-over disciplines, Internet service businesses, and lay individuals alike who are interested in understanding the effects (positive and negative) of social media on individual, interpersonal and societal behavior. Despite the continued rise of interest in the area of Cyberpsychology, there is currently a dearth of reference works that can be recommended for the rapidly increasing number of core and modular courses being offered at both the undergraduate and postgraduate levels. Even fewer books have the range of expertise offered by the contributing authors from diverse backgrounds to provide a good cross-over reference for other disciplines to which psychological theory and research is essential to understanding human behavior from a wide and varied perspective. In order to achieve this, a number of the chapters are contributed by experts from areas such as technology and the social sciences.

Firstly, Danilo Garcia et al. discusses “A Collective Picture of What Makes People Happy: Words Representing Social Relationships, not Money, are Recurrent with the Word ‘Happiness’ in Online Newspapers”, research which looks into the co-occurrence of the word “happiness” with other words in online newspapers. They examine differences between sets of articles including the word “happiness” and a random set of articles not including this word. Finally, the chapter summarizes that there is a relatively coherent understanding among members of a society concerning what makes us happy: relationships, not money.

D’Arcy J. Reynolds Jr. et al. follows with his paper “The Online Calming Effect: Does the Internet Provide a More Comfortable Modality for Conducting Psychotherapy?”, which focuses on a study in which the impact of online therapy was compared to previously published results obtained in face-to-face therapy. The study suggested that therapists and clients experience the online environment as more comfortable and less threatening than the face-to-face milieu.

Later, a paper by Hui-Tzu Grace Chou and Ron Hammond titled “Feeling Anxious without It: Characteristics of People Prone to Facebook Addiction” asserts that benefits provided by Facebook to its users may lead to gradual addictions which are related to gender, age, and marital status. Researchers concluded that those with high subjective well-being or high self-esteem are less likely to have Facebook addiction, while those who feel lonely, shy, or concerned with others' perceptions of them are prone to this kind of addiction.

Next, researchers Chun-Chia Lee and Jen-Wei Chang in their paper "Play with My Team – Modeling Online Game Players' Teamwork Model in Massively Multiplier Online Role Playing Games (MMORPGs)", present research which investigates the impact of trust on players' teamwork with affective commitment and normative commitment as mediators. This paper asserts that trust promotes teamwork for players with high experience through affective commitment compared to those with low experience.

José A. Carmona-Torres et al. provides "Assessment of Risk Behaviors Related to Substance Use, Bullying and Alterations in Body Image in Adolescents Through a 3D Simulation Program". Researchers demonstrate the relevance and importance that VR environments have in the field of applied psychology. Their study indicates that social networking within the educative system could take advantage of the utilities that this sort of program presents regarding the importance and implications that drug use behaviors, bullying, and eating disorders may have for schoolchildren.

Lee J. et al. then aims to identify attractive gamification features for collaborative storytelling websites in his paper titled "What Determinants Matter When Users Engage in Particular Collaborative Storytelling Websites? Exploring Attractive Gamification Features and Design Guidelines". The authors propose that collaborative storytelling website users pay more attention to feedback after conducting certain behaviors.

Next, Lina Gega et al. present a novel system of virtual environments (VEs) which were developed and evaluated in the context of cognitive behaviour therapy (CBT) for socially anxious patients recovering from psychosis. The study suggested that the VEs evoked the same responses as the real life alternatives for at least two-thirds of patients.

After that there is a paper "Sharing personal experiences and offering advice within online health-based social networks" by Elizabeth Sillence which explores notions surrounding experience, expertise, and advice. The author presents findings from a study exploring advice exchange within an online breast cancer support group and highlights the importance of personal experience as a form of advice giving. She concludes that the link between online advice and decision-making behavior is both subtle and complex and disentangling this relationship lies at the centre of our current research agenda.

Later, researchers Martin R. C. and Vieux L. E. examine "The Digital Rage: How Anger is Expressed Online". The study explores the limited research on online anger along with identifying psychological phenomena that make online anger more likely. The authors go on to offer suggestions on how to minimize the frequency of expressing anger online.

Meagan Ramsey then aims to analyze the socio-spatial aspects of how college students use a variety of communication channels to connect with their parents using both quantitative and qualitative methods in her paper "College Students' Use of

Communication Technology with Parents: Influences of Distance, Gender, and Social Presence". The study focuses on the use of ICT among college students and their parents, particularly in the early years of transitioning from dependence on family support and guidance to independence and autonomous decision-making.

Deborah Ko and Mike Z. Yao in their paper "Internet addiction: an cross-cultural perspective" review empirical studies on Internet addiction, identify a number of lingering theoretical and methodological issues, and offer some new thoughts on this line of research from a cross-cultural perspective. Researchers hold the view that excessive and unhealthy Internet use is a social phenomenon that is affected by environmental, cultural, and technological factors.

Next, Nicholas David Bowman et al. follow with the paper "My pixels or my friends? Game characters as a lens for understanding user avatars in social networks" which examines how our relationships with technology – specifically, the avatars that we craft, perform, experiment with, and reflect upon – moderate our online experiences. Researchers draw from current perspectives on a particular type of user-avatar pair – video game players and their graphical in-game characters – to theoretically and empirically contextualize the range of relationships users may have with their digital representations in a variety of social networking platforms, and how those relationships may differently influence social interactions online. The results indicate that the nature of the relationship between the player and the avatar (albeit as reported by the player) holds influence over the virtual experience itself.

Olatz Lopez-Fernandez in his paper titled "Problem Mobile Phone Use in Spanish and British Adolescents: A comparative study between two European countries and cultures" discusses cultural differences that have been detected between user's countries in relation to the addictive symptoms presented, finding both differences in regard to withdrawal symptoms, as well as commonalities within the psychosocial problem itself. The results of this study highlight the main addictive symptoms which appear in the use of mobile phones, which show similarities to other technological behavioural addictions.

Silvia Casale provides an update on previous findings regarding the psychometric properties of the GPIUS2 among young people in the paper "Generalized Problematic Internet Use Scale 2: update on the psychometric properties among Italian young adults". The study builds on previous research on the psychometric properties of the GPIUS2, supporting its use among young, non-clinical populations.

Finally, Cipresso et al. parsed methodological aspects in studying behavior with mobile social networking sites like Facebook. Current computational methods and the huge availability of sources and devices for psychophysiological recording allowed a deeper understanding of complex behavior and even more intense understanding of human emotions.

Giuseppe Riva, Brenda K. Wiederhold, Pietro Cipresso

1 Psychology Of Social Media: From Technology To Identity

Abstract: From a psychosocial viewpoint social networks can be defined as "digital spaces" allowing users to manage both their network of social relationships (organization, extension, exploration and comparison) and their social identity (description and definition). Moreover, social networks allow the creation of hybrid social networks, at the same time constituted by virtual connections and real connections giving rise to 'interreality', a new social space, more malleable and dynamic than preceding social networks.
The hybrid nature - both virtual and real - that characterises the social networks leads them to have two faces, made explicit with the following three paradoxes:
If it is possible to effectively use social networks to change our social identity (impression management) it is also true that external intervention can more easily modify the way in which the other members of the network receive our identity (reputation management);
If in the social network it is easier to decide how and what features to emphasize within the social identity (personal branding), it is also true that following the traces left by different virtual identities it is easier for others to rebuild our real identity (privacy management).
3. If the social networks, without making any distinction between strong bonds (close friends) and weak ones (acquaintances), enable us to manage with limited effort weak ties facilitating enlargement of the social network, at the same time the lack of difference may make us behave with weak ties alike with strong ties (disappearance of the division of social roles) with all the problems of this situation.
In conclusion, if social networks are used by mature people responsibly they provide an excellent opportunity to interact socially, improve their interpersonal relationships, and even conduct business. On the contrary, when used in an irresponsible way by people who are too young it can cause problems and difficulties that in some cases even time cannot erase.

1.1 The social media sites as digital places

Today, everyone knows what Facebook is - a social network. But what is a social network? There are three characteristics (Boyd & Ellison, 2007) to characterize a social network from an operational point of view:

1. The presence of a "virtual space" (forum), in which a user can create and present their own profile. The profile must be accessible, at least in partial form, to all users of the space.
2. The possibility to create a list of other users (network) with which one can get in touch and communicate.
3. The possibility to analyze the characteristics of the network, in particular, the connections of other users.

Thanks to these characteristics social networks are different from previous media in terms of two opportunities. The first is the ability to make visible and usable their own social networks. In fact, through them one can identify personal, social and professional opportunities that aren't otherwise immediately apparent (Ellison, 2007).

The second one is impression management, the possibility to decide how to present yourself to the people who make up the network (Krämer & Winter, 2008).

On the basis of these opportunities we can define the social network from a psychosocial point of view (Riva, 2010; Riva & Galimberti, 1998) as a "digital space" that allows users to manage both their social network (organization, extension, exploration and comparison) and their social identity (description and definition).

1.2 The opportunities offered by Social Networks

Why should we use social networks? The answer to this question is not trivial. As pointed out by American psychologists Prochaska and DiClemente (1982) subjects only change if forced or if the change represents a significant opportunity (*affordance*). More, research by American sociologist Everett Rogers underlines that every technological innovation requires a long and complex process characterized by different stages of adoption (Rogers, 2003):

1. *Phase of awareness.* Individuals discover the existence of a technological innovation but lack of complete information about it. At this stage there are just the "*innovators*" to adopt the technology, subjects with a high capacity to deal with uncertainty combined with the expertise required to address the technical and economic aspects;
2. *Phase of interest.* An interest for the innovation arises in individuals that leads to information seeking. At this stage of adopting the technology there are only "pioneers" (*early adopters*), subjects integrated into the social network where they play the role of an opinion leader willing to accept the innovation if they see an advantage;
3. *Phase of evaluation.* Individuals are able to understand the possible effects of the innovation on their present situation and the future. At this stage, adopting the technology is done by an "*early majority*"; subjects are often in *leadership*

positions who adopt a new idea only after having carefully considering the advantages and disadvantages;
4. *Phase of trial.* Individuals begin trying the innovation to verify directly its utility. At this stage, adopting the technology is done by the "*late majority*", subjects are normally skeptical, traditionally-minded with a low economic status, approaching the innovation because of the social pressure of peers;
5. *Phase of adoption.* Individuals decide to make full use of the innovation. At this stage, adopting the technology is done by the "*laggards*" - isolated, suspicious individuals with reduced social relationships (only neighbors or relatives) that are slow in making decisions and have limited resources.

In general, the model of Rogers points out that, regardless of the specific characteristics of a technology, the concept of "opportunity" (affordance) is crucial in order to assess the potential impact of the social network.

The concept of *opportunity* was originally introduced by Gibson, a cognitive psychologist (Gibson, 1979): an *opportunity* is a resource that the environment "offers" to a person who is able to seize it. According to Gibson, each object or environment is characterized by a set of properties that support a particular type of action and not others. Therefore, the opportunity may be considered as a kind of 'invitation' of the environment to be used in a certain way. For example, a level and smooth ground offers an opportunity to walk on it while this is not the case with a vertical wall.

In fact, according to Mantovani (1995) and Norman (1999), the relationship between a subject and *opportunity* is the result of an interpretation related to the context and culture, in which the person is a part. In practice, the individual may choose based on their own goals the type of property more useful to them from those that the social network has to offer. The level of utility depends not only on the type of objective, the physical structure of the medium (*direct affordance*), meanings and practices (*mediated affordance*) associated with the medium but also on the context in which it is placed. However, it should be emphasized that the *opportunities are not all the same* but vary in importance depending on the specific need which they refer to. In this regard, one of the most interesting contributions to this discussion is the analysis of the American psychologist Abraham Maslow (1987).

According to Maslow, the different needs that each of us experiences are not isolated and self-contained, but they tend to be arranged in a hierarchy of importance (see Figure 1.1):

1. *Physiological needs:* basic needs associated with survival.
2. *Safety needs:* ensure protection and tranquility to the individual.
3. *Associative needs:* the need to feel part of a group, to be loved and to love and cooperate with others.
4. *Needs for self-esteem:* the need to be respected, appreciated and approved, to feel competent and productive.

5. *Needs for self-realisation:* the need for realising one's own identity and fulfilling one's own expectations as well as taking a satisfactory position in their own group.

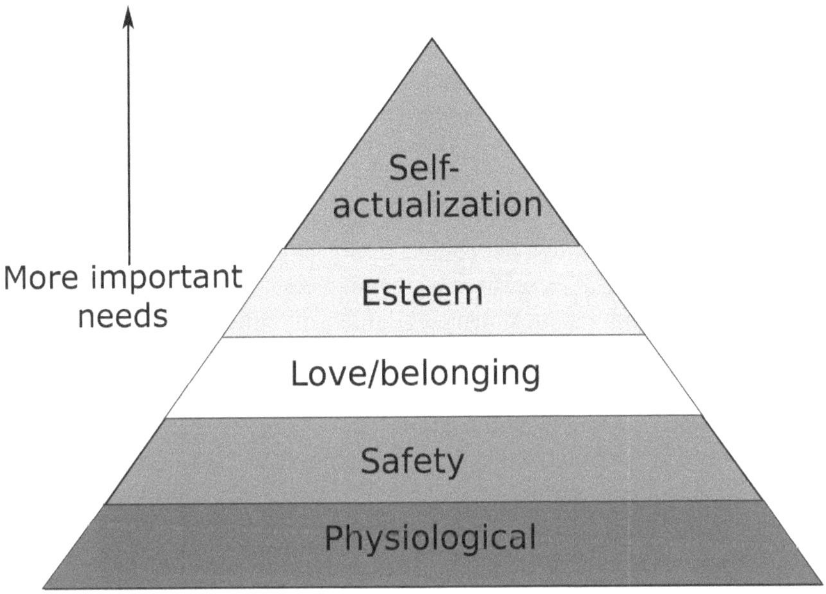

Figure 1.1 Maslows's hierarchy of needs

Characterizing the hierarchy of needs is a fundamental property: *in order to have a desire to meet the present needs at the highest level of the scale, the individual must first meet those needs located at lower levels.* This means, for example, that I don't feel the desire to be part of a group unless I have solved problems related to my survival beforehand.

In other words, if I'm on a certain step of the ladder of needs it will be the achievement of that goal (satisfaction of that need) to push me into action, nothing else (Inghilleri, Riva, & Riva, 2015). This means that the opportunity level is closely related to the characteristics of the subject, and in particular, to the need that initiates action.

At this point the question arises: to what degree does the social network meet these needs? To answer this question let us examine a set of examples.

Alessandra is a person who likes to know everything that happens to the people in her social network. As soon as she finds out that Paula has posted online a photo of her evening with Andrea she rushes to look and comment on them with Silvana.

Paolo is the type of person who likes letting all of her friends know what she is doing. Her *Twitter* page is updated every thirty minutes and full of messages such as "... I have just arrived from Rome" and photos of the various monuments photographed en route from the Piazza di Spagna to Termini railway station.

Marco is a manager of a large publishing company. He began posting on Twitter for fun using a style somewhere between ironic and professional. He is now followed by over hundred thousand users, making him one of the most popular Italians on the social network. Each week, he checks his ranking position on *TwitterCounter* (http://www.twittercounter.com) to see if he can get into the top one thousand most followed Twitter users in the world.

Daniela is a director of an association that offers support to those who have chronic alcohol addiction. Through her contact on social networks you can get help, even anonymously, and advice for addressing the problem.

Not only do Alessandra, Paolo, Marco and Daniela all differ in their use of social networking, but their reasons for using social networks also vary considerably. However, referring to their experience we can say that social networks can help its users meet the needs of the following categories:

1. *Safety needs*: In a social network the people I communicate with are just "friends" and not strangers. I can choose who a "friend" is, control what they tell about themselves and comment on it.
2. *Associative needs*: With these "friends" I can communicate and exchange ideas, resource applications. If needed, I can even look for a soulmate.
3. *Need to estimate*: I can choose the "friends", but others also can do it. Therefore, if many chose me as a "friend" then "I am worthwhile"
4. *Need for self-realization:* I can display myself (who I am and what I do) as I want, and I can use my skills to help some of my "friends" who listen to me.

Thanks to these possibilities, you can use social networks to meet two very different needs (Figure 1.2): *social support and self-expression.*

In fact, through the social network the digital native can develop both their own identity and their understanding of others (Riva, 2010). At the same time one can look for support or offer it. Furthermore, the social network is able to accompany the digital native in their own development. If a preteen uses the social network to stay in touch with their friends, then they can also use it to find new friends, later create professional contacts, and finally express themselves and fulfill their aspirations.

But the attraction towards social networks cannot be only explained by their ability to offer opportunities for its users. A number of studies conducted by psychologists of IULM and the Catholic University of Milan (Mauri, Cipresso, Balgera, Villamira, & Riva, 2011; Mauri et al., 2010) have shown social networks to have the capacity to produce the "*optimal experience*" defined as *'flow'*, capable of providing an intrinsic reward to their users (Csikszentmihalyi, 1990, 1997). As Dan Pink (2009) recently pointed out: the ability to be a rewarding experience, regardless of the reasons, is the most effective form of motivation, the joy of the task becomes the main reward that drives the person to repeat it.

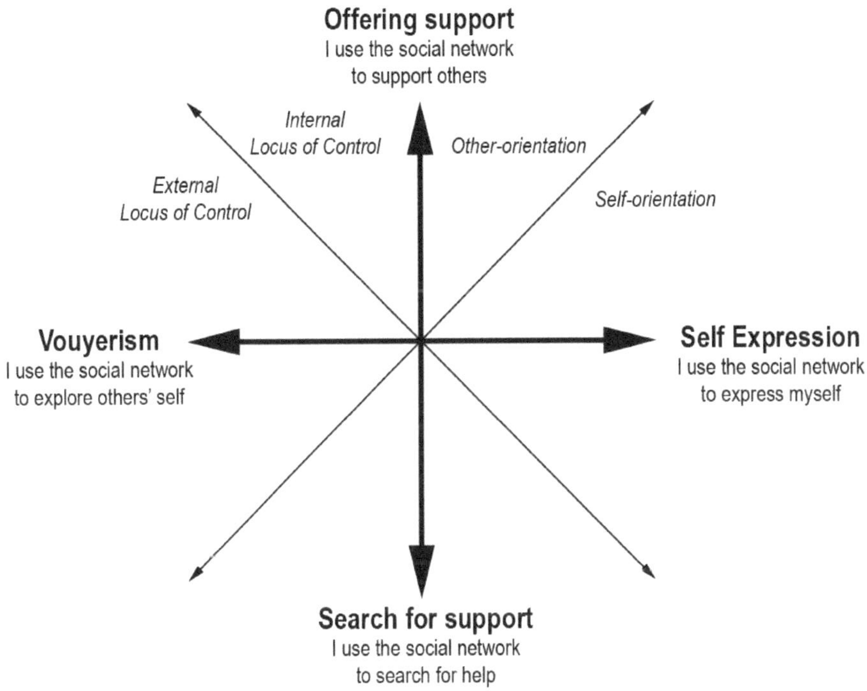

Figure 1.2 The needs met by a social network (Riva, 2012)

The research carried out by Wilson and colleagues (2010) has also shown that unlike other forms of mediated communication - the Internet, chat rooms and blogs, the user's personality traits are poorly correlated (explaining only 9% of the variance) to the frequency of using the social networks. This confirms that the main reasons pushing users to use social networks are, on the one hand, the possibility of finding the relevant opportunities in them, and on the other - a chance to get the best experience through them.

As such, it is possible to consider the social network as a social hybrid - the "interreality" (Riva, Raspelli, Algeri, et al., 2010; Riva, Raspelli, Pallavicini, et al., 2010; van Kokswijk, 2003) which allows the virtual to enter our real world and vice versa, giving all of us a powerful tool to create and/or modify our social experience. And thanks to the interreality we can use social networks either as a tool of support for our social net (organisation and extension),as a tool to express our social identity (description and definition) or as a tool to analyse the social identity of others (exploration and comparison).

1.3 From Social Media to Identity and back: The paradoxes of digital identities

The concept of "*digital place*" highlights how the social network is a hybrid of the social space since it is comprised of virtual links and real connections. This allows for the control and alteration of social experience and social identity in a manner completely different from before. Indeed, the nature of social networks as both providing opportunities and causing problems can be seen in three paradoxes which characterize social relationships through social networks(Aditi, 2014; Billedo, Kerkhof, & Finkenauer, 2015; Riva, 2012):

1. If it is possible to effectively use social networks to change our social identity (impression management) it is also true that external intervention can more easily modify the way in which the other members of the network receive our identity (reputation management);
2. If in the social network it is easier to decide how and what features to emphasize the social identity (personal branding) it is also true that by following the traces left by different virtual identities it is easier for others to rebuild our real identity (privacy management).
3. 3. If the social networks, without making any distinction between strong bonds (close friends) and weak ones (acquaintances), enable us to manage with limited effort weak ties facilitating enlargement of the social network, at the same time the lack of difference may make us behave with weak ties alike with strong ties (disappearance of the division of social roles) with all the problems of this case.

Let us examine the characteristics of these paradoxes in more detail.

1.3.1 The first paradox of the social network

One of the elements that characterize computer-mediated communication, and therefore, communication within social networks, is the absence of the physical body and the meanings that this brings. In face-to-face interaction the body is the subject. From facial expressions to gesticulations, every gesture reflects the subject and is observable to others within the vicinity. For example, I immediately understand that my friend Andrea wants her coffee sweeter just by seeing her hand moving towards the sugar bowl.

On the contrary, in social networks the physicality and immediacy of a real body is replaced by a virtual body consisting of a number of partial images and context: a disembodied head, a torso and legs in a bathing suit, and so on. In practice, the subject turns to their partners for what they communicate. In other words, in the social network the person can organize their presentation in a 'strategic' manner in order to convey an accurate self-image (Krämer & Winter, 2008).

However, the rules of social networks also allow other members of our network to be able to intervene in our social identity. And this can be done indirectly by posting a comment on the bulletin board or indirectly through the use of *tagging*, a feature of social networks with which you can associate a friend without their consentthrough a picture they is on or a text note referring to them. This can lead to unexpected changes in their social identity: the photo where I drink a bottle of vodka along with other friends at a party can transform me from a good boy into an inveterate alcoholic (Madden, 2012).

1.3.2 The second paradox of social networks

The majority of social network users don't only have a Facebook profile. In many cases, the same person can be on many different social networks - Facebook for daily relationships, LinkedIn for professional ones, Twitter to convey thoughts and ideas in real time, FourSquare to know where one's close friends are, and so on. In practice, participation in different social networks and the choice of what to post on each one becomes an advanced form of social identity management that can be called "*personal branding*" (Clark, 2013; Smith, 2009). Due to personal branding and the ability to bring out within the various social network elements that characterize the network itself, it becomes possible for users to promote themselves and their reputation within these networks with effective results both at the relational and professional levels (Wee & Brooks, 2010).

However, the ease with which social networks allow for the creation and sharing of content has made alarge amount of data and personal information available (Stutzman, 2006). This information ranges from personal data, tastes and favorite activities to places that have been visited. The result is that following the traces left by different virtual identities makes it easier for others to rebuild our real identity (Gross & Acquisti, 2005). Indeed, one can keep track of the different identities employed for various purposes, such as for business to evaluate a candidate in a job interview or fraudulent one, or for criminal purposes to take on the personality of another, as in *identity theft*. In many cases, simply entering a name and a last name into a search engine or on a social network can produce information related to thethe person's tastes, relationships and activities.

1.3.3 The third paradox of social networks

Through our daily experience we have learned how social bonds are not all the same (Haythornthwaite, 2002). In addition to a few 'true' friends you confide your problems to (the 'strong' bonds), there are hundreds of friends and acquaintances (the 'weak' bonds). It is clear that in everyday life the 'strong' bonds have a central role in supporting the subject, promoting the development of social identity through comparison and identification. However, if at individual level strong bonds are more important because they are more relevant to the experience of the subject; at the social level the opposite is true: the weak links are the bridges that allow us to get out of the perimeter bounded by strong bonds, to find new opportunities and meet other people (Granovetter, 1973; Silk et al., 2009).

In real life, however, we devote little time to the development of weak ties, with most free time being dedicated to strong bonds. For this reason, in many cases the attendance of weak bonds is linked to sporadic situations, a casual meeting, a random phone call. On the contrary, weak bonds in social networks have the same weight as strong bonds, within a social network a friend is the same as other friends. Moreover, social networks allow you to know the features of a individual you have a weak bond with, providing you with information and opportunities to improve the bond.

The lack of distinction between strong and weak bonds in social networks also represents a potential problem (Bakshy, Rosenn, Marlow, & Adamic, 2012; Grabowicz, Ramasco, Moro, Pujol, & Eguiluz, 2012). The relationship with weak bonds in real life is usually controlled by roles: I teach my students, I'm a parent like the other parents of my daughter's friends, I'm a fan when I go to the stadium, and so on. Given that each role always involves a description and a mode of behavior, I'm sure to behave in the ricorrect manner simply by following these rules. The problem with social networks is that there are some differences in roles with the members of the reference network: I'm always either a teacher or a parent or a fan and so on. But if I forget it, the problems begin. In other words, the lack of distinction between the friends of social networks does not allow me to clearly separate the different contexts that I attend and roles that take, with the risk of jeopardizing my reputation.

1.4 Conclusions

In summary, for the first time online social networks allow the creation of hybrid social networks, constituted by both virtual connections and real connections giving rise to 'interreality', a new social space, more malleable and dynamic than preceding social networks.

The hybrid nature - both the virtual and real that characterises the social networks leads them to have two faces, made explicit with three paradoxes that we have just described. These paradoxes have both positive and negative effects; one can create new opportunities and one can create new problems.

In conclusion, if social networks are used by mature people responsibly it is an important opportunity to talk about, improve their interpersonal relationships and even conduct business. On the contrary, when used in an irresponsible way by people who are too young it can cause problems and difficulties that in some cases even time cannot erase.

References

Aditi, P. (2014). Is Online Better Than Offline for Meeting Partners? Depends: Are You Looking to Marry or to Date? *Cyberpsychology, Behavior & Social Networking, 17*(10), 664-667.

Bakshy, Eytan, Rosenn, Itamar, Marlow, Cameron, & Adamic, Lada. (2012). *The role of social networks in information diffusion.* Paper presented at the Proceedings of the 21st international conference on World Wide Web.

Billedo, C.J., Kerkhof, P., & Finkenauer, C. (2015). The Use of Social Networking Sites for Relationship Maintenance in Long-Distance and Geographically Close Romantic Relationships. *Cyberpsychology, Behavior & Social Networking, 18*(3), 152-157.

Boyd, D.M., & Ellison, N.B. (2007). Social Network Sites: Definition, History, and Scholarship *Journal of Computer-Mediated Communication, 13*(1), Article 11. Online: http://jcmc.indiana.edu/vol13/issue11/boyd.ellison.html

Clark, D. (2013). *Reinventing You: Define Your Brand, Imagine Your Future.* Boston, MA: Harvard Business School Publishing.

Csikszentmihalyi, M. (1990). *Flow: The psychology of optimal experience.* New York: HarperCollins.

Csikszentmihalyi, M. (1997). *Finding flow.* New York: Basic Books.

Ellison, Nicole B. (2007). Social network sites: Definition, history, and scholarship. *Journal of Computer- Mediated Communication, 13*(1), 210-230.

Gibson, J.J. (1979). *The ecological approach to visual perception.* Hillsdale, NJ: Erlbaum.

Grabowicz, Przemyslaw A, Ramasco, José J, Moro, Esteban, Pujol, Josep M, & Eguiluz, Victor M. (2012). Social features of online networks: The strength of intermediary ties in online social media. *PloS one, 7*(1), e29358.

Granovetter, Mark S. (1973). The strength of weak ties. *American journal of sociology*, 1360-1380.

Gross, Ralph, & Acquisti, Alessandro. (2005). *Information revelation and privacy in online social networks.* Paper presented at the Proceedings of the 2005 ACM workshop on Privacy in the electronic society.

Haythornthwaite, Caroline. (2002). Strong, weak, and latent ties and the impact of new media. *The Information Society, 18*(5), 385-401.

Inghilleri, P., Riva, G., & Riva, E. (Eds.). (2015). *Enabling Positive Change. Flow and Complexity in Daily Experience.* Berlin: De Gruyter Open. Online: http://www.degruyter.com/view/product/449663.

Krämer, Nicole C, & Winter, Stephan. (2008). Impression Management 2.0. *Journal of Media Psychology: Theories, Methods, and Applications, 20*(3), 106-116.

Madden, Mary. (2012). Privacy management on social media sites. *Pew Internet Report*, 1-20.

Mantovani, G. (1995). Virtual reality as a communication environment: Consensual hallucination, fiction, and possible selves. *Human Relations, 48*(6), 669-683.

Maslow, A.H. (1987). *Motivation and personality, 3rd Edition.* New York: Harper and Row.

Mauri, M., Cipresso, P., Balgera, A., Villamira, M., & Riva, G. (2011). Why is Facebook so successful? Psychophysiological measures describe a core flow state while using Facebook. *Cyberpsychol Behav Soc Netw, 14*(12), 723-731.

Mauri, M., Magagnin, V., Cipresso, P., Mainardi, L., Brown, E. N., Cerutti, S., et al. (2010). Psychophysiological signals associated with affective states. *Conf Proc IEEE Eng Med Biol Soc, 2010*, 3563-3566.

Norman, D.A. (1999). Affordance, Conventions and Design. *Interactions*(5), 38-43.

Pink, D.H. (2009). *Drive: The Surprising Truth About What Motivates Us* (Vol. Riverhead Hardcover): New York.

Prochaska, J.O., & DiClemente, C.C. (1982). Transtheoretical therapy: Toward a more integrative model of change. *Psychotherapy Theory, Research and Practice, 19*(3), 212-216.

Riva, G. (2010). *I social network*. Bologna: Il Mulino.

Riva, G. (2012). *Psicologia dei Nuovi Media. Azione, Presenza, Identità e Relazioni nei Media Digitali e nei Social Media*. Bologna: Il Mulino.

Riva, G., & Galimberti, C. (1998). Computer-mediated communication: identity and social interaction in an electronic environment. *Genetic, Social and General Psychology Monographs, 124*(4), 434-464.

Riva, G., Raspelli, S., Algeri, D., Pallavicini, F., Gorini, A., Wiederhold, B. K., et al. (2010). Interreality in practice: bridging virtual and real worlds in the treatment of posttraumatic stress disorders. *Cyberpsychol Behav Soc Netw, 13*(1), 55-65.

Riva, G., Raspelli, S., Pallavicini, F., Grassi, A., Algeri, D., Wiederhold, B. K., et al. (2010). Interreality in the management of psychological stress: a clinical scenario. *Stud Health Technol Inform, 154*, 20-25.

Rogers, E.M. (2003). *Diffusion of innovations - 5th Ed.* New York: Free Press.

Silk, Joan B, Beehner, Jacinta C, Bergman, Thore J, Crockford, Catherine, Engh, Anne L, Moscovice, Liza R, et al. (2009). The benefits of social capital: close social bonds among female baboons enhance offspring survival. *Proceedings of the Royal Society B: Biological Sciences*, rspb20090681.

Smith, D. (2009). Personal branding. Success at last. *Health Serv J, 119*(6141), 24-25.

Stutzman, Frederic. (2006). An evaluation of identity-sharing behavior in social network communities. *International Digital and Media Arts Journal, 3*(1), 10-18.

van Kokswijk, J. (2003). *Hum@n, Telecoms & Internet as Interface to Interreality*. Hoogwoud, The Netherlands: Bergboek.

Wee, Lionel, & Brooks, Ann. (2010). Personal branding and the commodification of reflexivity. *Cultural Sociology, 4*(1), 45-62.

Wilson, K., Fornastier, S., & White, K.M. (2010). Psychological predictors of young adults' use of social networking sites *Cyberpsychology, Behavior and Social Networks, 13*(2), 173-177

Nieuwboer, Fukkink

2 Peer and Professional Online Support for Parents

Abstract: The Internet provides a popular and convenient source of information and support on parenting, offering many opportunities for both peer and professional support. Recent studies have also shown that both parents and children can benefit from online parenting support.

In this chapter, we describe the current variety of online services for parents, distinguishing between peer support and professional support. Specifically we will focus on the design characteristics of these web-based resources. Since Internet technology is still rapidly developing, many new opportunities for social networking are available. The provision of multilayered interaction (many-to-many, one-to-many, one-to-one) and the use of multiple components in websites may enhance the way parents feel supported. Also, training can be added to online programs, which aims to change parental knowledge, behavior and attitude. Furthermore, we discuss experimental results from recent meta-analytic study on the effects of online parental education.

Providing an overview of the past decade, we discuss two major trends which give direction to future research and development: missing aspects of research on online social networking and inspiring opportunities for online professional support for parents.

2.1 Parenting and Social Networking

Today's parents are known to be frequent users of the Internet in search of both information and support (Plantin & Daneback, 2009; Nieuwboer, Fukkink, & Hermanns, 2013a). The Internet is available to many families, especially in developed countries, (www.internetworldstats.com), and in recent years, its accessibility and availability has increased through the use of tablets and smartphones (www.pewinternet.org). Interestingly, reviewing the scholarly literature of studies on peer and professional parenting support on the Internet (Nieuwboer et al., 2013a, and complementing this study with 11 more recent studies up to October 2013), we found that the focus of studies is on pregnancy, first time parenting and young children, as well as on health related topics.

Professional support on the Internet is described with many different terms, like web-based therapy, e-health, online counseling, or cybertherapy; and practitioners in many disciplines are involved in providing support to parents, like psychologists, counselors, pediatricians and nurses. Peer support is often initiated by parents with specific experiences, like children's mental or physical health problems (such as autism, spina bifida, or cancer), or stages in parenting (like pregnancy or caring for young children), offering a social network for receiving and giving emotional support anonymously.

Web-based services include several components of online communication. More specifically, communication technology offers opportunities for multilayered mutual contact between other parents as well as with professionals (Barak & Suler, 2008). Examples of one-to-one communication are email and (video-)chat: a parent may submit a parenting question on a professional website concerning specific topics. One-to-many communication takes place in both information pages and email lists. Finally, discussion boards and forums are typical examples of many-to-many communication, in which peers support each other, sometimes moderated by a more experienced peer or professionals.

The relatively recent rise of broadband Internet and the increase in multimedia platforms offer even more opportunities for online communication. For example: an avatar can be used to provide the parent with daily tips and tricks, a parent may participate in an online test, troublesome parenting scenes from daily life can be logged or recorded and uploaded to a tutor, who can consequently live-coach the parent through an earpiece to handle the situation differently. Professionally designed training modules are mostly self-guided, with integrated in-between tests to assess progress. Blended forms of online support with face to face support have also been reported. For instance, pediatric hospitals have combined the usual check-ups of children with email consultation or a reference website. Hospitals have provided new mothers with online videos on breastfeeding, which they could access during and after their hospital stay. In some reports an online parenting course was combined with interaction with a therapist. Furthermore, as parenting practitioners have begun to acknowledge the opportunities of web-based communication, several well-known traditional parenting programs, such as Incredible Years (Taylor et al., 2008), Play and Learning Strategies Program (PALS, Feil et al., 2008) and the Positive Parenting Program (Triple P, Sanders, Calam, Durand, Liversidge, & Carmont, 2008) have been adapted for online dissemination and new services have been developed.

All these possibilities are available through Internet-based platforms, changing not only parenting but also professional parenting support. From the parents' point of view, these services are mostly free of cost, easily accessible, anonymous and beneficial, while also contributing to emotional well-being, confidence and self-efficacy (e.g., Bellafiore, Colón, & Rosenberg, 2004; Braithwaite, Waldron, & Finn, 1999; McKenna, 2008). Satisfaction reports show good results, without exceptions. From the professional perspective many advantages have been claimed such as how many target groups can be reached, content can be easily tailored, and services seem cost-effective (e.g., Daneback & Plantin, 2008; Funderburk, Ware, Altshuler, & Chaffin, 2009; Long, 2004; Self-Brown & Whitaker, 2008), although these still have to be verified by experimental studies. As well as this, organizations can offer a variety of guided, self-guided and non-guided, online and face-to-face support, as well as combinations of these support types. All in all, the Internet offers ample opportunities to support parents with all kinds of questions and needs .

2.2 Professional Support

In a recent meta-analysis of 12 studies (Nieuwboer, Fukkink, & Hermanns, 2013b) we found that web-based programs have indeed contributed to improvements in parental knowledge, behavior and attitude. Programs with relatively high positive outcomes (ES > 0.50) can be characterized as psycho-educational services, addressing a specific issue; the programs with a broad public health orientation on everyday parenting resulted in smaller effects. The provision of more types or layers of online communication was not related to study outcomes, although the combination between peer and professional support showed higher outcomes in parental attitude. Self-guided programs showed higher outcomes with regard to parental knowledge, whereas guided programs produced higher outcomes in parental attitude and behavior. Finally, more intensive programs, offering multiple training sessions, led to higher outcomes in all aspects.

2.2.1 Examples of Studies on Successful Online Parenting Programs

KidzGrow Online is an online parenting portal, offering an individualized tracking program about the development of children aged three months to 6 years old. The program contains a suite of age-appropriate activities, explained through text and animations. Parents' observations of their child performing these activities are compared with established developmental milestones. If delayed development is consistently observed parents are encouraged to seek professional help.

Na and Chia, 2007

This study describes a substance abuse intervention program, in which daughter-mother dyads interact in nine online sessions. Sessions contained voice-over narration, skills demonstration, and interactive exercises. Communication between mothers and daughters improved, family rules about substance use were better established and girls used less alcohol and marijuana compared to girls in the control group.

Schinke, Fang and Cole, 2009

> Single session email consultation is a very brief kind of intervention to support parents. This study evaluated the increase of parental empowerment between submitting a parenting question and after receiving professional email consultation a few days later. The findings from the study showed that parents showed more self-confidence in addressing the parenting situation after email consultation.
>
> Nieuwboer, 2014

> The I-interact intervention is designed to increase positive parenting skills and to improve stress management and coping for parents of children who have experienced traumatic brain injury and are between the ages of 3 and 8 years. The sessions consisted of self-guided didactic information, video modeling skills, exercises and videoconferences. Online sessions were followed by synchronous sessions providing coaching through a remote earpiece.
>
> Wade, Oberjohn, Burkhardt and Greenberg, 2009

> KopOpOuders (Chin Up, Parents) is an online group course aiming to improve parenting skills of parents with psychiatric problems. The online course consists of eight 90-minute sessions conducted weekly in a secured chat room. The chat room itself was divided in a part for interaction (peer support and direct professional interactions) and a part for materials (e.g., video's, outline or diagram). At the end of the course, a large proportion of parents had moved out of the clinical ranges of laxness and over-reactivity.
>
> Zanden, Speetjens, Arntz, and Onrust, 2010

Online professional parenting support has shown promising potential, and there are more reasons to implement these opportunities in regular parenting support programs. This kind of support is easily accessible, providing a suitable tool for prevention and primary care (Nieuwboer, Fukkink, & Hermanns, 2014). Current efforts in changing the youth care system in the Netherlands are aimed at reducing the high and often unnecessary claim on specialized secondary youth care (Bot et al., 2013) and strengthening easily accessible and low intensity primary care. For instance, single session email consultation is propagated and being employed as a professional tool, offered by more than 400 municipal centers for family support. Every parent can freely access a website, find validated information on parenting and submit parenting questions for tailored advice through email or instant messengers.

However, although we know that parenting programs are more effective when they are provided by well-trained practitioners (Dunst, Boyd, Trivette, & Hamby, 2002; Nation et al., 2003), there were only a few vague references to training or guidelines in the studies on online parenting support. For instance, we found that in approximately two thirds of the studies email consultation was offered, sometimes called ‘Help line’ or ‘Ask-a-nurse’; but we know little about the professional skills needed to respond to parental questions through this text-based medium. Yet it is plausible that online methods require specific communication skills, for instance, building rapport, interpreting, reflecting, confronting, and summarizing, in order to empower parents and families (Stofle & Chechele, 2004; Suler, 2000; Zelvin & Speyer, 2004). Recently, some initiatives have been undertaken to develop materials for higher vocational and in-company training, aiming to ground these online practices in long standing key concepts and goals of traditional parenting support.

2.3 Peer Support

Peers have been supporting one another in a range of informal experience-based Internet forums since the 1980s. Parents who share a specific experience in childrearing can meet in an online forum or discussion board, and can exchange messages in groups. Using ‘chat,’ parents can exchange experiences and opinions, typing short alternating texts in small groups or pairs. A unique feature is the shared social identity and the shared similar identity among ‘peers’, which creates a feeling of solidarity (see Fukkink, 2012). The social peer support also offers an online system of distributed expertise, interactivity, social distance and control, which may promote disclosure of personal problems (Paterson, Brewer, & Leeseberg, 2013). Users may value different aspects of online peer support and use the online support in different ways. An important distinction in this respect is the difference between actives users (“posters”) who often both give and receive support, and “lurkers” who follow the discussion but without contributing. This latter group is substantial; Patterson et al. (2013) reported a very rough estimate, varying from a low 50% to a high 90%.

The results of our recent review (Nieuwboer et al., 2013a) show that the Internet offers a variety of opportunities for sharing peer support among parents. Approximately a quarter of the studies which we analyzed were exclusively peer oriented. In the specific case of online peer support for parents, self-help support groups were included in our review. Also moderated electronic support groups were included. Two thirds of the content was analytic studies containg coded postings on e-mail lists, discussion boards, and group chat rooms, and thus focused on social networking among parents. One third of these studies analyzed peer support combined with professional support, whereby a professional functioned as a moderator of a peer group, or a professional consultation was offered in addition to peer support.

A few content-analytic studies defined a coding system based on a theoretical framework (e.g., the typology of social support, Braithwaite et al., 1999). Whereas some researchers have used well-known classifications, other studies adopted an inductive or ethnographic approach, identifying new emerging themes and highlighting main topics in the discourse. Mostly, the authors in these studies evaluated postings and messages without a predesigned observational tool; they noted the most mentioned words and opinions. These qualitative studies have revealed the wide variety of topics on different Internet forums. Content analyses of peer support in various online groups have demonstrated that parental peer support usually includes informational support, esteem support, and network support, as distinguished by Braithwaite et al. (1999); only tangible support, as distinguished in the framework of Braithwaite is relatively rare in online contexts. A repeated finding from these content-analytic peer support studies is that social networking was appreciated because it contributed actively to reaching meaningful goals, for instance to be acknowledged, be empowered, adjust to changes, seek encouragement, seek a sense of belonging, or to help others.

2.4 Evaluations of Peer Support

Meta-analytic reviews have confirmed the positive effects of social support in computer-mediated support groups in general (see Fukkink, 2012 for a summary). This line of study also suggests moderators are necessary for optimal support. Effects are presumably larger when people participate for a relatively long period in a relatively small support group that offers both synchronous and asynchronous media, as the meta-analysis of Rains and Young (2009) suggests. However, these conclusions are largely based on Internet-based group health interventions, and we cannot generalize the modest, but positive results of this type of online peer support to the specific domain of online peer support for parents, which include both specific health-related interventions and other general parental services. The fact is that the effects of peer support for parents have been evaluated in only a small number of studies so far. Experimental evaluation of the effect of electronic support is also difficult, because most parents may complement the online support with other sources of support, both on the Internet and in their personal networks, which complicates a straightforward interpretation of experimental results. It should also be noted that many peers tend to participate only for brief periods of time or sporadically in an online social support environment (Paterson et al., 2013).

2.4.1 Examples of Studies on Web-Based Peer Support Amongst Parents

> In an online maternity clinic, conversations between expectant families were analyzed, finding that families developed a sense of virtual community, which gradually evolved into a real-life community. Novice parents felt supported and better informed through this online medium. Furthermore, the postings offered maternity care providers a deeper insight into daily family life, concerns about pregnancy and the transition to parenthood, which they used to personalize their interactions with parents-to-be.
>
> Kouri, Turunen, Toassavainen and Saarikoski, 2006

Postings on an online chat forum on vaccination of children were analyzed, finding that parents distinguished between healthy and vulnerable children, criticizing parents who did not vaccinate their healthy children and urging them to take social responsibility in order to protect the larger community. The authors suggest that providers of vaccination promotion material could pay more attention to this dominant perspective of parents to successfully motivate parents to participate in herd immunity.

Skea, Entwistle, Watt and Russell (2008)

One of the topics on an Internet discussion board for parents was children's obesity. A discourse analysis revealed that parents, especially mothers, were viewed as the main cause of fatness, and in postings negative images were constructed with mothers having 'lousy characters, being unable to create an adequate emotional bond with their child, and using faulty child-rearing practices'. Findings suggest that in the public debate fault-finding and blaming is dominant, as opposed to public care guidelines.

Kokkonen, 2009

The postings of divorced fathers, living apart from their children, on an unmonitored Internet chat room were analyzed and compared to findings in previous studies. Fathers expressed an acute sense of powerlessness and anger towards the mothers of their children, family courts, lawyers and helping professionals, and these feelings were much more intensely conveyed compared to focus group or individual interviews. It is suggested to offer professional support using the same medium through which they express their concerns most intensely: Internet support groups.

Erera and Baum, 2009

2.5 Trends and Future Developments

The use of Internet-based programs is relatively recent and with the availability of more bandwidth and devices this trend is progressing in an almost furious tempo. The digital divide, indicating that some populations are denied access to these resources because they are too expensive or too high-tech (Steyaert & Gould, 2009), also seems to be rapidly narrowing. However, the availability of web-based devices is not the only component which defines the problems which make a digital divide: it is also the need for skills to be a productive and responsible Internet user, which is a concern of many providers and educators (e.g., Bernhardt en Feiter, 2004). In this chapter, we have showed several examples of the benefits of professional and peer social networking on the Internet. We will conclude with some recommendations for professionalizing web-based interventions and programs and will begin with some general concerns about online social networking.

2.6 More Insight in Dynamics in Online Peer Support

In most content analyses of online support among parents, posted messages were analyzed at an aggregate level of the site, without distinguishing between the different and often anonymous parents. With this analysis strategy, we still have little information about individual parents. The visitors of parenting sites are anonymous in most studies and little is known about the background of the different visiting parents. More research is therefore needed to describe the differences between the users of parent-related sites.

Studies of social support for different populations (e.g., Bambina, 2007) have shown that there are layers of social support operating in an electronic support group with active users who offer rich support and less-active users who offer limited support. Future studies should also provide insight into how users first visit a site, join an Internet forum, perhaps lurk in the beginning, post their first message, react to other messages and, finally, round off their participation in online support. Put differently, new studies should start to chart the process of how parents use online support over a period of time. The current content-analytic studies of online support are 'timeless' in that a time dimension is lacking. Little is still known, therefore, in terms of the dynamic process of social support (see also Fukkink, 2012; Paterson et al., 2013). The first generation of studies have described, often with fine-grained detail, the content of online support, showing the rich content of parental sites. However, parents have been relatively anonymous in this 'timeless' line of study. The next generation of studies should provide more insight into the dynamics of peer support for various users, including active users and lurkers, fathers and mothers, first-time and experienced parents, and parents with children with or without health-related issues.

2.7 Taking Professional Online Parenting Programs to the Next Level

We have that self-guided programs can enhance the level of knowledge on certain subjects, especially when they are combined with intersession assessments. Parents may need knowledge about, for instance, basic child care, safety measures in and around the house, the educational system, child development or rights and obligations in case of divorce an online course may be an easy and accessible way to learn more (e.g., Na & Chia, 2008). Short online courses and tests could be a way to disseminate knowledge in an attractive and interactive manner, reaching a wide audience in a public health approach. However, parental behavior and attitudes show more improvements with guided programs. The recent reviewing studies (Nieuwboer et al., 2013a; 2013b) show many inspiring possibilities for integrating multi-layered, multi-medium and blended program components, offering a large array of support to parents. More specifically, complementing informal experience-based Internet forums with more didactic methods to support parents (Salzman-Erikson & Eriksson, 2013) seems a feasible way to help parents with their interactions in their families as well as raising their own self-confidence (e.g., Baggett et al., 2009).

The next level of online parenting support is a more methodical and systematic approach to offering these services to parents: while employing technological innovations, professionals will need to focus on the goals of such services. If the aim is to enhance knowledge, several options for interactive dissemination of information are available; if the aim is to improve other facets of competencies, professionals should choose a method of teaching or training, blend it with face to face or telephone support and be skilful in online communication through email or chat consultation.

References

Baggett, K. M., Davis, B., Feil, E. G., Sheeber, L. L., Landry, S. H., Carta, J. J., & Leve, C. (2010). Technologies for expanding the reach of evidence-based interventions: Preliminary results for promoting social-emotional development in early childhood. *Topics in Early Childhood Special Education, 29*(4), 226-238.

Barak, A., & Suler, J. (2008). Reflections on the Psychology and Social Science of Cyberspace. In A. Barak (Ed.), *Psychological Aspects of Cyberspace. Theory, Research, Applications.* (Vol. 1, pp. 228). New York: Cambridge University Press.

Bambina, A. (2007). *Online social support; The Interplay of social networks and computer-mediated communication*. Youngstown, NY: Cambria Press.

Baum, L. S. (2004). Internet parent support groups for primary caregivers of a child with special health care needs. *Pediatr Nurs, 30*(5), 381-388, 401.

Bellafiore, D. R., ColÃ³n, Y., & Rosenberg, P. (2004). Online Counseling Groups. In R. Kraus, J. S. Zack & G. Stricker (Eds.), *Online Counseling. A Handbook for Mental Health Professionals* (pp. 197-215). London: Elsevier.

Bernhardt, J. M., & Felter, E. M. (2004). Online pediatric information seeking among mothers of young children: Results from a qualitative study using focus groups. *Journal of Medical Internet Research*, 6(1), e7.

Bot, S., Roos, S. de, Sadiraj, K., Keuzenkamp, S., Broek, A. van den, Kleijnen, E. (2013), *Terecht in de jeugdzorg, voorspellers van kind- en opvoedproblematiek en jeugdzorggebruik.* Den Haag, Sociaal en Cultureel Planbureau. Retrieved from SCP website: http://www.scp.nl/content.jsp?objectid=33372

Braithwaite, D. O., Waldron, V. R., & Finn, J. (1999). Communication of social support in computer-mediated groups for people with disabilities. *Health Communication, 11*(2), 123-151.

Daneback, K., & Plantin, L. (2008). Research on Parenthood and the Internet: Themes and Trends. *Journal of Psychosocial Research on Cyberspace, 2*(Journal Article), article 2.

Dunst, C. J., Boyd, K., Trivette, C. M., & Hamby, D. W. (2002). Family-oriented program models and professional helpgiving practices. *Family Relations, 51*(3), 221-229.

Erera, P. I. (2009). Chat-room Voices of Divorced Non-Residential Fathers. *Journal of Sociology & Social Welfare, XXXVI*(2), 63-83.

Feil, E. G., Baggett, K. M., Davis, B., Sheeber, L., Landry, S., Carta, J. J., & Buzhardt, J. (2008). Expanding the Reach of Preventive Interventions Development of an Internet-Based Training for Parents of Infants. *Child Maltreatment, 13*(4), 334-346.

Finn, J. (1999). An exploration of helping processes in an online self-help group focusing on issues of disability. *Health & Social Work, 24*(3), 220-231.

Fukkink, R. G. (2011). Peer counseling in an online chat service: A content analysis of social support. *Cyberpsychology, Behavior and Social Networking, 14*(4): 247-251.

Fukkink, R.G. (2012). Peer counseling behaviors. In Z. Yan (Ed.), *International Encyclopedia of Cyber Behavior* (pp. 714-716). Hershey, PA: IGI Global

Funderburk, B. W., Ware, L. M., Altshuler, E., & Chaffin, M. (2008). Use and Feasibility of Telemedicine Technology in the Dissemination of Parent-Child Interaction Therapy. *Child Maltreatment, 13*(4), 377-382.

Kokkonen, R. (2009). The Fat Child-A Sign of 'Bad' Motherhood? An Analysis of Explanations for Children's Fatness on a Finnish Website. *Journal of Community & Applied Social Psychology, 19*(5), 336-347.

Kouri, P., Turunen, H., Tossavainen, K., & Saarikoski, S. (2006). Pregnant families' discussions on the net - From virtual connections toward real-life community. *Journal of Midwifery & Womens Health, 51*(4), 279-283.

Long, N. (2004). E-Parenting. In M. Hoghughi & N. Long (eds.), *Handbook of parenting; Theory and research for practice* (pp. 369-379). London, UK: Sage Publications.

Na, J. C., & Chia, S. W. (2008). Impact of online resources on informal learners: Parents' perception of their parenting skills. *Computers & Education, 51*(1), 173-186.

Nation, M., Crusto, C., Wandersman, A., Kumpfer, K. L., Seybolt, D., Morrissey-Kane, E., & Davino, K. (2003). What works in prevention - Principles of effective prevention programs. *American Psychologist, 58*(6-7), 449-456.

Nieuwboer, C.C. (2014). *Online parenting support. Guiding parents towards empowerment through single session email consultation.* Doctoral dissertation. Amsterdam: University of Amsterdam.

Nieuwboer, C. C., Fukkink, R. G., & Hermanns, J. M. A. (2013a). Peer and Professional Support on the Internet: A systematic review. *Cyberpsychology, behavior and social networking, 16*(7), 518-528.

Nieuwboer, C. C., Fukkink, R. G., & Hermanns, J. M. A. (2013b). Online Programs as Tools to Improve Parenting: A meta-analytic review. *Children and Youth Services Review, 35*, 1823-1829.

Nieuwboer, C.C., Fukkink, R.G., & Hermanns, J.M.A.. Practitioner Response to Parental Need in Email Consultation: How do They Match? A Content Analysis. *Child Youth Care Forum* (2014), doi: 10.1007/s10566-014-9253-2

Paterson, B.L., Brewer, J., & Leeseberg Stamler, L. (2013). Engagement of parents in on-line social support interventions. *Journal of Pediatric Nursing, 28*, 114-124.

Plantin, L., & Daneback, K. (2009). Parenthood, information and support on the internet. A literature review of research on parents and professionals online. *Bmc Family Practice, 10*(Journal Article), 12.

Rains, S.A., & Young, V. (2009). A meta-analysis of research on formal computer-mediated support groups: Examining group characteristics and health outcomes. *Human Communication Research, 35*, 309-336.

Salzmann-Erikson, M., & Eriksson, E.H. (2013). Fathers sharing about early parental support in health-care – Virtual discussions on an Internet forum. *Health & Social Care in the Community, 21*(4), 381-390.

Sanders, M., Calam, R., Durand, M., Liversidge, T., & Carmont, S. A. (2008). Does self-directed and web-based support for parents enhance the effects of viewing a reality television series based on the triple P--Positive Parenting program? *Journal of Child Psychology and Psychiatry, 49*(9), 924-932.

Schinke, S. P., Fang, L., & Cole, K. C. (2009). Preventing substance use among adolescent girls: 1-year outcomes of a computerized, mother-daughter program. *Addictive Behaviors, 34*(12), 1060-1064.

Self-Brown, S., & Whitaker, D. J. (2008). Introduction to the Special Issue on Using Technology to Address Child Maltreatment Prevention, Intervention, and Research. *Child Maltreatment, 13*(4), 319-319.

Skea, Z. C., Entwistle, V. A., Watt, I., & Russel, E. (2008). 'Avoiding harm to others' considerations in relation to parental measles, mumps and rubella (MMR) vaccination discussions - An analysis of an online chat forum. *Social Science & Medicine, 67*(9), 1382-1390.

Steyaert, J., & Gould, N. (2009). Social Work and the Changing Face of the Digital Divide. *British Journal of Social Work, 39*(4), 740-753.

Stofle, G. S., & Chechele, P. J. (2004). Online Counseling Skills: In-Session Skills. In R. Kraus, J. S. Zack & G. Stricker (Eds.), *Online Counseling. A handbook For Mental Health Professionals* (pp. 164). San Diego / London: Elsevier Academic Press.

Suler, J. R. (2000). Psychotherapy in cyberspace: A 5-dimensional model of online and computer-mediated psychotherapy. *Cyberpsychology & Behavior, 3*(2), 151-159.

Taylor, T. K., Webster-Stratton, C., Feil, E. G., Broadbent, B., Widdop, C. S., & Severson, H. H. (2008). Computer-Based Intervention with Coaching: An Example Using the Incredible Years Program. *Cognitive Behaviour Therapy, 37*(4), 233-246.

Wade, S. L., Oberjohn, K., Burkhardt, A., & Greenberg, I. (2009). Feasibility and Preliminary Efficacy of a Web-Based Parenting Skills Program for Young Children With Traumatic Brain Injury. *Journal of Head Trauma Rehabilitation, 24*(4), 239-247.

Winzelberg, A. (1997). The analysis of an electronic support group for individuals with eating disorders. *Computers in Human Behavior, 13*(3), 393-407.

Zanden, R., Speetjens, P., Arntz, K., & Onrust, K. (2010). Online group course for parents with mental illness: development and pilot study. *Journal of Medical Internet Research, 12*(5), e50.

Zelvin, E., & Speyer, C. M. (2004). Online Counseling Skills: Treatment Strategies and Skills for Conducting Counseling Online. In R. Kraus, J. S. Zack & G. Stricker (Eds.), *Online Counseling. A handbook For Mental Health Professionals* (pp. 164). San Diego / London: Elsevier Academic Press.

http://www.pewinternet.org/Reports/2013/Tablets-and-ereaders.aspx Retrieved 10-28-2013

http://www.internetworldstats.com/ Retrieved 10-28-2013

Table 2.1: Characteristics of Online Interventions and Support for Parents (1998-2010, $N = 75$)*

First author	Year	Name of resource[a]	Types of Internet Communication							
			Synchr.	**Prof.**	**E-mail**	**List-serv**	**Conf.chat**	**Gr. chat**	**Gr. forum**	**Info**
Ahmed	2007	Antenatal Screening Web Resource (AnSWeR)	A	Pr	-	-	-	-	-	+
Anand	2005	Email communication in pediatric care	A	Pr	+	-	-	-	-	-
Askins	2009	Problem-solving skills training[a]	A	Pr	-	-	-	-	-	+
Baggett	2009	Infant net[a]	A	Pr + P	-	-	-	-	+	+
Baum	2004	Internet Parent Support Groups	A	P	-	-	-	-	+	-
Beck	2005	Research on Birth Trauma	A	Pr	+	-	-	-	-	-
Bergman	2009	New Model of Well-Child Care	A	Pr	+	-	-	-	-	-
Bert	2008	Adventures in Parenting[a]	A	Pr	-	-	-	-	-	+
Borowitz	1998	Email consultations	A	Pr	+	-	-	-	-	-
Brent	2009	Health Physics Website	A	Pr	+	-	-	-	-	+
Britto	2009	MyCare Connection	A	Pr	+	-	-	-	-	+
Buzhardt	2006	Training modules	A	Pr	-	-	-	-	-	+
Campbell	2009	New Mothers Network	A	Pr + P	+	-	-	-	+	-
Capitulo	2004	Perinatal Loss Listserv	A	P	-	+	-	-	-	-
Carpenter	2004	Parent–Adolescent Conflict Training PACT	A	Pr	-	-	-	-	-	+
Chan	2008	Happy Land	A + S	P	-	-	-	+	+	-
Christakis	2006	MyHealthyChild (Bright Futures)[a]	A	Pr	-	-	-	-	-	+
Christian	2005	Saafamilies.org	A	P	-	-	-	-	+	+
Cook	2003	Strategies for Preschool Interv. in Everyday Settings[a]	A	Pr	-	-	-	-	-	+
d'Alessandro	2004	Information Prescriptions	A	Pr	-	-	-	-	-	+

First author	Year	Name of resource[a]	Types of Internet Communication							
			Synchr.	Prof.	E-mail	List-serv	Conf.chat	Gr. chat	Gr. forum	Info
Deitz	2009	Youth Mental Health A Parent's Guide	A	Pr	-	-	-	-	-	+
Demaso	2006	Experience Journal, Depression	A	P	-	-	-	-	+	+
Downing	1999	Missouri Development. Disability Resource Center	A + S	Pr + P	-	+	-	+	+	+
Drentea	2005	Mothering Board	A	P	-	-	-	-	+	-
Dunham	1998	Staying Connected	A	P	-	-	-	-	+	-
Erera	2009	alt.dads.rights	S	P	-	-	-	+	-	-
Ewing	2009	The Web site	A	Pr + P	+	-	-	-	+	+
Feil	2008	Infant Net (Playing and Learning Strategies, PALS)[a]	A + S	Pr + P	-	-	-	-	+	+
Fletcher	2007	New Fathers Information Project	A	Pr	-	+	-	-	-	-
Gray	2000	Baby CareLink	A	Pr	+	-	-	-	-	+
Hall	2009	Online group	A	Pr + P	-	+	-	-	-	-
Han	2001	N-BLASTOMA; PED-ALL; PED-ONC	A	P	-	+	-	-	+	-
Herman	2005	Healthy Pregnancy Website	A	Pr + P	+	-	-	-	+	+
Huang	2007	Breastfeeding Education Program	A	Pr	-	-	-	-	-	+
Hudson	1999	Young Parents Project	A	Pr + P	+	+	-	-	-	+
Hudson	2003	New Fathers Network	A	Pr + P	+	-	-	-	+	+
Hudson	2008	New Mothers Network	A	Pr + P	+	-	-	-	+	+
Huws	2001	An International List serv	A	P	-	+	-	-	-	-
Kibar	2009	Email consultations with specialists	A	Pr	+	-	-	-	-	-
Kokkonen	2009	A Finish website	A	P	-	-	-	-	+	-
Kouri	2006	Net Clinic	A	P	+	-	-	-	+	+
Kuo	2009	Internet newborn-care education program	A + S	Pr + P	+	-	-	+	+	+
Leonard	2004	Rettnet	A	P	-	+	-	-	-	-

First author	Year	Name of resource[a]	Types of Internet Communication							
			Synchr.	Prof.	E-mail	List-serv	Conf.chat	Gr. chat	Gr. forum	Info
Mackert	2009	Child Care Center Web Site	A	Pr	-	-	-	-	-	+
Madge	2002	Babyworld	A + S	Pr + P	-	-	-	+	+	+
Madge	2005	Babyworld	S	P	-	-	-	+	-	-
Magee	2009	Ucanpooptoo	A	Pr	-	-	-	-	-	+
Mankuta	2007	Internet consultations forum Hadassah Medical Org.	A	Pr + P	-	-	-	-	+	-
Mertensmeyer	2000	Parentlink[a]	A + S	Pr	+	+	-	-	-	+
Na	2008	Kidz Grow Online	A	Pr	-	-	-	-	-	+
Nelson	2003	Healthy Steps over Telemedicine	S	Pr	-	-	-	-	-	+
Nicholas	2004	Spina Bifida Father Group	A	P	-	-	-	-	+	-
Nyström	2006	Parental Support e-meeting portal (mothers)	S	Pr + P	-	-	-	+	-	-
Nyström	2008	Parental Support e-meeting portal (fathers)	S	P	-	-	-	+	-	-
O'Connor	2004	Babyworld	A + S	Pr + P	-	-	-	-	+	+
Ritterband	2005	Ucanpooptoo	A	Pr	-	-	-	-	-	+
Rosen	2007	PPEM, patient–physician email	A	Pr	+	-	-	-	-	-
Salonen	2008	Vauvankaa	A	Pr + P	+	-	-	-	+	+
Salovey	2009	Head Start Community Technology Centers	A	Pr	-	-	-	-	-	+
Sanders	2008	Triple P[a]	A	Pr	+	-	-	-	-	+
Sanghavi	2005	Bright Futures	A	Pr	-	-	-	-	-	+
Sarkadi	2005	FöräldraNätet	A	P	-	-	-	-	+	-
Scharer	2005	Internet Discussion Board	A	Pr + P	-	-	-	-	+	+
Scharer	2009	Web-based Social Support Group	S	Pr + P	-	-	+	+	-	-
Schinke	2009	Daughter-mother substance abuse program	A	Pr	-	-	-	-	-	+

First author	Year	Name of resource[a]	Synchr.	Prof.	E-mail	List-serv	Conf.chat	Gr. chat	Gr. forum	Info
			Types of Internet Communication							
Skea	2008	Mumsnet	S	P	-	-	-	+	-	-
Taylor	2008	Incredible Years Adapted[a]	A	Pr + P	+	-	-	-	+	+
Thomas	2007	Breastfeeding Support	A	Pr	+	-	-	-	-	-
Thompson	2007	Touchscreen Computer Kiosk	A	Pr	-	-	-	-	-	+
Thompson	2008	Parent–Teacher Email communication	A	Pr	+	+	-	-	-	-
Wade	2006	Family Poblem-solving Group (FPS)	A + S	Pr	-	-	-	-	-	+
Wade	2009	I-InTERACT[a]	A + S	Pr	-	-	-	-	-	+
Wallace	2005	Vaccination Decision Aid	A	Pr	-	-	-	-	-	+
Wang	2006	VBAC program	A	Pr + P	+	-	-	-	+	+
Wilson	2003	Hepatitis B and You	A	Pr	-	-	-	-	-	+
			A	Pr	32.0%	13.3%	1.3%	13.3%	36.0%	61.3%
Percentage			78.7%	49.3%						
			S	P						
			9.3%	22.7%						
			A+S	Pr+P						
			12%	28.0%						

Note. Synchr. A / S = asynchronous / synchronous; Prof. Pr / P = professional / peer; E-mail = email one-to-one; List-serv. = online mailing list; Conf. chat = confidential chat; Gr. chat = group chat; Gr. forum = group forum / discussion board; Info = information pages. An "+" indicates that the criterion has been met.

[a]Adaptation of or similar to a traditional parent training program

* For references to all studies, see Nieuwboer, 2014

Ma. Regina M. Hechanova, Antover P. Tuliao, Arsenio S. Alianan, Jr., Lota Teh

3 Online Counseling for Migrant Workers: Challenges and Opportunities

Abstract: The advent of globalization and the changing landscape of international social and economic conditions have led to the rise of transnational labor migration. Among countries that export labor, the Philippines ranks as the second largest, with an estimated 11 million, or 10% of the population, leaving the country to work in various parts of the globe (Asian Migrant Centre, 2000; Philippine Overseas Employment Agency [POEA], 2012). Although overseas Filipino workers (OFWs) have helped uplift their families from poverty and improve the Philippines' economy, there are social costs to labor migration. OFWs commonly report depression, loneliness, increased stress, discrimination, homesickness, and, for those illegally staying in the host country, experience abuse and being persistently fearful of possible deportation (e.g., Ayalon, 2012; Briones, 2008; Lee, 2006). The families of OFWs also experience psychological distress as well. For instance, children whose mothers have left the country to work tend to be more angry, confused, and apathetic, and feel different from other children (Battistella & Conaco, 1998).

This chapter summarizes research on online counseling, particularly for Filipino migrant workers. Using data from an online counseling site created for overseas Filipino workers (OFWs), it reports the profile of the consumers that use these services as well as their drives for seeking counseling support online. It also discusses the common issues migrant workers attempt to address during online counseling. We present the opportunities and challenges encountered by both counselees and counselors in online counseling. The chapter ends with a discussion of the prospects for online counseling and other technology-mediated interventions in addressing the psychosocial needs of migrant workers.

3.1 Online Counseling Among OFWs: The OFW Online Project

3.1.1 Project Rationale

Migrant workers and their families experience psychological distress, particularly in terms of workers' separation from their families and their sources of social support. Unfortunately, research indicates that Filipinos are generally reluctant to seek professional help for their psychological and emotional distress (Hechanova, Tuliao, Teh, Alianan, & Acosta, 2013; Tuliao, in press). Furthermore, among Filipinos living abroad, several barriers compound the reluctance to seek mental health services, such as cultural mistrust, acculturation, limited English proficiency, and the lack of Filipino-proficient service providers (David, 2010; U.S. Department of Health and Human Services, 2001). Thus, online counseling can be used to reach populations that do not have access to traditional mental health services (Tait, 1999).

The use of online resources for counseling cuts through both physical and economic barriers. Offering free online counseling service allows OFWs and their family members access to these services. The nature of an online environment allows the person to express more of one's thoughts or feelings compared to face-to-face interactions (Suler, 2004), which may enhance help seeking among the overseas Filipino population. These two advantages to the online counseling medium were thought to be integral in creating this project.

There is also emerging literature on the effectiveness of online counseling for various problems (Richards & Vigano, 2013). Online exchanges enable the client and the counselor to build a relationship. This is integral in establishing the online therapeutic alliance (Martin, Garske & Davis, 2000) that is linked to greater success in therapy (Horvath & Greenberg, 1989; Horvath & Luborsky, 1993). There is also evidence that online counseling has positive physical and psychological outcomes, such as, decreased anxiety, depression, and emotional reactions to stress and trauma (Cavanagh & Shapiro, 2004; Christensen, Griffiths & Jorm, 2004; Campbell & Pennebaker, 2003; Soper & Bergen, 2001; Ulrich, & Lutgendorf, 2002).Given this, the Department of Psychology of the Ateneo de Manila University launched OFW Online in 2009, an Internet site that provides free online counseling for OFWs and their families. Online counselors who were either graduate students of or those with Masters degree in Counseling Psychology conducted counseling through Internet messaging/synchronous chat and (asynchronous) e-mail format. All counselors underwent training on online counseling, labor migration, and OFW issues, and were under direct supervision of the Clinical Psychology faculty of the university.

3.1.2 User Profile and Predictors of Use of Online Counseling

Between July 2009 and October 2010, a total of 191 OFWs registered on the online counseling website. The mean age of those who registered was 40.69 (SD = 8.69), and the majority were males (65%) with at least a Bachelor's Degree (n = 125, 65%). Geographically they were distributed between working in the Middle East (n = 117, 61%), East/Southeast Asia (n = 24, 13%), as well as Europe and North America (n = 25, 13%). Most were also engaged in white-collar professions such as Business, Engineering/Architecture, Information Technology, and Health-related occupations (n = 127, 66%). Of registered users, a smaller number (n = 36, 19% of the total registered users) actually availed of counseling within the time period surveyed, with 35 preferring online counseling through chat and one preferring email exchanges only.

Chat counseling sessions typically ran an average of 60.73 minutes and counselees had an average of 2 sessions (Hechanova, Tuliao, & Ang, 2011).

The profile of users was similar to that of registered users with the majority being male and based in the Middle East. It is important to note that the profile of the users is different from the general profile of OFWs. The majority of OFWs are involved in blue-collar work (e.g., domestic workers, factory and production workers, agricultural workers, and other service workers) and white-collar occupations (defined as professional, technical, managerial, clerical and sales occupation) only account for 18% of the total OFW population. In addition, only 13% of online users were from Asia even though 20% of all OFWs are based in Singapore and Hong Kong. However, the geographical representation may be explained by the predominantly white-collar sample of users, with the majority of OFWs in Asia hold blue-collar jobs (POEA, 2012). The profile of users suggests that access to facilities and technology is an important contributor to the utilization of online counseling. Similarly, Parreñas's (2005) study on parenting among Filipino OFW women found that the frequency of transnational communication is dependent upon the resources available. She reports that mother and child transnational communication is better for those with higher paying occupations (e.g., nurse versus domestic helpers) in countries with better access to technology.

3.1.3 Issues Raised in Online Counseling

The majority of Filipinos leave the Philippines to work overseas for economic reasons. For many of these Filipinos, working overseas is also their first time travelling out of the Philippines. This context of migration cuts across the various issues encountered in the OFW Online counseling service.

A content analysis of counseling exchanges on the OFW Online site revealed five areas of concern brought forth in counseling: family, marital and relationship issues; homesickness and loneliness issues; work-related issues; adjustment issues; and financial issues. Those who came with family, marital and relationship issues talked about conflict, decision-making and power struggles, infidelity, and lack of communication. Those who reported homesickness and loneliness felt the loss of their social support. Work-related issues often involved interpersonal problems with colleagues and superiors, which sometimes included felt prejudice or discrimination. Adjustment problems included the challenges of living in a new, and sometimes more restrictive, environment. Financial issues relate to their concerns in providing well or having enough savings for their families back home (Hechanova et al., 2011).

Work migration necessarily impacts the family structure. When one or both parents leave their children to work overseas, long distance marital relationships and parenting issues ensue (Parreñas, 2005; Madianou, 2012). A reconfiguration within these transnational families is then necessary, with this happening in different ways for different people (Asis, Huang, & Yeoh, 2004). Indeed, OFWs raised these issues in the online counseling sessions.

For migrants, living and working in an unfamiliar environment can cause undue stress. Living alone and away from one's natural support system is often enough of a challenge. Adjusting to a new work culture with colleagues from different parts of the world can then exacerbate this already difficult situation. As previously mentioned, the majority (61%) of those who registered in the OFW Online site between July 2009 and October 2010 were based in the Middle East (Hechanova et al., 2011). This suggests that adjusting to living in a Muslim-dominant culture presented a substantial social change for Filipino migrant workers who are predominantly Christian.

The problems raised with OFW Online counselors are not surprising in light of the social context of the OFW's experience, as well as the demographic information of those who intended to use these services. These have implications for the delivery of counseling and psychotherapy services to this group, both in terms of the training for counselors and the possibilities of psycho-education for migrant workers.

3.2 Challenges in Online Counseling

3.2.1 Attitudes Towards Help-Seeking

One of the biggest barriers to online counseling amongst migrant workers is the stigma attached to seeking professional help. A study of 365 Filipino migrant workers showed that the intent to seek online counseling among OFWs is fairly low (Hechanova, et al, 2013). The same study found that problem severity is the greatest predictor of seeking online counseling. That is, OFWs who view their problems as severe are those who are likely to seek professional help. This is consistent with the stage model of help-seeking behaviors, suggesting that the help-seeking processes generally begin with problem acknowledgment and appraisal (Broadhurst, 2003).

Another study reveals that OFWs would only consider seeking online counseling when there was no immediate source of social support from family or friends. The interviews suggested a general discomfort in asking for help or sharing one's problem with a stranger. Interestingly, some participants were reluctant to seek counseling because they did not want to burden others. Others indicated a preference for spiritual rather than professional support (Hechanova et al., 2011).

3.2.2 Access to Technology

Beyond attitudes towards help-seeking, access is another barrier for potential users. The study of OFWs and their families revealed that lack of access was an often-cited reason for non-use. Furthermore, OFWs said that they were more inclined to seek online counseling if they have the resources for it (Hechanova, et al 2013). About half reported having an Internet connection at work (56%) and their domicile (49%) in their host countries. Those with the least access to computers or Internet are domestic helpers in Asia. Others even report that their employer confiscates their phone. Beyond access to suitable technology, there is also the issue of time. Some domestic helpers reported that they have no weekly rest days. In addition to this, access also requires resources and blue-collar OFWs report that they cannot afford to pay for Internet access (Hechanova et al., 2011).

There also appears to be an interaction between problem severity and facilitating conditions. Those who have organizational and technological infrastructure support have a higher intent to use online counseling even when their problems are not severe. However, when problems are more severe, the effect of facilitating conditions seems to disappear (Hechanova, et al, 2013).

3.2.3 Capacity to Use and Comfort with Technology

A third challenge from the perspective of counselees is the skills necessary to utilize online services. Migrant workers and their families reported lack of capability to use technology as a reason for non-use. Although majority report that they use the Internet, 16% do not use or do not know how to use (Hechanova et al., 2011).

Non-users also prefer face-to-face rather than online counseling because it is seen as more personal (Hechanova et al., 2011). However, it must be noted that the OFW Online project utilized email or chat as medium. Skype or similar technologies was not used because of technological and resource limitations. One area for future research might be to explore whether technology-mediated visual communication would be perceived as more personal than email or chat.

3.2.4 Openness and Capability of Counselors

The issues of openness and capability are mirrored in those who provide online counseling. A study on the attitudes of 134 clinical and counseling psychologists found preferred preference for face-to-face counseling over online counseling (Teh, Acosta, Garabiles, Hechanova, & Alianan, 2013). Counselors believed face-to-face counseling provides greater opportunities for genuine empathy and emotional support that are necessary to establishing a therapeutic connection between counselor and client. They cited that a major disadvantage of online counseling is the lack of nonverbal cues. This makes it difficult to manifest empathy, ascertain clients' feelings and build a therapeutic relationship.

However, despite a preference for face-to-face counseling, respondents still reported a generally positive attitude toward online counseling. They acknowledged its advantages, and indicated their openness, albeit with minor reservations, to give this new counseling modality a try. They cited the following advantages of online counseling: accessibility or availability, convenience as a means to provide immediate help, anonymity and confidentiality, less stigma, suitability for certain types of clients, and as an adjunct to face-to-face counseling. The minor reservations are with regard to the difficulty in establishing a genuine counselor-client relationship, lack of competence in conducting online counseling, technical difficulties, and ethical concerns (Teh, et al, 2013).

A look into the composition of the study's sample may explain the results. Although the respondents of this research ranged from 20 to 62 years, the majority were graduate students. Eighty-three percent of the respondents had less than 4 years of experience in conducting counseling/therapy. A great majority (93%) spend an average of 23 hours using the Internet every week. Being Internet users themselves, they are open to using technology-mediated counseling. On the other hand, it must also be noted that respondents were trained to do counseling in a face-to-face context and only 23% of the respondents have experience doing online counseling. The lack of training and exposure to online counseling may explain their hesitation to adapt to the changes brought about by new technology (Teh, et al, 2013).

To summarize, two factors emerged as significant predictors of openness to conducting online counseling. These are attitude towards online counseling/therapy and ability to use various online services. Counselors who are more open to conducting online counseling are those with more positive attitudes towards online vis-à-vis face-to-face counseling and have the ability to use such online services.

The good news is that the concerns expressed by respondents may actually be addressed. The lack of competence in conducting online counseling may be resolved by providing specialized training via regular courses and seminar-workshops on online counseling. Guidelines for assessment, selection, and intervention including protocols during crisis situations, or when client's concerns can no longer be handled online can be formulated. Given the possibility of electronic glitches (such as getting disconnected during a session), an alternative means of communicating (such as mobile phones) may be established.

Ethical guidelines have to be formulated and provided to ensure the integrity and qualifications of online counselors, given that some competencies expected from online counselors are different from those required of traditional counselors. For instance, online counselors need to be Internet-savvy and proficient in writing, which are not essential when doing face-to-face counseling. Hence, additional qualifications in terms of skills in using the Internet and in written language are imperative.

Although not yet an immediate need because online counseling services in the country are not yet at the point of online counselors charging a professional fee, advocates of online counseling should also anticipate the concern about how online counselors will be paid for their services. Prearranged and agreed-upon payment schemes will have to be worked out.

Counselors have suggested that that combining online counseling with face-to-face counseling may be a better alternative to treating them independently. For example, clients can undergo face-to-face counseling first, and then use online counseling as a follow-up. Another approach is for clients to have initial sessions online if they feel uncomfortable about meeting the counselor face-to-face, and then have face-to-face counseling when they feel more at ease (Teh et al., 2013). In addition, the emergence of technologies such as Skype and Facetime may also provide the 'face-to-face', albeit virtual, dimension.

3.2.5 The Issue of Risk

The issue of client risk, particularly in terms of the potential for self-harm or injury to others, cannot be extricated from mental health counseling. Kraus, Zack, and Stricker (2004) warned mental health workers that such issues are best left to face-to-face interventions rather than online counseling. Responding to such risks in online interventions can prove to be tricky, particularly given the distance between counselor and counselee and the presumable lack of knowledge of the resources available in the counselee's locality.

As part of the volunteer counselors' training program, risk assessment and response protocols were set in place. This included exclusion of these clients in the consent forms of the website, which registrants are required to submit. Nevertheless, there were a number of instances when clients who initially did not present a risk of self-harm revealed such a risk. Their lack of willingness or inability to seek face-to-face-mental health services also occasionally raised this risk. The counselor handling such cases was instructed to break confidentiality and contact next-of-kin in the Philippines to transfer responsibility of care.

Such issues are a challenge even for the most experienced counselors, and more so for the counselors-in-training who usually volunteered for the OFW Online counseling service. Adequate training and close supervision of these counselors are necessary steps in making sure that both the needs of the counselor and the counselee are adequately met.

3.3 Opportunities in Social Networking

Limitations notwithstanding, online counseling is a promising means to providing psychosocial support to a population who may not have immediate access to mental health services. In particular, the emergence of social networking can provide the infrastructure and platform, as well as be a means to promote online counseling itself, and also act as a mechanism in providing additional psycho-educational support for migrant workers.

3.3.1 Platform and Access

The effectiveness of online counseling to support migrant workers hinges on their ability to use technology. Although we often assume that Internet use is ubiquitous and pervasive, such may not always be the case. The profile of OFW online counseling users and the results of the study among migrant workers (Hechanova, Tuliao, Teh, Alianan, & Acosta, 2013) suggest that there is a segment of the OFW population (blue-collar workers, particularly in Asia) that does not have the competence to use or access to online counseling. However, the emergence of smart phones poses a great opportunity to improve such capabilities. In addition, the emergence of technologies such as instant messaging, forums and social networking sites may motivate non-users to adopt these technologies.

Initially, the OFW Online site was created as a stand-alone site with a built-in chat function. However, the emergence of Yahoo Messenger, Facebook, and Skype eliminated the need for a separate site and infrastructure. As the use of these sites became more popular among migrant workers, it was easier for counsellors to set-up chats using these technologies. Still, the issue of protecting the counselees' identity and records when using these platforms should be of the utmost importance, and steps should be taken to preserve confidentiality (Joint Task Force for the Development of Telepsychology Guidelines for Psychologists, 2013).

3.3.2 Promotion

Beyond the access and capability in technology-use, social networking may also provide mechanisms to promote awareness of online counseling. Although the OFW Online project continues to exist independently, the team created its own Facebook page to generate more awareness of its service.

3.3.3 Psycho-education

OFWs are a diverse group of people with varying mental health needs with online counseling being one way respond to these needs. Furthermore, beyond facilitating and promoting online counseling, social networking can provide a means to help educate migrant workers on help-seeking. Asians, in particular, appear to underutilise mental health services (Matsuoka, Breaux, & Ryujin, 1997; Zhang, Snowden, & Sue, 1998), however, if online counseling can be promoted within their social networks, people may become more open to its use. Social network sites can also provide relevant materials online that focus on preventive-mental health and enhance self-care.

3.3.4 Peer Support

Given that Asians tend to avoid using mental health services, another way to harness social networking is by using it to provide peer support. Chang (2005) suggests that the majority of people are using the Internet for psycho-education, self-help, and mutual support. Thus, sites that will allow migrant workers to interact and provide help to one another might be beneficial for those who are reluctant to seek professional help.

3.3.5 Apps on Mobile Devices

Another emerging opportunity in serving the-mental health needs of OFWs is the use of free and downloadable smartphone apps. The recent years have seen an emergence of such applications for health including those at risk for HIV to seek help (Hood, et.al, 2012) and those with Type II Diabetes to monitor their health habits (Ribu, et.al., 2013). In mental health, some initial evaluations of app usability have also been done in strengthening face-to-face rational-emotive therapy (Warren, 2012) and in monitoring wellness habits of those diagnosed with schizophrenia (Ben-Zeev, Kaiser, Brenner, Begale, Duffecy, & Mohr., 2013).

Echoing the previous point on psycho-education, these apps may be vehicles that promote such information and link users with appropriate mental health services. These apps may be viewed either as stand-alone services or complementary self-help resources that enhance counseling interventions.

3.4 Conclusion

This chapter sought to summarize literature and our present our own experiences in providing online counseling for Filipino migrant workers. We highlight the difficulties faced by migrant workers and how online counseling may be used to provide psychosocial support to a population that may not have access to it. However, we also present the challenges to providing such services, such as issues of access, the stigma associated with help-seeking, as well as resource and technological barriers. From the perspective of counselors, although there is openness to it, the barriers appear to be lack of training and exposure to online counseling. Furthermore, the absence of guidelines and protocols for online counseling may be a problem, especially in relation to clients who are high-risk. Finally, we summarize the possibilities of harnessing social networking as a platform in order to provide greater access to online counseling. Social networking can also be used as a means to promote online counseling, provide psych-education and peer support to migrant workers. We also view the emergence of mobile applications as potentially useful in addressing issues of resource and technological barriers to online counseling.

References

Asis, M.M.B., Huang, S., & Yeoh, B.S.A. (2004). When the light of the home is abroad: Unskilled female migration and the Filipino family. *Singapore Journal of Tropical Geography, 25, 2,* 198-215.

Ayalon, L. (2012). Suicidal and depressive symptoms in Filipino home care workers in Israel. *Journal of Cross Cultural Gerontology, 27,* 51 – 63.

Asian Migrant Centre (2000). *Asian Migrant Yearbook: Migration Facts, Analysis and Issues in 1999.* Hong Kong: Asian Migrant Centre Ltd.

Ben-Zeev, D., Kaiser, S.M., Brenner, C.J., Begale, M., Duffecy, J. & Mohr, D.C. (2013). Development and usability testing of FOCUS: A smartphone system for self-management of schizophrenia. *Psychiatric Rehabilitation Journal, 36, 4,* 289-296.

Battistella, G., & Conaco, M. (1998). The impact of labor migration on the children left behind: A study of elementary school children in the Philippines. *Sojourn: Journal of Social Issues in Southeast Asia, 13,* 220 – 241.

Briones, L. (2008). Beyond trafficking, agency and rights: A capabilities perspective on Filipina experiences of domestic work in Paris and Hong Kong. *Wagadu: A Journal of Transnational Women's and Gender Studies, 5,* 49 – 72.

Broadhurst K. (2003). Engaging parents and careers with family support services: What can be learned from research on help-seeking. *Child and Family Social Work, 8,* 341–50.

Campbell, S., & Pennebaker, J. (2003). The secret life of pronouns: Flexibility in writing style and physical health. *Psychological Science, 14, 1,* 60-65.

Cavanagh, K., & Shapiro, D. (2004). Computer treatment for common mental health problems. *Journal of Clinical Psychology, 60* (3), 239-251, doi: 10.1002/jclp.10261

Chang, T. (2005). Online counseling: Prioritizing psychoeducation, self-help, and mutual help for counseling psychology research and practice. *Counseling Psychologist, 33* (6), 881-890.

Christensen, H., Griffiths, K., & Jorm, A., (2004). Delivering interventions for depression by using the Internet: Randomised controlled trial. *Primary Care*, 1-5, doi:10.1136/bmj.37945.566632.EE

Chung, I., & Shibusawa, T. (2013). Contemporary clinical practice with Asian immigrants: A relational framework with culturally responsive approaches. USA: Routledge.

David, E.J.R. (2010). Cultural mistrust and mental health help-seeking attitudes among Filipino Americans. *Asian American Journal of Psychology, 1* (1), 57 – 66.

Hechanova, M.R.M., Tuliao, A.P., Ang, P.H. (2011). If you build it, will they come?: Prospects and challenges in online counseling for overseas migrant workers. *Media Asia, 38* (1), 32 – 40.

Hechanova, M.R.M., Tuliao, A.P., Teh, L.A., Alianan, A.S., & Acosta, A. (2013). Problem severity, technology adoption, and intent to seek online counseling among overseas Filipino workers. *Cyberpsychology, Behavior, and Social Networking, 16* (8), 613 – 617.

Hood J.E., MacKellar, D., Spaulding, A., Nelson, R., Mosiakgabo, B., Sikwa, B., Puso, I., Raats, J., Loeto, P., Alwano, M.G. & Monyatsi, B. (2012). Client characteristics and gender-specific correlates of testing HIV positive: a comparison of standalone center versus mobile outreach HIV testing and counseling in Botswana. *AIDS and Behavior, 16* (7), 1902-16.

Horvath, A. O., & Greenberg, L. S. (1989). Development and validation of the Working Alliance Inventory. *Journal of Counseling Psychology, 36,* 223-233.

Horvath, A., & Luborsky, L. (1993). The Role of the therapeutic alliance in psychotherapy. *Journal of Consulting and Clinical Psychology, 61*(4), 561-573.

Joint Task Force for the Development of Telepsychology Guidelines for Psychologists (2013). Guidelines for the practice of Telepsychology. *American Psychologist 68* (9), 791 – 800.

Kraus, R., Zack, J. & Stricker, G. (2004). *Online counseling: a handbook for mental health professionals.* San Diego, CA: Elsevier Academic Press.

Lee, M. (2006). Invisibility and temporary residence status of Filipino workers in South Korea. *Journal for Cultural Research, 10* (2), 159 – 172.

Madianou, M. (2012). Migration and the accentuated ambivalence of transnational families. *Global Networks, 12, 3,* 277-295.

Martin, D., Garske, J., & Davis, K. (2000). Relation of the therapeutic alliance with outcome and other variables: A meta-analytic review. *Journal of Consulting and Clinical Psychology, 68*(3), 438-450, doi: IO.I037//0022-006X.68.3.438

Matsuoka, J. K., Breaux, C, & Ryujin, D. H. (1997). National utilization of mental health services by Asian Americans/Pacific Islanders. *Journal of Community Psychology*, 25, 141-145.

Parreñas, R. (2005). Long distance intimacy: Class, gender and intergenerational relations between mothers and children in Filipino transnational families. *Global networks, 5, 4,* 317-336.

Philippine Overseas Employment Administration (2012). *2008 – 2012 Overseas Employment Statistics*. Retrieved from http://www.poea.gov.ph/stats/2012_stats.pdf

Richards, D. & Vigano, N. (2013). Online counseling: A narrative and critical review of literature. *Journal of clinical psychology, 69* (9), 994-1011.

Ribu, L., Holmen, H., Torbjornsen, A., Smastuen, M.C., Elind, E., Wahl, A.K., . . . Arsand, E. (2013). Low-intensity self-management intervention for persons with type 2 diabetes using a mobile phone-based diabetes diary, with and without health counseling and motivational interviewing: Protocol for a randomized controlled trial. *Journal of Medical Internet Research*, 15, 8, e34.

Soper, B., & Bergen, C.W. (2001). Employment counseling and life stressors: coping through expressive writing. *Journal of Employment Counseling, 38*, 150-160.

Suler, J. (2004). The online disinhibition effect. *Cyberpsychology and Behavior, 7, 3*, 321-326.

Tait, A. (1999). Face-to-face and at a distance: The mediation of guidance and counseling through the new technologies. *British Journal of Guidance and Counseling, 27*, 113 – 122.

Teh L., Acosta A., Garabiles, M., Hechanova, R., Alianan, A. (2013). Attitudes of counseling psychologists and counseling psychologists-in-training towards face-to-face and online counseling and the predictors of their openness to conducting online counseling. Paper presented at the 50th Annual Convention of the Psychological Association of the Philippines on 25 October 2013, at Miriam College, Quezon City, Philippines.

Tuliao, A.P. (in press). Mental health help seeking among Filipinos: A review of the literature. *Asia Pacific Journal of Counseling and Psychotherapy.*

Ulrich, P., & Lutgendorf, S. (2002). Journaling about stressful events: Effects of cognitive processing and emotional expression. *The Society of Behavioral Medicine, 24*(3), 244-250.

U.S. Department of Health and Human Services (2001). *Mental Health: Culture, Race, and Ethnicity – A Supplement to Mental Health: A Report of the Surgeon General.* Retrieved from http://www.ncbi.nlm.nih.gov/books/NBK44243/pdf/TOC.pdf.

Warren, J. (2012). Mobile mind mapping: **Using mobile** technology to enhance rational emotive behavior therapy. *Journal of Mental Health* **Counseling**. *34, 1,* 72-81.

Zhang, A. Y.,Snowden, L. R, & Sue, S. (1998). Differences between Asian and White Americans' help seeking and utilization patterns in the Los Angeles area. *Journal of Community Psychology*, 26, 317-326.

Ron Hammond, Hui-Tzu Grace Chou

4 Using Facebook: Good for Friendship But Not So Good for Intimate Relationships

Abstract: This research examines the impact of using Facebook on the satisfaction with and quality of intimate relationships among those who were married, dating, or living together. Using a probability sample of both current and non-returning students at a state university in Utah, participants were solicited to take an online survey in April and May 2012. The results of a multivariate analysis, based on 509 respondents, indicated that using Facebook is negatively related to the satisfaction with and quality of intimate relationships. First, the more often respondents updated their Facebook, the less satisfied they were with their spouses or partners. Second, the more years respondents used Facebook, the more likely it was for them and their partners or spouses to see defects in each other and to be defensive with each other. Third, the more "friends" respondents added to their Facebook, the more likely it was that they and their partners or spouses withdrew from each other. Fourth, those who spent more time with friends offline were more satisfied with their relationships with their partners/spouses, and they were also less likely to withdraw from their partners/spouses. The implications of these findings are discussed.

4.1 Introduction

The purpose of this research was to examine the impact of using Facebook on the quality of and satisfaction with intimate relationships. One contribution Facebook has made on society is that it helps people build and maintain social relationships (Bonds-Raacke & Raacke, 2010; Ellison, Steinfield, & Lampe, 2007). People can easily update their Facebook "status" and share with significant others or individuals they do not know personally, both near and far away. Compared with traditional offline interactions (Hill & Dunbar, 2003), Facebook dramatically increases the speed of communications and the size of social networks (Acar, 2008). People can now be connected with each other or with larger communities more efficiently than through traditional offline interaction, which is often limited by time, space, and cognitive resources.

4.1.1 Differences Between Online and Offline Interaction

Facebook users share with close friends, acquaintances, or even strangers, who are connected through different areas of life, such as family, schools, religious groups, the workplace, and clubs. One consequence of indiscriminately sharing with many people at the same time is that it becomes less likely for people to present information that might damage their public image. In contrast to traditional offline interactions, where people might share some true feelings or challenges in life with their close friends, interactions through Facebook are under the surveillance of others (Brandtzæg, Lüders, & Skjetne, 2010; Muise, Christofides, & Desmerais, 2009), which might include current and future colleagues or employers (Caers & Castelyns, 2011). Therefore, people are less likely to share information that might be socially undesirable; instead, users of computer-mediated communication tend to adopt several techniques to optimize their image (Adkins & Brashers, 1995; Dominick, 1999; Lea & Spears, 1992; Schau & Gilly, 2003; Tidwell & Walther, 2002; Walther, 2007).

4.2 Theoretical Argument

Goffman (1973) identified the public presentation of the self that is made via impression management, especially in the specific roles we take on in life. Although the Online Social Networks (OSNs) were not part of Goffman's original work, the core concepts can be readily applied to Facebook and the everyday interaction users experience while using it. Bullingham and Vasoncelos (2013) identified Goffman's concepts of the impressions made (intentional "given" and unintentional "given off") while on the front stage that Facebook has made so readily available in this digital age. Interestingly, someone has set up an Erving Goffman Facebook webpage which had over 3,900 likes as of 10 June 2014. One has to question if the black and white photo used on this page would actually reflect the Faceboook image Goffman might like to present if he were alive today. This truly is a serious question to raise given that Goffman is not actually alive to create his own Facebook image and manage how others perceive him on it. Some researchers of Facebook have utilized Goffman's concept of self-presentation (Junghyun, & Jong-Eun Roselyn, 2011; Strano & Wattai Queen, 2012; Wallace, Buil, & Chernatony, 2014). Given that Facebook users regularly post their photos on their pages and tag an identifier to those who often times did not grant permission for their image to be used, Strano and Wattai Queen (2012) identified how and why Facebook users untag themselves in others photos or simply ask others to remove photos of them from their Facebook wall in an effort to most precisely manage their public presentation of self on their own and on other's Facebook pages.

Previous research found that those who spend more time on Facebook daily are more likely to believe that others have better lives and are happier, and those who have been active on Facebook for longer are more likely to perceive that others are happier, and are less likely to agree that life is fair (Chou & Edge, 2012). When people perceive that others are happier and have better lives, they may have higher and unrealistic expectations in various areas of life, including their intimate relationships. Viewing others' photos with their spouses or partners on Facebook—disproportionately happy ones—may lead users to assume that others have ideal relationships. Therefore, while many people encounter some challenges with their partners or spouses, those more involved with using Facebook might be less satisfied with their partners or spouses than those less involved, because of higher and less realistic expectations formed by viewing others' happy photos with their partners or spouses on Facebook.

Disclosing one's intimate information with many people at the same time may impair the maintenance of closeness for couples. Previous research has documented how Facebook contributes to the experience of jealousy and partner surveillance in romantic relationships (Elphinston & Noller, 2011; Gershon, 2011; Muise. Christofides, & Desmerais, 2009), and how jealousy and surveillance behaviors relate to relationship dissatisfaction (Elphinston & Noller, 2011). Some college students reported during interviews that "Facebook transformed them into anxious, jealous, and monitoring selves that they did not want to be," and to preserve their romantic relationships, some of them had deactivated their Facebook accounts (Gershon, 2011).

In addition, based on the displacement hypothesis, when one puts more effort into a particular task (e.g., Facebook), it usually displaces needed efforts to engage in other tasks (e.g., relationship maintenance) (Coyne, et al., 2012; Kraut, et al., 1998). Therefore, those more involved with using Facebook might have less time and energy to maintain their offline intimate relationship than those using Facebook less. Furthermore, if people experience great satisfaction from using Facebook, such as a feeling of belongingness (Nadkarni & Hofmann, 2012), gaining the perceived social support from many online friends (Zhang, Tang, & Leung, 2011), or entertainment (Speical & Li-Barber, 2012; Yesil, 2014), they might also be less motivated to maintain their intimate relationships. When encountering problems with their spouses or partners, those more involved with using Facebook might withdraw from intimate relationships rather than put effort into improving them, because they can get some satisfaction from online interaction through Facebook, such as a sense of being popular or feeling accepted.

Based on the arguments above, the hypothesis was formulated:

Hypothesis: Those more involved with using Facebook are less likely to have quality intimate relationships when compared with those less involved with using Facebook.

4.3 Method

4.3.1 Sample and Procedure

To test this hypothesis, an online questionnaire was developed and sent to undergraduate students at a state university in Utah through the university Institutional Research department in April and May 2012. These university students collectively provided a unique insight into the impact Facebook has on intimate relationships, given that university records identified that about 40 percent of their current students were married at the time (Unpublished Institutional data). The university research office drew a random probability sampling, 8,000 current and non-returning students enrolled in Fall 2011; of these, 1,059 filled out the survey. The majority of respondents (95%) had used Facebook; 36.8% were married, 10.0% were single with a steady dating partner, 22.4% were single without a steady dating partner, 2.9% were divorced, and 3.5% chose other categories. Since the focus of this research was intimate relationships, only those with a spouse or partner were included in the final sample. The ethnic composition of the sample was similar to the distribution of the university: 84.3% of respondents were White, 6.4% were Hispanic, 2% were Asian and Pacific Islander, and 1.8% were African American. The mean age of respondents was 28.01.

4.3.2 Measures

4.3.2.1 Dependent Variables

Given that studies have already measured how Facebook use impacts intimate relationships (Ledbetter, et al., 2011; Monden, 2007; Muise, Christofides, & Desmarais, 2009; Papp, Danielewicz, & Cayemberg, 2012; Sheldon, Abad, & Hinsch, 2011), we wanted to test the impact on marital and relationship instability. To test the hypothesis, five measures of the quality of intimate relationships were adapted from Gottman's research on common divorce predictors (Gottman, 1993; 1999). Respondents were asked how much they agreed with these statements about their relationship: "We have been critical of each other, seen defects in each other, been defensive with each other, and withdrawn from each other." In addition, respondents were also asked to rate how satisfied they were with their relationship, which was measured by a 5-point Likert-scale, with 1 indicating being strongly dissatisfied with the relationship, and 5 strongly satisfied. Although these five variables are highly consistent (the Cronbach's α=.80), they were examined individually in the multivariate analysis to see whether using Facebook might affect different aspects of intimate relationships.

4.3.2.2 Independent Variables

The use of Facebook was measured by the number of years of having used Facebook, frequency of updating Facebook, hours spent on Facebook each week, number of Facebook friends, and number of Facebook friends who were total strangers. This research also controlled for several variables, including hours spent with friends offline, religious service attendance, whether they had kids, marital status, gender, and age. Detailed descriptions of all variables, including measurement, means, and standard deviations, are presented in the Appendix.

4.4 Results

The results of the multiple-regression analysis on the satisfaction with and quality of relationships with partners/spouses are presented in Table 4.1. The results showed that the more often respondents updated their Facebook, the less satisfied they were with their partners/spouses (β=0.10, $p<0.05$), compared with those who updated their Facebook less often. In addition, the results indicated that the more years respondents used Facebook, the more likely they were to see defects in their partners (β=0.11, $p<0.05$) and to be defensive with their partners (β=0.08, $p<0.10$). Furthermore, the more friends respondents added to their Facebook, the more likely they were to withdraw from their partners (β=0.09, $p<0.10$). The results of this research also indicated that the satisfaction with and quality of intimate relationships were affected by the number of hours spent with friends offline: Those who spent more time with friends offline were more satisfied with their relationships with their partners/spouses (β=0.09, $p<0.05$), and they were also less likely to withdraw from their partners/spouses (β=-0.13, $p<0.01$).

Other variables were also found to have impacts on the satisfaction with and quality of intimate relationships. Religious-service attendance showed positive impacts: Those attending religious services more often were less critical of (β=-0.08, $p<0.10$), less defensive of (β=-0.17, $p<0.001$), and less withdrawing from (β=-0.13, $p<0.01$) their partners/spouses. The quality of and satisfaction with relationships were also related to some demographic factors: married people were more likely to be defensive (β=.10, $p<0.10$); however, they were also more satisfied with their partner (β=-.65, $p<0.001$), compared with those who were not married.

Table 4.1: Correlation Coefficient Matrix for All Variables Used (n=510)

Variables	1.	2.	3.	4.	5.	6.	7.	8.
1. Satisfied with the relationship	1.00							
2. Frequency of updating Facebook	-.11*	1.00						
3. Hours spent on Facebook	-.07	.45***	1.00					
4. Number of Facebook friends	-.01	.23***	.19***	1.00				
5. Number of strangers on Facebook	-.07	.08	.02	.31***	1.00			
6. Hours spent with friends offline	-.09*	.13**	.09*	.22***	-.01	1.00		
7. Religious service attendance	.10*	-.12**	-.06	.18***	.03	-.04	1.00	
8. Married	.54***	-.09*	-.10*	-.10*	-.05	-.36***	.14**	1.00
9. Having kids	.16***	-.04	-.05	-.20***	-.03	-.31***	-.06	.55***
10. Gender (male)	-.08	-.18***	-.20***	-.06	.08	-.02	-.04	.02
11. Age	.01	-.13**	-.06	-.21***	.01	-.29***	-.06	.34***

Note: +: p<.10; *: p<.05 **: p<.01 ***: p<.001 (two-tailed)

Variables	9.	10.	11.	Min.	Max.	Mean	S.D.
1. Satisfied with the relationship				1	5	4.03	1.10
2. Frequency of updating Facebook				1	6	3.12	1.66
3. Hours spent on Facebook				0	50	4.67	5.47
4. Number of Facebook friends				0	2893	339.07	568.88
5. Number of strangers on Facebook				0	1000	11.68	62.87
6. Hours spent with friends offline				1	4	2.63	.95
7. Religious service attendance				1	5	3.67	1.53
8. Married				0	1	.37	.46
9. Having kids	1.00			0	1	.41	.49
10. Gender (male)	-.02	1.00		0	1	.39	.49
11. Age	.63***	.01	1.00	18	73	28.01	8.96

Note: +: p<.10; *: p<.05 **: p<.01 ***: p<.001 (two-tailed)

Table 4.2: Multiple Regression Analysis of the Quality Relationship on Selected Independent Variables (Standardized Coefficients)

Independent variables	**Satisfied with my partner**			
Frequency of updating Facebook	-.10**			
Hours spent on Facebook		-.05		
Number of Facebook friends			-.01	
Number of strangers on Facebook				-.05
Hours spent with friends offline	.08*	.07⁺	.07⁺	.07⁺
Religious service attendance	-.02	-.01	-.01	-.01
Married	.64***	.63***	.65***	.65***
Having kids	-.07	-.06	-.10⁺	-.10*
Gender (male)	-.07	-.07⁺	-.07*	-.05
Age	-.15***	-.17***	-.11*	-.13**
F-value	42.11***	34.76***	41.24***	41.55***
R^2	.32	.31	.33	.33
N	624	544	595	613

⁺ $p<0.10$; * $p<0.05$; ** $p<0.01$; *** $p<0.001$

4.5 Discussion and Conclusions

4.5.1 Implications

This research found that the use of Facebook is related to the satisfaction with and quality of intimate relationships among current and former college students who participated in this study. The results of this study have some implications. First, those frequently updating their status or profiles on Facebook were more likely to set their minds on Facebook, rather than on their partners/spouses. Therefore, they might be more interested in sharing with their online friends than maintaining a good relationship with their partners/spouses. Maintaining a good relationship takes some effort, and those frequently keeping their mind on Facebook interactions may be less likely to put effort into maintaining their relationships with partners/spouses, compared with those updating their Facebook statuses less often.

Second, having more friends listed on the Facebook might make people perceive that they have stronger social connections. Therefore, when encountering problems with partners/spouses, Facebook could be a place to withdraw, where people might feel that they are loved and accepted by many friends. In contrast to offline interactions with partners or spouses, who might see each others' weaknesses, online interactions tend to reveal individuals' positive parts and conceal their negative ones, thus making Facebook an attractive place to withdraw when encountering problems with partners or spouses.

The impact of online interactions through Facebook might differ from offline interactions in building relationships with partners/spouses. This study found that, while online interaction through Facebook increases the likelihood that people will withdraw from their partners/spouses, offline interactions with friends decrease the likelihood of withdrawing, and increase satisfaction with intimate relationships. Although both Facebook friends and real-life friends provide social and emotional support, offline interactions, especially with fewer people at the same time, make it easier for people to share some of their challenges in life. Acknowledging each other's challenges in life—rather than just seeing each other's happy Facebook persona online—prompts people to be more content with their life, including their intimate relationships.

4.5.2 Alternative Interpretation of the Findings

This research collected surveys and found a negative correlation between the frequency of updating one's status on Facebook and satisfaction with intimate relationships. Although it is possible to state that those frequently updating their status on Facebook are more interested in sharing with online friends, and thus are less likely to put the effort into maintaining the relationship with their spouses/partners, as discussed previously, it is also possible to argue the other way around. That is, those who are not satisfied with the relationships with their partners/spouses update their Facebook more often, trying to find some satisfaction from sharing with online friends. Future research might need to use an experimental design to find the real causal mechanism between these two factors.

4.5.3 Limitations and Suggestions for Future Research

This research, borrowing and adapted from Gottman's work on predictors of divorce, found significant impacts of using Facebook on some specific issues of intimate relationships, including seeing defects, being defensive, and withdrawing. It explored some, but not all dimensions of intimate relationships. Future research might want to use other theories or measurements of intimate or interpersonal relationships to see whether using Facebook affects other aspects of relationships. In addition, future research might want to include other variables, such as the length of relationship, and collect data dyadically so that it includes both partners' Facebook usage and feelings about their relationship. Finally, the majority of respondents in this study were young adults who are White, affiliated with the Mormon church, and live in Utah. Future research might want to see whether similar patterns exist among people of different ages, ethnicities, religious affiliations, geographic areas, and cultures.

References

Acar, A. (2008). Antecedents and consequences of online social network behavior: The case of Facebook. *Journal of Website Promotion*, 3, 62-83.

Adkins, M., & Brashers, D. (1995). The power of language in computer-mediated groups. *Management Communication Quarterly*, 8, 289-322.

Bonds-Raacke, J. & Raacke, J. (2010). MySpace and Facebook: Identifying dimensions of uses and gratifications for friend networking sites. *Individual Differences Research*, 8, 27-33.

Brandtzæg, P. B., Lüders, M., & Skjetne, J. H. (2010). Too many Facebook "Friends"? Content sharing and sociability versus the need for privacy in social network sites. *International Journal of Human-Computer Interaction*, 26, 1006-1030.

Bullingham, L., & Vasconcelos, A. (2013). 'The presentation of self in the online world': Goffman and the study of online identities. *Journal of Information Science*, 39, 101-112.

Caers, R., & Castelyns, V. (2011). Linkedln and Facebook in Belgium: The influences and biases of social network sites in recruitment and selection procedures. *Social Science Computer Review*, 29, 437-448.

Chou, H.-T.G., & Edge, N. (2012). "They are happier and having better lives than I am": The impact of using Facebook on perceptions of others' lives. *CyberPsychology, Behavioral & Social Networking*, 15, 117-121.

Coyne, S. M., Busby, D., Bushman, B. J. Gentile, D. A., Ridge, R. & Stockdale, L. (2012). Gaming in the game of love: Effects of video games on conflict in couples, *Family Relations*, 61, 388-396.

Dominick, J. (1999). Who do you think you are? Personal home pages and self-presentation on the world wide web. *Journalism & Mass Communication Quarterly*, 76, 646-658.

Ellison, N., Steinfield, C., & Lampe, C. (2007). The benefits of Facebook "Friends:" Social capital and college students' use of online social network sites. *Journal of Computer-Mediated Communication*, 12, 1143-1168.

Elphinston, R. A., & Noller, P. (2011). Time to face it! Facebook intrusion and the Implications for romantic jealousy and relationship satisfaction. *CyberPsychology, Behavior & Social Networking*, 14, 631-635.

Gershon, I. (2011). Un-friend my heart: Facebook, promiscuity, and heartbreak in a neoliberal age. *Anthropological Quarterly*, 84, 865-894.

Goffman, E. (1973). *The Presentation of Self in Everyday life.* Overlook Press.

Gottman, J. (1993). A theory of marital dissolution and stability. *Journal of Family Psychology*, 7, 57-75.

Gottman, J. (1999). *The seven principles for making marriage work.* New York: Three Rivers Press.

Hill, R. A., & Dunbar, R. I. M. (2003). Social network size in humans. *Human Nature*, 14, 53-72.

Junghyun, K., & Jong-Eun Roselyn, L. (2011). The Facebook paths to happiness: Effects of the number of Facebook friends and self-presentation on subjective well-being. Cyberpsychology, Behavior & Social Networking, 14, 359-364.

Kraut, R., Patterson, M., Lundmark, V., Kiesler, S., Mukopadhyay, T., & Scherlis, W. (1998). Internet paradox: A social technology that reduces social involvement and psychological well-being? *American Psychologist*, 53, 1017-1031.

Lea, M., & Spears, R. (1992). Paralanguage and social perception in computer-mediated communication. *Journal of Organizational Computing*, 2, 321-341.

Ledbetter, A.M., Mazer, J.P., DeGroot, J.M., Meyer, K.R., Yuping, M., & Swafford, B. (2011). Attitudes toward online social connection and self-disclosure as predictors of Facebook communication and relational closeness. *Communication Research*, 38:27–53.

Muise, A., Christofides, E., & Desmerais, S. (2009). More information than you ever wanted: Does Facebook bring out the green-eyed monster of jealousy? *CyberPsychology & Behavior*, 12, 441-444.

Monden, C. (2007). Partners in health? Exploring resemblance in health between partners in married and cohabitating couples. *Sociology of Health and Illness*, 29:391–411.

Nadkarni, A., & Hofmann, S. (2012). Why do people use Facebook? *Personality and Individual Differences*, 52, 243-249.

Papp, L. M., Danielewicz, J., & Cayemberg, C. (2012). 'Are We Facebook Official?' Implications of Dating Partners' Facebook Use and Profiles for Intimate Relationship Satisfaction. Cyberpsychology, Behavior & Social Networking, 15, 85-90.

Schau, H. J., & Gilly, M. C. (2003). We are what we post? Self-presentation in personal web space. *Journal of Consumer Research*, 30, 385-404.

Sheldon, K.M., Abad, N., & Hinsch, C. (2011). A two-process view of Facebook use and relatedness need-satisfaction: Disconnection drives use, and connection rewards it. *Journal of Popular Media Culture*, 1(S), 2-15.

Special, W. P., & Li-Barber, K. (2012). Self-disclosure and student satisfaction with Facebook. *Computers in Human Behavior*, 28, 624-630.

Strano, M. M., & Wattai Queen, J. (2012). Covering your face on Facebook: Suppression as identity management. *Journal of Media Psychology: Theories, Methods, and Applications*, 24, 166-180.

Tidwell, L. C., & Walther, J. B. (2002). Computer-mediated communication effects on disclosure, impressions, and interpersonal evaluations: Getting to know one another a bit at a time. *Human Communication Research* 2002; 28:317-348.

Wallace, E., Buil, I., & Chernatony, L. (2014). Consumer engagement with self-expressive brands: Brand love and WOM outcomes. *Journal of Product & Brand Management*, 23, 33-42.

Walther, J. B. (2007). Selective self-presentation in computer-mediated communication: Hyperpersonal dimensions of technology, language, and cognition. *Computers in Human Behavior*, 23, 2538-57.

Yesil, M. (2014). The relationship between facebook use and personality traits of university students. *International Journal of Academic Research*, 6, 75-80.

Zhang, Y., Tang, L. S. T., & Leung, L. (2011). Gratifications, collective self-esteem, online emotional openness, and traitlike communication apprehension as predictors of Facebook uses. *Cyberpsychology, Behavior & Social Networking*, 14, 733-739.

Appendix

Operationalization of Variables, Mean, and Standard Deviation

	Survey items and coding	Min.	Max.	Mean	S.D.
Overall Satisfaction	How much would you agree with the following statements about your relationship? "Overall, I am very satisfied with my spouse/intimate partner." (1: strongly disagree; 5: strongly agree)	1	5	4.03	1.10
Be critical of one another	How much would you agree with the following statements about your relationship? " My date/spouse/partner and I have never been critical of one another." (5: strongly disagree; 1: strongly agree)	1	5	3.37	1.09
See defects in one another	How much would you agree with the following statements about your relationship? "My date/spouse/partner and I have never seen defects in one another." (5: strongly disagree; 1: strongly agree)	1	5	3.50	.94
Be defensive with one another	How much would you agree with the following statements about your relationship? "My date/spouse/partner and I have never been defensive with one another." (5: strongly disagree; 1: strongly agree)	1	5	3.49	1.04
Withdraw from one another	How much would you agree with the following statements about your relationship? "My date/spouse/partner and I have never withdrawn from one another." (5: strongly disagree; 1: strongly agree)	1	5	3.27	1.15
Years of using Facebook	How many years have you been using Facebook?	0	8	3.63	1.55
Frequency of updating Facebook	About how often do you update your Facebook? 1. Seldom update; 2. Several times a year; 3. Several times a month; 4. Once a week; 5. 2-3 times a week; 6. Almost every day.	1	6	3.12	1.66

	Survey items and coding	Min.	Max.	Mean	S.D.
Hours spent on Facebook	How many hours do you spend on Facebook each week?	0	50	4.67	5.47
Number of Facebook friends	How many friends do you currently have on Facebook?	0	12006	339.07	568.88
Number of strangers on Facebook	How many of your Facebook friends are total strangers?	0	1000	11.68	62.87
Hours spent with friends offline	How many hours do you usually spend out with friends each week (not online)? 1. Never; 2. 1-3 hours; 3. 4-6 hours; 4. 7 hours or more.	1	4	2.63	.95
Religious service attendance	How much would you agree with the following statement? "I attend religious service every week." (1: strongly disagree; 5: strongly agree)	1	5	3.67	1.53
Having kids	Do you have any children? 1. Yes; 0. No.	0	1	.41	.49
Married	What is your current marital status: married	0	1	.37	.46
Dating	What is your current marital status: single with a steady dating partner	0	1	.10	.30
Gender (male)	What is your gender? 1. Male; 0. Female	0	1	.39	.49
Age	What is your age?	18	73	28.01	8.96

Gregor Petrič

5 Communicatively Integrated Model of Online Community: A Conceptual Framework and Empirical Validation on a Case of a Health-Related Online Community

Abstract: This paper proposes that sustaining quality of communication is vital for the reproduction of online communities in terms of social integration, reliable knowledge accumulation, and empowered group identity. By building on Habermas' concept of communicative action and Friedland's model of a communicatively integrated community, this paper provides an alternative perspective on one of the key questions in online community research—How is online community possible? It is asserted that online communication, which is reciprocal, justified, sincere, emphatic, and reflexive, essentially constitutes social glue and plays a key role in sustaining online communities. Hypotheses are derived from the theoretical framework mentioned above, suggesting that quality of online communication in an online community is associated with supportive ties, the credibility of the exchanged information in the online community, the sense of belonging to the online community and individual empowerment. The hypotheses are tested on a sample of users from the biggest online health community in Slovenia (n=742). The data were collected via a web survey in June 2013 and January 2014. With the use of a linear structural equation modeling approach, insight is given into the proposed hypotheses and some theoretical and practical considerations are offered.

5.1 Introduction

This chapter focuses on one of the essential questions in the research of online phenomena, that is, how online community is possible, with this concept being defined as any online domain where people come together with different purposes, from having conversations with others to exchanging support and advice, learning, playing or just being with each other. Moreover, online communities range from small online groups to social networking sites with millions of users (Resnick & Kraut, 2012). More specifically, the issue of what the "social glue" might be that holds together an online community and enables its sustainability and reproduction has not yet been definitively resolved. It has been argued that most of the studies that tackle this question rest on a general model of human behavior that considers social actors as rational and self-interested, striving to maximize gains and minimize efforts (e.g., Matzat, 2009). Such a model has been criticized within the social sciences in general (Eder, 2007; Miller, 1992) and in the field of internet research in particular, where it has been argued that such theories do not provide a satisfactory account of the behavior exhibited in online communities (Resnick & Kraut, 2012). In this paper, we aim to present a model of online community based on an alternative understanding of the general nature of human behavior, elaborated through the concept of communicative rationality. This was introduced in the framework of the theory of communicative action (Habermas, 1984, 1987) and then further elaborated on by researchers who have followed this stream, primarily via Friedland's (2001) concept of communicatively integrated model of community.

The core idea of communicatively integrated community is that communicative rationality is inherent in communicative action through which common understandings, social bonds, and collective identities are formed. The communicative model of community is also relevant for online domains, as in this framework, community is understood as a communication network where communication is essential for the constitution of the community (Friedland, 2001). From this perspective, it is close to Wellman's (2001) understanding of community as a network of interpersonal ties that allows important resources to be built such as social support, knowledge, and social identity. Although the communicatively integrated model of community pertains to complex relations among various societal levels (Shin, 2007), in this paper we limit ourselves to the micro-level of interpersonal networks, through which we can study the dynamics of integration processes in online communities.

Of course, internet research does not ignore communication processes in online domains. On the contrary, communication has been at the center of discussions since the early theories of computer-mediated communication emerged (Postmes et al., 2001; Sproul & Kiesler, 1986). Moreover, as pioneers of online community research, Preece et al. (2003) and Rheingold (2000) explicitly emphasized interaction and communication as building blocks of online communities. However, while communication is often implicit or even self-evident in terms of its essential role in the existence of online social phenomena, it has only rarely been placed at the center of analysis. The research that exists predominantly focuses on the question of what types of communication are destructive for online communities (Caspi & Gorski, 2006; Suler & Phillips, 1998; Wagner et al., 2005), while the qualities of communication that are constitutive of online communities are rarely discussed, conceptualized, operationalized, and/or empirically investigated. This gap was also observed by Preece (2000), who found it necessary to acquire more knowledge on interactions in online communities. However, the question of what kind of communication is essential for the sustainability and reproduction of online community has not received much theoretical or empirical attention.

The intention of this paper is thus to introduce the idea of communicatively integrated community and the concept of quality of communication. Moreover, our aim is to test the proposal that quality of communication is an important factor in the key building blocks of online communities - empowered community identity, supportive relations, and credibility of online community knowledge.

5.2 Communicatively Integrated Online Community

The idea that quality of communication is a constitutive element of a healthy community and democratic life goes back to such eminent thinkers as Dewey (1927) and Mead (1962), and was probably best elaborated by Habermas (1984) in the context of his theory of communicative action. These ideas were further investigated and resulted in the concept of communicatively integrated community and social capital (Friedland, 2001; Rojas et al., 2011), while with rare exceptions (Petrič, 2006; Petrič et al., 2011; Petrič & Petrovčič, 2014a), internet research field did not work on these grounds. One of the main concepts in this stream of ideas is communicative rationality, which refers to the experience of "unlimited, unifying and consensus building force of argumentative speech, in which participants transcend their subjective views [...] and implicitly refer to validity claims in their speech acts" (Habermas, 1984, p. 10). Communicative action is consequently a social action based on communicative rationality and is separate from strategic rational action, which is governed by rules of rational choice and is oriented toward maximizing the effectiveness of influencing the decisions of other participants. Communicatively acting participants are coordinating themselves and achieving their goals on the basis of mutual strive for reaching understanding (Habermas, 1984). Moreover, when people communicatively act in social contexts, they are implicitly claiming that the facts they are providing are real, that they are acting correctly according to existing normative context, and that their expressions of purposes, desires, and experiences are sincere.

Communicative rationality is not an idealist concept, but rather an inherent attribute of human communication, which is oriented toward understanding. Moreover, the "discursive quality" constitutes the micro-level of social order, since it guarantees that the speaker's utterances will be understood by the listener and the two parties will derive their cooperative relationship from it (Habermas, 1987). Friedland (2001) built on this idea and claimed that communicatively based interactions are important for the continuation and reproduction of community knowledge and culture, integrative social relations, as well as the establishment of participants' competences. In other words, communicative action is the central social action that ties together various social actors and is at the same time the medium for the reproduction of solidarities, identities, and knowledge as central anchors of community (Friedland, 2011). If social integration is based only on strategic rational action, which is manipulative and founded on self-interest, community becomes unstable, relations become transient, and identities are threatened (Habermas, 1987). Communicatively integrated community thus refers to a community that through the medium of communicative action fosters social integration, democratic selves, and competent personalities. While this model originally referred to interrelations of macro-level networks of power and influence, meso-level networks of organizations and associations, and micro-level of personal networks (Friedland, 2001), only the latter level is relevant for our analysis. On the micro-level, communicative action is understood as a certain type of interpersonal communication that involves careful and serious employment of reason to support or criticize the claims of the other, respectful listening to the other, reflection on one's own claims, and orientation to understanding of the other (Rojas et al., 2011; Shin, 2007). The qualities of such communication can be more closely operationalized by referring to research on deliberative speech, which to a large extent is derived from the Habermasian school of thought, but in a way that is limited to political communication. Some authors have suggested that qualities of deliberative speech are not only attributes of political communication, but also of everyday talk (Graham & Hajru, 2011; Wright, 2011). Consequently, we argue that the characteristic attributes of the quality of communication, which is essential for communicatively integrated model of online community, are mutuality, reciprocity, rationality, openness, perspective taking, empathy, and sincerity.

If we take only the micro-level of the model of the communicatively integrated community and assume that communicative action is manifested through quality of communication, then the model can be quite straightforwardly applied at the level of online domains. In other words, as already mentioned, communication processes are constitutive for online communities. Furthermore, based on the above reasoning, it is safe to say that communication, which is based on communicative rationality, flows through online social networks, reinforces them, and leads to important psycho-social online outcomes and structures. It is thus a certain quality of communication that is not only constitutive for online communities, but also for their reproduction and sustainability. Empirical research has clearly demonstrated the importance of various interactional accomplishments and structures, which are important resources for participants and reasons for their membership and participation in the online community: Solidarities in terms of social support exchange (Coulson & Malik, 2012) and online trust (Blanchard et al., 2011); Identity in terms of belonging to the online community (Blanchard, 2008) and psychological empowerment (Barak et al., 2008); Knowledge in terms of exchange of information (Hara & Hew, 2007), learning (Luck & Norton, 2006), and medical help (Tanis, 2008). However, the question of how the (quality of) communication is related to these important resources has not yet been systematically investigated. Nevertheless, partial aspects of this question have been investigated and provide support for at least parts of the proposed model. Namely, it is argued that communication between participants plays an important function in (re)creating the social glue that holds together an online community (Rollman et al., 2000) and to allow its sustainability (Koh & Kim, 2003). More specifically, Rollman et al. (2000) argued for the relevance of respectful, open, and reciprocal communication for the formation of group identity. Furthermore, casual conversation often leads to building social relationships and helps construct a sense of community (Kim & Kim,

2008; Stromer-Galley, 2007). Regarding the association of quality of communication with psychological empowerment as an important dimension of online identity, we can also find some support in the literature. That is, certain types of participation in an online community and communication exchanges through which reciprocity and empathy flows can lead to greater self-confidence and feelings of greater competences, which are typical dimensions of psychological empowerment (Tanis, 2008). That certain styles of communication in an online community are associated with trustworthy and supportive relationships has been demonstrated by Jarvenpaa et al. (1998). Ultimately, it seems plausible to claim that quality of communication is associated with credibility of exchanged information, as information processes in online communities are inherently linked to communication processes by the fact that a certain type of communication among members in terms of posting messages, tagging, and responding produces certain types of information and knowledge in online communities (Hara & Hew, 2007).

Based on the above ideas, we claim that communicatively integrated online community is characterized with vital interactional outcomes on the personal, interpersonal, and knowledge levels that depend on the quality of communication processes in the online community. More precisely, the hypotheses we propose are as follows:

H_1: Quality of communication is associated with individual empowerment and a sense of virtual community.

H_2: Quality of communication is associated with supportive social relations.

H_3: Quality of communication is associated with credibility of exchanged information.

Before empirically testing these hypotheses, it should be noted that interactive outcomes in online communities do not only depend exclusively on the quality of communication, but also on many other factors, which are probably best grasped within the concept of online community as a socio-technical system. This informs us that online community represents a complex network of technical infrastructure and administrators' decisions, as well as norms, policies, communicative practices and dispositions of users who are embedded into wider spheres of social interaction (Kling & Courtright, 2003; Lamb et al., 2000). To take this into account in the empirical research in totality is practically impossible, but we want to consider at least to some extent the fact that the structural conditions of online community, most often grasped through the concepts of usability and sociability (Preece, 2000), provide an important context for the communicative processes described in the above hypotheses. For this reason, we additionally address an exploratory research question:

RQ: How are quality of communication and psycho-social outcomes associated with ease of use, usefulness, and sociability in the online community?

5.3 Method

5.3.1 Sample

Although the above hypotheses and research question are conceived as general communicative processes in online domains, this research focuses on one specific type of online communities—health-related online support communities. These are popular spaces of group communication, where people inform themselves about health-related issues, exchange social support with other users (Demiris, 2006; Fox, 2011; Preece, 1998), as well as acquire self-efficacy and competences for handling health-relates issues (Author, 2014b; Lemire et al., 2008; Menon, 2002; van Uden-Kraan et al., 2008). The data for this research come from a web survey that was conducted in collaboration with the owners of the largest health-related online community in Slovenia, Med.over.net. Established in 2000, this consists of a series of web forums in which users have posted more than 8 million of messages about health, everyday life, parenting, partnerships, social issues, and so on. A random sample of 7,500 users was drawn from the list of all registered members of the online community, and the survey was administered in two time slots—one in July 2013 and the second in January 2014. In total, 742 respondents completed the survey out of 7,500 members of the sample, which means that the aggregate response rate was 9.9% (American Association for Public Opinion Research [AAPOR], 2011). The sample consisted of 119 (16%) males and 623 (84%) females, which is a typical distribution for health-related online communities (Couslon & Malik, 2012). Respondents ranged in age from 16 to 85 years ($M = 37.1$, $SD = 10.5$). Almost half (47%) had a university degree and most were married or de facto married (76%). After the exclusion of item non-response on model variables, the final sample size was 536 units.

5.3.2 Measures

Sense of virtual community. An established scale for measuring sense of virtual community (e.g., “I feel at home in this online community”) was used (Blanchard, 2008), where responses were collected on a dichotomous scale (0 = false; 1 = true) and summed in an index, demonstrating good reliability (.71).

Social support exchange. A one-dimensional scale tapped into the degree to which members of the online community are involved in exchanging social support with other members in terms of advice, consolation, sharing experiences (e.g., “Other community members offer me advices regarding my health-related issues”). An established scale with nine items on a 5-point Likert-type scale was used (van Uden-Kraan et al., 2009) and demonstrated good to excellent reliability (.88).

Credibility of exchanged information. Five items on a 5-point Likert-type scale were used to assess respondents' perception of how reliable, trustworthy, and credible the information exchanged in the online community is (e.g., "Information published by users of the online community is reliable"). The scale demonstrated good reliability (0.87).

Individual empowerment. This was measured with a short, adapted version of Zimmerman's (1995) intrapersonal component of the psychological empowerment scale. Respondents assessed the role of the online community in raising self-efficacy, control, and competences regarding their health-related issues on a 7-point semantic differential describing change regarding the above elements. The wording was as follows: "Due to my use of the Med.over.net community, I have..." and the sample item was a semantic differential ranging from -3 (...less control over my health condition) to +3 (...more control over my health condition). Good internal reliability (alpha = .86) was shown for this measure according to Brown's (2006) criteria.

Quality of communication in the online community. An adapted version of the perceived quality of conversations in online community scale (Petrič, 2014) was used. The original scale, which showed good levels of reliability and validity, was shortened due to the overall length of the questionnaire. Eight items on a 5-point Likert-type scale were used, aiming to grasp perceived reciprocity, justification, reflexivity, ideal role taking, and sincerity (e.g., "Members of the community usually explain why they don't agree with someone or something") and demonstrated good reliability (alpha = .71).

Ease of use. This is a dimension of various service quality instruments (Loiacono et al., 2007) that taps into the issue of how easy it is to use various online community features (e.g., "The site of online community is easy to navigate"). Nine items on a 5-point Likert-type scale showed good reliability (alpha = 0.75).

Usefulness. This dimension of the instrument was employed to assess the quality of web sites (Loiacono et al., 2007), and pertains to the question of how reliable the site of the online community is, the level of trust toward managers of the site, and the extent to which the information fits the needs of the individual (e.g., "On the web site I can quickly find relevant information"). This is an eight-item scale that demonstrated good reliability (alpha = 0.80).

Sociability. Sociability refers to the extent to which the technical design of the online community supports establishing and interacting with other users of the community (Preece, 2000; Rizavi et al., 2011). The four-item scale (e.g., "Online community offers good conditions for communicating with other users") demonstrated good to excellent reliability (alpha = 0.89).

5.4 Analysis and Results

Descriptive analysis of the variables used in the hypotheses reveals that the health-related online community under investigation had managed well when it came to developing structural, communicative, and psycho-social resources that were available to their users. Specifically, as Table 1 shows, there was an above average level of sense of virtual identity (M=5.84, SD=2.17), feelings of individual empowerment (M=3.33, SD=0.85), and perceived credibility of exchanged information among users of the online community (M=3.12, SD=0.84). Only the intensity of social support exchange was somewhat below average (M=2.49, SD=0.89). The variable that pertains to the main integrative mechanisms of online community—communication quality—was present to an average extent (M=3.02, SD=0.46). Furthermore, the managers of the online community had obviously been successful in establishing usability and sociability as all three related variables performed well in the eyes of users: They were satisfied with the possibilities for interaction (M=3.50, SD=0.51), and the perceived usability of the online community (M=3.56, SD=0.60) and ease of use (M=3.45, SD=0.49) were high.

Table 5.1: Descriptive statistics of variables in the hypotheses and research question

Variables	Scale	Mean	SD
Sense of virtual community (SVC)	0–9	5.84	2.17
Individual empowerment	1–5	3.33	0.85
Social support	1–5	2.49	0.89
Credibility of information	1–5	3.12	0.84
Quality of communication	1–5	3.02	0.46
Sociability	1–5	3.50	0.51
Ease of use	1–5	3.45	0.49
Usefulness	1–5	3.63	0.59

To test our hypotheses, we used a structural equation modeling approach, which is a suitable statistical technique for cases where the same variable simultaneously acts as a dependent and independent variable (Joreskog, 1993). For statistical analysis, we used the standard computer program for structural equation modeling, LISREL 8.7 (Joreskog & Sorbom, 2004), where the maximum likelihood method was used for parameter estimation. The initial model, where parameters that pertain to the impact of usability and sociability variables were fixed to zero, demonstrated bad fit to the data. After taking into account the values of modification indices, we inserted several parameters that pertain to the association between exogenous and endogenous variables. In addition, two error correlation terms between two endogenous variables were relaxed. The final model, which is presented in Figure 1, demonstrated good fit to the data (χ^2=23.28, df=13, RMSEA=0.039, RMR=0.027, NFI=0.98, AGFI=0.97) according to various criteria as suggested by Browne and Cudeck (1993).

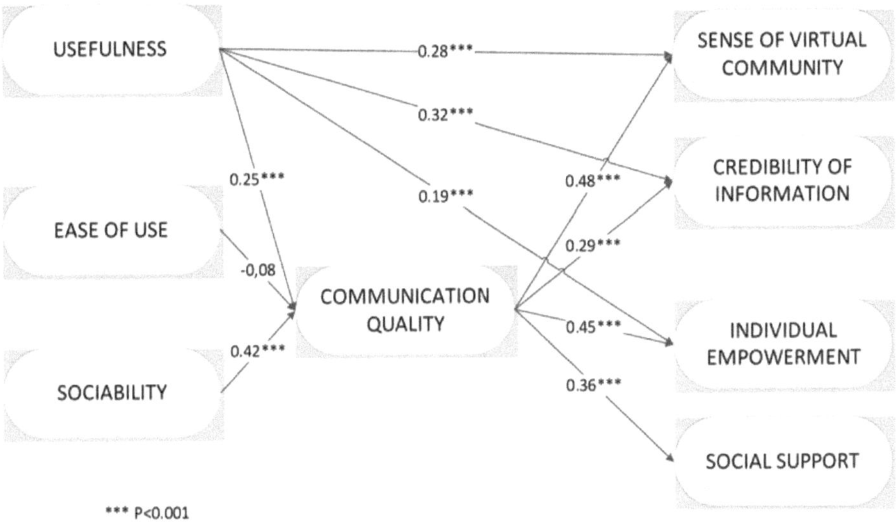

Figure 5.1: Estimated communicatively integrated model of online community

The results confirmed the important role of the quality of communication. Specifically, quality of communication was found to have a statistically significant impact on all dependent variables. The strongest was the influence on the sense of virtual community (β=0.48, p<0.001), followed by the influence on individual empowerment (β=0.45, p<0.001). Somewhat weaker, but still significant, was the influence on social support exchange (β=0.36, p<0.001) and the credibility of exchanged information (β=0.29, p<0.001). On the other hand, the data suggested that there were also associations with usability and sociability variables. Communicative quality was thus significantly dependent on the perceived sociability of the online community (γ=0.42, p<0.001) and its usefulness (γ=0.25, p<0.001), but was not associated with ease of use. Sense of virtual community seemed to be associated with usefulness (γ=0.28, sig<0.001), but not with sociability or ease of use. Usefulness also had some impact on individual empowerment (γ=0.19, p<0.001) and credibility of exchanged information (γ=0.32, sig<0.001). Social support, however, did not seem to be associated with usability and sociability factors, at least those included in the model.

5.5 Discussion and Conclusion

The intention of this chapter was to introduce the concept of communicatively integrated online community and empirically test it on the case of a specific online community. The results confirmed all three hypotheses and showed the validity of the proposed model. The interactive psycho-social outcomes, which the literature often points out as main building blocks of successful and sustainable online communities (Chu, 2009; Kraut & Resnick, 2011), are obviously to a large extent dependent on the type of communication that is present in an online community. Our results show that sense of virtual community, which is often pointed out as key social glue of online community (Blanchard et al., 2011; Kraut & Resnick, 2011), is strongly associated with the quality of communication in that community. Not only is the group aspect of identity related to quality of communication, but so too are personal competences and self-worth, as demonstrated by the strong association with individual empowerment. Thus, the first hypothesis was supported. The second and third hypotheses were also supported by our data, although the associations were somewhat weaker. In any case, the data confirmed that both supportive interactions and credibility of knowledge in the community are to some extent dependent on the quality of communication. In this way, we provided support for the idea that communicative action is vital for the healthy reproduction of identity, solidarities, and knowledge (Habermas, 1984), applied on the level of online communities. A healthy reproduction of online community is achieved through a) empowered community identity, anchored in the sense of virtual community and individual empowerment; b) fulfilling interpersonal relationships, manifested through social support among members of the online community; and c) the establishment of community knowledge that can be trusted and relied on. All these resources are especially important for an online health community, where people make important health-related decisions on the basis of the support and knowledge they receive (Tanis, 2008).

As already suggested, these outcomes do not depend only on the quality of communication, but also on a wider set of factors, which are implied in the socio-technical nature of the online community. At the empirical level, we managed to provide a limited insight into this issue by showing that both communicative quality and interactional outcomes are associated with usability and sociability which are provided by the managers and structure of the online community. Quality of communication was strongly associated with the structural conditions for users of the community to communicate smoothly. Interestingly, however, interactive outcomes were most intensively associated with the usefulness of the site hosting the online community, which suggests that beyond quality of communication, community owners have to ensure that users put trust in them and their ability to provide useful, credible information and an efficient user experience.

This part of our research also has some limitations, as consideration of the whole socio-technical network would demand inclusion of other important structural conditions and factors, such as management of norms (Petrič & Petrovčič (2014b)), online community policies (Preece, 2003), external factors and also psychological dispositions. When thinking about the external factors of the social glue of online communities, we could build on the aspects of Friedland's model of communicatively integrated community that has been neglected in our research—the macro- and meso-levels. This would, among others, necessitate consideration of the business model of online community, issues of online-offline integration, associations with other social actors such as sponsors, local community, media and politics, and in the case of the online health community, the healthcare system itself.

There are other limitations that warrant further research. For one, we focused on a specific type of online community in the empirical part of our research, while the proposed model of communicatively integrated community in principle should be valid for other types of communities, as well as social networking sites. In this case, the socio-technical nature of the community should be also taken into account, as different online platforms provide different affordances regarding the structure of communication between participants, clarity of membership, community boundaries, and so on.

This study should be understood as an attempt to put the (quality) of interaction at the center of analysis of online social domains, as already advised by Preece (2000) or Kraut et al. (2002), who noted a gap in conceptualization of the quality of online relations. Such analysis could also prove profitable for online community owners, as the management of online interactions might move its predominant focus from prevention of undesirable types of communication, such as hate speech, to the question of how to stimulate certain qualities of communication that have important psycho-social outcomes.

References

American Association for Public Opinion Research. (2011). Standard definitions: Final dispositions of case codes and outcome rates for surveys. Retrieved on Feb 14th 2014 from http://www.aapor.org/ethics/stddef.html#mail

Barak, A., & Dolev-Cohen, M. (2006). Does activity level in online support groups for distressed adolescents determine emotional relief? *Counselling and Psychotherapy Research*, *6*(3), 186–190.

Blanchard, A.L. (2008). Testing a model of sense of virtual community. *Computers in Human Behavior, 24*, 2107-2123.

Blanchard, A. L., Welbourne, J. A., & Boughton, M. A. (2011). A model of online trust: the mediating role of norms and sense of virtual community. *Information, Communication, and Society*, 14(1), 76-106.

Brown, T. A. (2006). *Confirmatory Factor Analysis for Applied Research*. New York: Guilford Press.

Browne, M.W., Cudeck, R.(1993). Alternative ways of assessing model fit. In K.A. Bollen & J.S. Long (Eds.), *Testing Structural Equation Models* (pp. 136–162). Beverly Hills, CA: Sage.

Caspi, A., Gorsky, P. (2006). Online deception: Prevalence, motivation and emotion. *Cyberpsychology & Behavior*, 9, 54-59.
Chu, K.M. (2009). A study of members' helping behaviors in online community, *Internet Research*, 19(3), 279-292.
Coulson, N. S., & Malik, S. (2012). Health-related online support communities. In *Encyclopedia of cyber-behaviour* (pp. 671–688). Hershey, PA: IGI Global.
Graham, T., Hajru, A. (2011). Reality TV as a trigger of everyday political talk in the net-based public sphere. *European Journal of Communication*, 26,18-32.
Demiris, G. (2006). The diffusion of virtual communities in health care: concepts and challenges. *Patient Education and Counseling, 62*, 178-88
Dewey, J. (1927). *The public and its problems*. New York: Holt-Rinehart & Winston.
Eder, K. (2007). Cognitive Sociology and the Theory of Communicative Action: The Role of Communication and Language in the Making of the Social Bond. *European journal of social theory*, 10(3), 389-408.
Ellison, N.B., Steinfield, C., Lampe, C. (2007). The benefits of facebook friends: social capital and college students' use of online social network sites. *Journal of Computer-Mediated Communication*, 12, 1143–1168.
Fox, S. (2011). *Medicine 2.0: Peer-to-peer healthcare. Report.* Washington, DC: Pew Internet & American Life Research Center.
Hara, N., Hew, K.F. (2007). Knowledge-sharing in an online community of health-care professionals. *Information Technology & People*, *20*(3), 235 – 261.
Jarvenpaa, S.L., Sirkka, L., Knoll, K. & Leidner, D.E. (1998). Is Anybody Out There? Antecedents of Trust in Global Virtual Teams, *Journal of Management Information Systems* 14(4), 29–64.
Jöreskog, K.G. & Sörbom, D. (2004). *LISREL 8.7 for Windows [Computer software]*. Skokie, IL: Scientific Software International, Inc.
Kim, J., Kim, J.E.. Theorizing Dialogic Deliberation: Everyday Political Talk as Communicative Action and Dialogue. Communication theory, 18, 51-70.
Koh, J., Kim, Y.G.(2003). Sense of virtual community: a conceptual framework and empirical validation. *International Journal of Electronic Commerce*, 8, 75-93.
Kraut, E.R., & Resnick, P. (2011). Encouraging Contribution to Online Communities. In R.E. Kraut & P. Resnick (Eds.), *Building successful online communities: Evidence-based social design (pp.*21-77). MIT Press, Cambridge, MA.
Lemire, M., Sicotte, C., Paré, G. (2008). Internet use and the logics of personal empowerment in health. Health *Policy, 88*, 130-40.
Loiacono, E.T., Watson, R.T., Goodhue, D.L. (2007). WebQual: An Instrument for Consumer Evaluation of Web Sites. *International Journal of Electronic Commerce*, 11(3), .
Luck, P., Norton, B. (2006). Collaborative management education: an online community in Europe? *International Jounral of Web Based Communities, 2*, 45 – 58.
Matzat, U. (2009). A theory of relational signals in online groups. *New Media & Society, 11*, 375-394.
Mead, G.H. (1962). *Mind, self, and society*. Chicago, London: The University of Chicago.
Menon, S.T. (2002). Toward a model of psychological health empowerment: implications for health care in multicultural communities. *Nurse Education Today, 22*, 28-39.
Miller, B. (1992). Collective action and rational choice: Place, community and the limites to individual self-interest. *Economic Geography*, 68(1), 22-43.
Petrič, G. (2006). Conceptualizing and measuring the social uses of the Internet: The case of personal web sites. The Information Society, 22(5), 291-301.
Petrič, G., Petrovčič, A., & Vehovar, V. (2011). Social uses of interpersonal communication technologies in a complex media environment. European Journal of Communication, 26(2), 116-132.

Petrič, G. (2014). Perceived Quality of Conversations in Online Communities: Conceptual Framework, Scale Development, and Empirical Validation. Cyberpsychology, Behavior, and Social Networking, 17(2), 82-90.

Petrič, G., & Petrovčič, A. (2014a). Individual and collective empowerment in online communities: the mediating role of communicative interaction in web forums. The Information Society, 30(3), 184-199.

Petrič, G., & Petrovčič, A. (2014b). Elements of the management of norms and their effects on the sense of virtual community. Online Information Review, 38(3), 436-454.

Postmes, T., Spears, R., Sakhel, K., & De Groot, D. (2001). Social influence in computer-mediated communication: The effects of anonymity on group behavior. *Personality and Social Psychology Bulletin*, *27*, 1242–1254.

Preece, J. (1998). Empathic communities: reaching out across the web. *Interactions*, 2, 32-43.

Preece, J. (2000). *Online Communities: Designing Usability, Supporting Sociability*. Chichester: John Wiley.

Preece, J., Maloney-Krichmar, D., Abras, C. (2003). History and emergence of online communities. In H.Rheingold (Ed.), *The virtual community: homesteading on the electronic frontier*. Cambridge, London: MIT.

Rizavi, S.S., Rizavi, A.L., & Mustafa, S.H. (2011). User perceived quality of social networking websites: A study of Lahore region. *Interdisciplinary Journal of Contemporary Research in Business*, 2(12).

Rojas, H., Shah, D.V., Friedland, L.A. (2011). A Communicative Approach to Social Capital. *Journal of Communication*, 61(4), 689-712.

Rollman, B.J., Krug, K., Parente, F. (2000). The Chat Room Phenomenon: Reciprocal Communication in Cyberspace . *CyberPsychology & Behavior*, 3, 161-166.

Sproul, L. & Kiesler, S. (1986). Reducing social context cues: Electronic mail in organizational communication. *Management Science*, 32, 1492-1512.

Stromer-Galley, J. (2007). Measuring Deliberation's Content: A coding Scheme. *Journal of Public Deliberation, 3*(1):1-37.

Suler, J.R., Phillips, W. (1998). The Bad Boys of Cyberspace: Deviant Behavior in Multimedia Chat Communities. *CyberPsychology and Behavior,1*, 275-294.

Tanis, M. (2008). Health-related online forums: what's the big attraction? Journal of Health Communication, 13, 698–14.

van Uden-Kraan, C.F., Drossaert, C.H.C., Taal, E. & et al. (2008). Empowering processes and outcomes of participation in online support groups for patients with breast cancer, arthritis, or fibromyalgia. *Qualitative Health Research*, 18, 405–17.

van Uden-Kraan, C.F., Drossaert, C.H.C., Taal, E., & et al. (2009). Participation in online patient support groups endorses patients' empowerment. Patient Education and Counseling, 74, 61–69.

Wagner, C, Ip, R.K.F., Cheung, K.S.K., Lee, F.S.L. (2005). Deceptive Communication in Virtual Communities. *Proceedings of the 38th Annual Hawaii International Conference on System Sciences (HICSS'05)*, 1, 21-23.

Wellman, B. (2001). Physical place and cyberplace: The rise of personalized networking. *International Journal of Urban and Regional Research, 25*, 227-252.

Wright, S. (2011). Politics as usual? Revolution, normalization and a new agenda for online deliberation. *New Media & Society, 14, 244-261.*

Zimmerman, M. A. (1995). Psychological empowerment: issues and illustrations. *American Journal of Community Psychology*, 23(5), 581–599.

Jamie E. Guillory, Jeffrey T. Hancock

6 Effects of Network Connections on Deception and Halo Effects in Linkedin

Abstract: On social networking websites (SNS) there is a general goal to convey desirable self-presentations, which can be achieved in many ways, from lying about qualifications in one's Linkedin profile to posting flattering Facebook profile photos. In this chapter we use two experiments to explore the pervasive influence that our social relationships have on how we construct our self-presentations and how others form perceptions of our self-presentations in SNS. In the first experiment, participants' deception was compared across three self-presentational resume settings: a traditional resume, private Linkedin profile, or publicly available Linkedin profile. Findings suggest that the public nature of Linkedin resume claims affected the kinds of deception used, such that public Linkedin resumes were less deceptive about the kinds of information that count most to employers, namely an applicant's prior work experience and responsibilities, but were more deceptive about interests and hobbies. In a second experiment, we explore how halo effects, defined as global impressions about an individual formed using a single characteristic (e.g., physical attractiveness), can extend beyond the individual and become "extended halo effects" (EHEs). In SNS, EHE predicts that tie strength and status will affect global impression formation of the individual. Participants in a second study evaluated online Linkedin profiles, which manipulated the strength and status of a tie to a recommender. Impressions were positively biased in the presence of strong, high-status ties, despite actual job experience, supporting EHE.

Many of the decisions that we make everyday are driven by the desire to convey positive impressions to others. We carefully consider our wardrobe choices or choose to eat at a trendy restaurant to impress a date. We choose to wear a suit and practice a presentation to appear competent to our supervisor and work colleagues. The desire to convey positive impressions is a major force driving human behavior (Goffman, 1959) and is often referred to as a self-presentational goal. In online contexts, self-presentational goals range as widely as they do face-to-face, from wanting to appear qualified for a job on Linkedin, to wanting to appear romantically desirable on Match.com, and typically involve the desire to elicit a positive impression (Curtis, 1992; Donath, 1999; Roberts & Parks, 1999).

Opportunities for self-presentation online are abundant and understanding impression formation via studies of self-presentation has long been a focus of computer-mediated communication research. In computer-mediated spaces we can share a wide variety of information that reflects who we are to a number of different audiences. In a short period of time personal profiles for SNSs have become common. SNS profiles link individuals' profiles to the profiles of friends, acquaintances and colleagues. SNS include friendship-oriented profiles, such as profiles on Facebook, and more professionally-oriented profiles, such those seen on Linkedin, in which people upload online versions of their resume and form connections with former and current colleagues, supervisors and friends. SNS link our self-presentations with known and unknown others, providing the opportunity to widely disseminate self-presentations.

While the self-presentations that we craft, both online and face-to-face, are largely our own, the information that we share about ourselves and indeed the way this information is perceived by others is heavily influenced by our social networks. In the chapter that follows, we examine the ways in which our social relationships influence how people construct self-presentations and how others form perceptions of these self-presentations in SNS. We demonstrate these relationships with two experiments. The first explores how social relationships influence deceptive behavior on the professional SNS Linkedin. The second investigates the influence that information about social network connections (e.g., characteristics of and relationships with ties) has on others' perceptions of online self-presentations on Linkedin.

6.1 The Effect of Linkedin on Deception in Resumes

From a self-presentation management perspective, the fundamental desire to maintain positive impressions suggests that social networks are important to shaping the information that people choose to include in self-presentations. Because SNS profiles are virtual self-presentations and are not physically connected to the self, there is frequently concern that the desire to maintain positive impressions will lead people to engage in deception in order to accomplish self-presentational goals. Indeed self-presentational goals are a common and important motivator for deception (DePaulo et al., 2003). SNS profiles offer novel opportunities for deception not possible face to-face. Walther (1996, 2007) argues that in computer-mediated settings, users take advantage of the affordances of the medium, such as the reduced cues and the ability to edit, to enhance self-presentations and inflate others' positive impressions of the self.

Though the online environment may facilitate the use of deception to accomplish self-presentational goals, features of this context also have the potential to constrain deception and foster honesty. SNS profiles make self-presentations publicly available and link individuals to the profile who can verify whether information is deceptive. Researchers both on and offline have long demonstrated the importance of social relationships in fostering honesty between individuals (Resnick & Varian, 1997; Resnick, Kuwabara, Zeckhauser, & Friedman, 2000; Zimmerman & Kurapati, 2002). For example, recommender systems on websites like eBay help to ensure that transactions remain honest by providing users, who may have no previous history with a seller, with valuable information about the seller's trustworthiness.

Affordances that allow for social links between the virtual representation of self that one encounters online and the face-to-face, offline self can improve the likelihood of honesty in SNS.

In the first experiment we investigate how social connections in the professional SNS Linkedin influence the way that we use deception in resume profiles (Guillory & Hancock, 2012). We predicted that people would take a profile's potential audience into consideration when crafting resume profiles so as to avoid being caught in a lie by network members who can verify information as deceptive. More specifically, we predicted that people would lie less about objective information that network members could verify as truthful (or deceptive) (e.g., job experience and responsibilities), but would instead seek to meet self-presentational goals by lying more about subjective information that would be difficult for former employers or colleagues to recognize as lies (e.g., interests, hobbies) while enhancing self-presentations. For example, if applying for a job requiring large amounts of travel a person might lie in their resume about being interested in travel to appear to be a better fit for the position. The opposite should be true for people creating private profiles that their social network cannot access.

Linkedin provides an ideal context for exploring how the publicness of a SNS profile affects self-presentation and deception. Undergraduate participants came to our lab where they were randomly assigned to create a resume in one of the following three conditions: 1) a traditional resume created in Microsoft Word, 2) a completely private Linkedin resume profile that only the user and researchers could access, and 3) a completely public Linkedin resume profile available to anyone online via a web search. Participants were asked to create the resume based on a job description for a consultant position that would be very difficult for a student to attain. Participants were not explicitly encouraged to lie, but were asked to craft their profile to best fit the job description and were offered the added incentive of receiving a $100 gift card if their resume was determined to be the best fit for the position. Once participants completed their resumes, we revealed to students the study's true purpose of exploring deception in resumes. Participants then identified all lies (i.e., any information intended to create false belief) and described more truthful versions of the deception to provide us with a better idea of the types of lies that participants used in their profiles.

Deceptions identified by participants were coded based on how verifiable information was. Verifiable information included aspects of the self-presentation that could be conceivably confirmed by others online. Lies in this category were related to responsibilities, information describing responsibilities at a job or activity; abilities, information indicating an ability to use software, language, or anything involving expertise; and involvement, information indicating level of participation in an activity or job. Unverifiable information made up a smaller subset of lies and included information typically unknown to colleagues. These lies related to interests, and indicated an interest, motivation, or concentration in some aspect of life. These lies included information about interests or hobbies.

We found that participants lied about three times on average. The number of lies that people told did not differ between the experimental conditions, suggesting that whether resume information is publicly available does not influence the frequency of deception in resumes. In line with our predictions we found that it was the type of lies that differed between the self-presentational conditions. Participants who created public Linkedin resumes lied less about responsibilities relative to participants who created private Linkedin and traditional resumes. Participants in the public condition instead lied more about interests relative to participants in the two private profile and traditional resume conditions. Comparisons for abilities and involvement deception categories did not differ.

The findings from this study are consistent with claims that self-presentational motivations drive deception (Levine et al., 2010). Participants in the three conditions used deception to accomplish the same self-presentational goal of appearing qualified for a job, but did so using different types of deception. When resumes were private, participants lied about things that were important to helping them get the job, such as the amount of time spent at a job, in order to appear to have more experience. While lies such as these more directly accomplished the self-presentational goal of appearing qualified for the job, using this type of deception when a resume was publicly available online would risk detection by members of the social network. Therefore, people creating public resumes chose to lie about information that would make them appear to be a good fit for the job without the risk of being caught lying. In these cases participants lied more about hobbies or interests, for example being interested in travel and learning new languages because the job requirements included travel and fluency in a second language. Websites such as Linkedin, which make resume information public and link to social networks, can encourage honesty for resume claims that are most important to getting a job, such as claims about experience and responsibility. However, participants considered publicness strategically, adapting lies based on whether information could be verified by others online, suggesting that public availability of information does not guarantee honesty. Instead, the availability of SNS self-presentations to our networks shapes how we use deception to accomplish self-presentational goals.

6.2 Impact of Social Networks on Impression Formation in Linkedin

The first experiment illustrates the importance of our social network in shaping how people construct self-presentations. How might social networks influence the way that others perceive the self-presentations that people share in SNS? People often use multiple sources of information to form impressions of an individual. While the most important source of information is often what individuals say about themselves, our first experiment and other research suggests that the veracity of self-presentations in SNS is suspect because individuals can craft inflated or deceptive self-presentations (e.g., Guillory & Hancock, 2012, Herring & Martinson, 2004; Walther, 2007). People expect this type of manipulation and rely not only on personally shared information, but also on information learned from other sources in forming impressions in SNS (Ellison, Heino, & Gibbs, 2006).

One such source is what others say about a person. Consider, as an example, the process of forming an impression of someone based on his or her Facebook profile. These profiles contain self- and other-generated comments and content (e.g., links, videos, photographs) provided by friends, family and acquaintances. Other-generated information about the individual (e.g., others' Facebook wall posts) is more influential for impression formation than personally generated information (Walther, Van Der Heide, Kim, Westerman, & Tong, 2008). As Will Rogers once said: "Get someone else to blow your horn, and the sound will carry twice as far."

A third source of information that is used in impression formation goes beyond what others say about a target individual, and instead pertains to who the other person is and how they are connected to the individual. Technically, people with whom the individual is connected are referred to as "ties" (Granovetter, 1983). SNS make this third source of information readily available by capturing and making visible relationships with and characteristics of ties (boyd & Ellison, 2007). This third source of information is both external to the individual (i.e., it is information about the individual's ties) and is not easily subject to manipulation.

Research exploring impression formation on Facebook and other SNS suggests that people use information about our ties' characteristics (e.g., extroversion, physical attractiveness) to form parallel impressions of our characteristics (Walther et al., 2008; Utz, 2010). Thus social network information (i.e., information pertaining to our network connections and our relationships with these connections) should play a role in impression formation that goes above and beyond information that is shared by the self or by others about the self. That is, to follow the Will Rogers aphorism, who blows the horn should also matter.

Social network ties clearly have effects on how an individual is perceived. For example, having a referral from a current employee leads to more positive perceptions of a job candidate's resume and a greater likelihood of being offered an interview and employment compared to candidates without referrals (Fernandez & Weinberg, 1997). When supervisors in an organization perceive that an individual has a friendship with a prominent person in the same organization, their performance reputation improves (Kilduff & Krackhardt, 1994). In SNS, people with attractive friends who post on their Facebook profile's "wall" are rated as more physically and socially attractive (i.e., likeable) than people with less attractive friends who post on their wall (Walther et al., 2008).

These research findings are consistent with the well-established halo effect (Thorndike, 1920; Nisbett & Wilson, 1977). Halo effects occur when global evaluations of an individual are made based on impressions of specific attributes. Thorndike's (1920) original conception of the halo effect suggests that people are unable to resist the affective impact that global perceptions of an individual (i.e., forming a generally positive or negative impression of an individual based on a given attribute) have in influencing subsequent evaluations of specific, often unrelated, attributes. This biasing process occurs outside of conscious awareness and these effects occur even when there is sufficient information to allow for more accurate assessments (Nisbett & Wilson, 1977).

The halo effect has been applied strictly to how an individual's characteristics in one dimension affect perceptions of that individual in another dimension. We expand on that original concept and argue that the network cases described above (Fernandez & Weinberg, 1997; Kilduff & Krackhardt, 1994; Walther et al., 2008), in which people were judged based on the characteristics of their ties, are examples of a term we've coined called the "extended halo effect" (referred to as EHE from here on). In particular, EHE should occur when the qualities of network ties (rather than qualities of the individual) globally affect impressions formed about the individual. EHE is distinct from the halo effect in that impression formation is influenced by reactions to information that is in some way external to the individual (e.g., information about their relationship with ties in their network, or about the characteristics of their ties), rather than information about their personal characteristics. While the halo effect would predict that a job candidate's high status should lead an interviewer to judge the candidate's other qualities (e.g., competence) more positively, EHE predicts that the high status of a job candidate's tie (e.g., a friend, boss, or family member) should lead the interviewer to judge the candidate more positively. Importantly, these effects should operate regardless of whether the interviewer has more pertinent information to assess a given quality.

While previous studies have demonstrated EHEs in showing that judgments about a tie's quality, such as extroversion, are used to make parallel judgments of the same quality for the target individual (i.e., extroversion) (Walther et al., 2008; Utz, 2010), research has yet to demonstrate EHEs that affect global impressions by influencing the general valence of impressions of a person's characteristics. We believe that this is an important extension of EHE, allowing us to predict the impact of tie characteristics on impression formation more broadly.

Two points are crucial to the conceptualization of EHE. First, we don't conceive of EHE as being the sole influence driving impression formation (i.e., overriding effects of self- and other-generated information), but rather identify it as one of multiple sources of bias that contributes to impression formation. Second, in line with the halo effect, EHE does not suggest a universally positive or negative reaction to information for all people, as certain qualities (e.g., physical attractiveness) can elicit different affective reactions based on individual differences (e.g., gender) (Försterling, Preikschas, & Agthe, 2007).

Linkedin provides a useful context to explore how EHEs influence impression formation. Understanding impression formation in the context of a resume is particularly important, as specific information about ties in one's network may have the potential to influence perceptions of the individual as a qualified job candidate. Both the strength and status of ties in a person's network are important characteristics for studying social networks in organizational settings (Bian, 1997; Granovetter, 1983) and should be important factors driving EHEs.

The status of a tie provides information about the network member's status in an organization and is defined in relative terms based on the status of the individual being evaluated. Ties can have relatively high status, such as a supervisor or professor, or low status, such as a subordinate or student. Making information about ties visible along with more traditional sources of impression-bearing information (e.g., self- and other-generated information) in online resume profiles (e.g., Linkedin profiles) should impact perceptions of the profile holder. The status of one's ties can have important implications for an individual across a broad spectrum of personal outcomes. For instance, the status of ties in an individual's social network can influence career outcomes, including promotions and advancement to senior-level positions (Podolny & Baron, 1997). A tie's high status also conveys positive information about their success in organizations (Judge, Higgins, Thorensen, & Barrick, 1999), suggesting that they are seen as more qualified for positions than their lower status counterparts. High-status ties should also be seen as more credible or trustworthy than low-status ties, given that the costliness of engaging in untrustworthy behaviors is higher for these individuals (Kidwell, 2004). One reason for this is that high-status members of organizations are often products of a history of trusting relationships with others, which allowed them to achieve their status (Kramer, 1999; Lewicki & Bunker, 1995; Shapiro, Sheppard, & Cheraskin, 1992). We predict that positive perceptions formed of high status ties should positively bias perceptions of an individual's professional credibility, defined here as the degree to which an individual is seen as trustworthy and qualified for employment.

Social network research also demonstrates the importance of strong ties for personal outcomes. Tie strength refers to the closeness of a person's relationship with ties. More specifically, strength of ties is defined in terms of emotional intensity, intimacy, reciprocity, and time spent with ties (Granovetter, 1983) irrespective of status. Research on the process of obtaining employment highlights the importance of strong ties. Most people found their first job with substantial support from helpers with whom they held strong ties (Bian, 1997).

Strong ties should also have a positive EHE on impression formation. Strong ties are likely to know a person well and have the ability to validate information in their profile, suggesting that their presence in the network should provide information for impression formation that is higher in value. Although strength of ties does not provide direct information about an individual's professional credibility or integrity, we predict that the value that their presence conveys should carry over to affect global impressions of the individual.

In our second experiment, we explored EHE by systematically comparing the impact of tie status and strength on impression formation (Guillory & Hancock, 2011). Fictitious versions of Linkedin profiles were created that varied the strength (strong versus weak) and status (high versus low) of a tie to the profile holder. To understand how EHE operates in conjunction with self-generated information, the level of experience shared in the profile was also manipulated (high versus low experience).

Each participant viewed either low or high-experience versions of four fictitious Linkedin profiles (between-subjects factor). Low-experience profiles included one internship and membership in two groups or associations. High-experience profiles included four internships and participation in four or more groups or associations. Experience in all profiles was comparable in quality (e.g., from the same or similar caliber organizations). Other profile information was held constant across profiles.

Each profile had a recommendation from a tie that varied in status and strength of connection to the profile holder. Strength of tie was manipulated within subjects, with participants viewing two profiles with strong ties and two with weak ties. Tie strength was operationalized within the text of each profile's recommendation. Strong-tie recommendations indicated a close, professional relationship with the profile holder, suggesting that the recommender knew the profile holder well and that the two interacted frequently (Granovetter, 1983). Weak-tie recommendations indicated infrequent interaction and suggested that the recommender did not know the profile holder well due to circumstances beyond the profile holder's control (e.g., working in different departments, overseas travel, etc.). The text of recommendations from strong and weak ties was carefully controlled to ensure the only differences were in information about the strength of tie to the profile holder.

Status of ties was also manipulated within subjects with participants seeing two profiles with a low status tie recommendation and two with a high status tie recommendation. Status was operationalized with a high or low-status job title of the recommender for the profile. Low-status ties were operationalized using a low-status job title (e.g., Intern) at an organization where the profile holder interned. High-status ties were operationalized using a high status title at an organization (e.g., Vice President) where the person interned.

After viewing each profile participants completed measures indicating their perceptions of the profile holder's professional credibility. Professional credibility was assessed using a single scale that included the following: two original items that assessed the person's quality of job experience and likelihood of being hired for an entry-level job and an established scale of items assessing the person's overall credibility or trustworthiness (Leathers, 1992).

Upon analysis we found that high-status ties elevated perceptions of professional credibility relative to low-status ties, indicating that the presence of high-status ties leads to higher ratings of professional credibility. We also found that strong ties elevated perceptions of professional credibility in profiles relative to weak ties, suggesting that the presence of strong ties leads to higher ratings of a person's professional credibility. These effects emerged regardless of whether the profile holder had a high or low level of job experience. Information provided by the profile holder was important, as high experience profile holders were rated as significantly higher in professional credibility than low experience profile holders, but this factor did not interact with the strength and status of ties. This finding indicates that strength and status of ties influence perceptions of online self-presentations beyond the effects of self-generated profile information. These findings demonstrate EHEs, in which global impressions about professional credibility were biased by specific attributes of the network ties (strength and status of ties).

The findings from this study are consistent with other theoretical frameworks, which explain the impact of others' characteristics on perceptions of the individual. Heider's (1958) balance theory, for example, suggests that people strive for cognitive consistency between related objects or entities when imbalance exists in the perceptions of these related objects. Our finding that profile holders with a high-status tie were perceived as more professionally credible is consistent with balance theory. Participants' motivation to maintain balance in the valence of their cognitions between the perceptions of the tie and the profile holder may have resulted in their evaluation of both entities as similar.

Walther et al. (2008) indicate assimilation as an explanation for their research finding that Facebook profile holders with physically attractive friends are evaluated as more physically and socially attractive. In this case, assimilation suggests that characteristics of network ties are incorporated into evaluations of the individual on the same characteristic via the perception of friendship. Utz (2010) also demonstrated assimilation effects in SNS, with profile holders being judged as more popular when they had friends who appeared to be extraverted in profile photographs. Both balance theory and assimilation suggest that information about related individuals is used to evaluate targets.

While these explanations are consistent with the majority of the findings from the second experiment, they do not explain all of them. For instance, neither of these theories can explain why a strong, low-status tie led to more positive impressions of the target's professional credibility. According to either balance theory or assimilation, the low-status of the tie should be negatively biasing for judgments about the target. Instead, we found that both tie strength and status made independent contributions to the global assessments of the target, as predicted by EHE.

Importantly, early work on the original halo effect suggests that this process occurs outside of conscious awareness (Nisbett & Wilson, 1977). If EHE indeed biases perceptions unconsciously it makes sense that participants formed positive impressions based on the positive information conveyed by the relationship to the tie (e.g., strong tie), without more carefully considering how strength might be perceived more negatively in the context of other qualities (e.g., low-status tie). While this study did not test whether bias occurred consciously or unconsciously, we speculate that EHE is likely the outcome of a person perception heuristic. Heuristics are-mental shortcuts for perception formation that allow users to make judgments without carefully evaluating all of the available information (Chaiken, 1980). It is possible that the presence of these positive characteristics (e.g., high-status and strong ties) provided users with a heuristic for forming perceptions about an individual's professional credibility. While this study did not measure whether EHEs were the result of conscious (or unconscious) processing, it will be important for future research to explore whether the processing that produces these effects occurs at a conscious or unconscious level.

6.3 Conclusions

Taken together, these findings from both experiments demonstrate the importance of considering information from multiple sources in understanding judgments of self-presentations in networked contexts. Experiment 1 calls into question the veracity of claims made about the self in Linkedin profiles, suggesting that other sources of information are also important to impression formation. Experiment 2 highlights network tie information as a source of information that has bearing on impression formation in a professional context. SNS make salient information about our social network ties and our relationships with these individuals. Although this network information has always been available, these sites emphasize and make this information visible. EHEs thus have the potential to dramatically change the dynamics of impression formation in SNS due to the abundance of available information about network members (Tufekci, 2008). Although earlier studies have demonstrated people's tendency to use network connections as social resources to elicit positive personal outcomes (e.g., Bian, 1997; Podolny & Baron, 1997), this research suggests that the simple presence of these connections in one's network biases interpersonal impression formation.

We leave you to consider the emergence of additional sources of information influencing impression formation in SNS that go beyond the sources identified in this chapter. As self-presentations become increasingly mediated, new sources of information identified by Tong, Van Der Heide, Langwell and Walther (2008) as system-generated information, also bias impression formation. Researchers have identified the number of friends on SNS as one type of system-generated information that biases impressions of the individual (Tong et al, 2008; Utz, 2010). While the present data clearly indicate that information about the characteristics of network ties is important for impression formation, these emergent sources should also be considered in future work exploring EHEs.

References

Bian, Y. (1997). Bringing strong ties back in: Indirect connection, bridges, and job search in China. *American Sociological Review, 62*, 355-385.

Chaiken, S. (1980). Heuristic and systematic information processing and the use of source versus message cues in persuasion. *Journal of Personality and Social Psychology, 39*, 752-766.

Curtis, P. (1992). Mudding: Social phenomena in text-based virtual realities. In D. Schuler (Ed.), *DIAC-92: Directions and implications of advanced computing* (pp. 48-68). Palo Alto, CA: Computer Professionals for Social Responsibility.

DePaulo, B.M., Lindsay, J.J., Malone, B.E., Muhlenbruck, L., Charlton, K., & Cooper, H. (2003). Cues to deception. *Psychology Bulletin, 129*, 74-118.

Donath, J.S. (1999). Identity and deception in the virtual community. In M.A. Smith & P. Kollack (Eds.), *Communities in Cyberspace*. (p. 29-59). New York, NY: Routledge.

Ellison, N.B., Heino, R., & Gibbs, J. (2006). Managing impressions online: Self-presentation process in the online dating environment. *Journal of Computer-Mediated Communication, 11*, 415-441.

Fernandez, R.M., & Weinberg, N. (1997). Sifting and sorting: Personal contacts and hiring in aretail bank. *American Sociological Review, 62*, 883-899.

Försterling, F., Preikschas, S., & Agthe, M. (2007). Ability, luck, and looks: An evolutionary look at achievement ascriptions and the sexual attribution bias. *Journal of Personality & Social Psychology, 92*, 775-788.

Goffman, E. (1959). *The Presentation of Self in Everyday Life*. Garden City, NY: Doubleday.

Granovetter, M. S. (1983). The strength of weak ties: A network theory revisited. *Sociological Theory, 1*, 201-233.

Guillory, J., & Hancock, J.T. (2011, May). The Extended Halo Effect in social networking websites: The impact of social ties on impression formation. Paper presented at the 61st annual conference of the International Communication Association, Division: Communication and Technology, Boston, MA.

Guillory, J. & Hancock, J.T. (2012). The effect of Linkedin on deception in resumes. *Cyberpsychology, Behavior, & Social Networks, 15*, 135-140.

Heider, F. (1958). *The psychology of interpersonal relations*. New York: Wiley.

Herring, S.C., & Martinson, S. (2004). Assessing gender authenticity in computer-mediated language use: Evidence from an identity game. *Journal of Language & Social Psychology, 23*, 424-446.

Judge, T.A., Higgins, C.A., Thoresen, C.J., & Barrick, M.R. (1999). The Big Five personality traits, general mental ability, and career success. *Personnel Psychology, 52*, 621- 652.

Kidwell, R.E. (2004). "Small" lies, big trouble: The unfortunate consequences of resume padding. *Journal of Business Ethics, 5*, 175-184.

Kilduff, M., & Krackhardt, D. (1994). Bringing the individual back in: A structural analysis of the internal market for reputation in organizations. *Academy of Management Journal, 37*, 87-108.

Kramer, R.M. (1999). Trust and distrust in organizations: Emerging perspectives, enduring questions. *Annual Review of Psychology, 50*, 569-598.

Leathers, D.G. (1992). *Successful Nonverbal Communication: Principles and Applications*. (2nd ed.) New York: Macmillan.

Levine, T.R., Kim, R.K., & Hamel L.M. (2010). People lie for a reason: An experimental test of the principle of veracity. *Communication Research Reports, 27*, 271–285.

Lewicki, R.J., Bunker, B.B. (1995). Trust in relationships: A model of trust development and decline. In B. B. Bunker & J. Z. Rubin, J. Z. (Eds.), *Conflict, Cooperation, & Justice*. San Franciso: Jossey-Bass.

Nisbett, R.E., & Wilson, T.D. (1977). The halo effect: Evidence for unconscious alteration of judgments. *Journal of Personality & Social Psychology, 34*, 250-256.

Podolony, J. M., & Baron, J. N. (1997). Resources and relationships: Social networks and mobility in the workplace. *American Sociological Review, 62*, 673-693.

Resnick, P., Kuwabara, K., Zeckhauser, R., & Friedman, E. (2000). Reputation systems. *Communications of the ACM, 43*(12), 45–48.

Resnick, P., & Varian, H.R. (1997). Recommender systems. *Communications of the ACM, 40*(3), 56–58.

Roberts, L.D., & Parks, M.R. (1999). The social geography of gender-switching in virtual environments on the Internet. *Information Communication, & Society, 2*, 521- 540.

Shapiro, D. L., Sheppard, B. H., & Cheraskin, L. (1992). Business on a handshake. *Negotiation Journal, 8*, 365-377.

Thorndike, E. L. (1920). A constant error in psychological ratings. *Journal of Applied Psychology, 4*, 25-29.

Tong, S., Van Der Heide, B., Langwell, L. & Walther, J. B. (2008). Too much of a good thing? The relationship between number of friends and interpersonal impressions in Facebook. *Journal of Computer-Mediated Communication, 13*, 531-549.

Tufekci, Z. (2008). Can you see me? Audience and disclosure regulation in online social network sites. *Bulletin of Science, Technology, & Society, 28*(20), 20-37.

Utz, S. (2010). Show me your friends and I will tell you what type of person you are: How one's profile, number of friends, and type of friends influence impression formation on social network sites. *Journal of Computer-Mediated Communication, 15*, 314-335.

Walther, J. B. (1996). Computer-mediated communication: Impersonal, interpersonal, and hyperpersonal interaction. *Communication Research, 23*, 3-43.

Walther, J. B. (2007). Selective self-presentation in computer-mediated communication: Hyperpersonal dimensions of technology, language, and cognition. *Computers in Human Behavior, 23*, 2358-2557.

Walther, J. B., Van Der Heide, B., Kim, S., Westerman, D., & Tong, S. T. (2008). The role of friends' appearance and behavior on evaluations of individuals on Facebook: Are we known by the company we keep? *Human Communication Research, 34*, 28-49.

Zimmerman, J., & Kurapati, K. (2002). Exposing profiles to build trust in a recommender. In: Proceedings of the Conference on Human Factors in Computing Systems CHI 2001 Extended Abstracts. ACM Press, New York, pp. 608–609.

Jesse Fox

7 The Dark Side of Social Networking Sites in Romantic Relationships

Abstract: Social networking sites (SNSs) enrich many aspects of our relationships, yet they also have the potential for harm. Although considerable research has focused on the benefits of SNSs, there is a "dark side" to online social networks, particularly in romantic relationships. Distinctive affordances of SNSs (e.g., visibility and connectivity) enable new types of negative communication outcomes in romantic relationships as news about the couple is made visible to both partners' networks, including friends, family, and ex-partners. Thus, SNSs can be a source of stress and relational turbulence for romantic partners from the early stages of dating to the post-breakup phase. When dating, users may sense disinterest based on a lack of SNS interaction or perceive competition among other network "friends" observed interacting on the romantic partner's page. Once the romantic relationship becomes exclusive, partners may experience pressure from the partner or the network to establish the relationship as "Facebook official" and advertise it on his/her page. In the relationship, techno-incompatibility may be source of conflict as partners have different patterns of use (e.g., one partner is constantly on and the other rarely is). Partners may also maintain different perceptions of appropriateness and privacy for communication within and about the relationship on SNSs, leading to conflict about what is shared publicly on the site. Partner monitoring on SNSs (i.e., "Facebook stalking"), a common practice influenced by attachment style, can be deleterious during and after romantic relationships. SNSs also provide unique sources of distress in the process and wake of relationship dissolution.

7.1 Introduction

Social networking websites (SNSs) have become an integral medium for communicating both within and about interpersonal relationships (Stafford & Hillyer, 2012; Turkle, 2011). The SNS Facebook is ubiquitous with over 1 billion active monthly users worldwide, and nearly half of Facebook users visit the site at least six days a week (Facebook, 2013). China's Qzone hosts over 700 million users, and several others (Google+, Tumblr, Weibo, and Twitter) boast at least a quarter of a million users globally (Smith, 2013). Given the widespread nature of use and the time users devote to them, it is imperative to examine the effects of SNSs on relationships.

Traditionally, SNSs have been lauded for their ability to unite distal friends, maintain relational ties, and promote social capital (e.g., McEwan, 2013; Valenzuela,

Park, & Kee, 2009). Some users claim that SNSs facilitate relationships by lowering the barriers to initiation and development (Fox, Warber, & Makstaller, 2013). Although considerable research has focused on these benefits of using SNSs, it is also important to examine the "dark side" of computer-mediated communication (DeAndrea, Tong, & Walther, 2011). For example, although positive feedback on SNSs yields benefits for users, negative feedback leads to decreased self-esteem and psychological well-being in users (Valkenburg, Peter, & Schouten, 2006). Scholars have noted negative psychological outcomes when users experience rejection on SNSs, either through others ignoring "friend requests" (i.e., attempts to link profiles on the site) or "unfriending" the user (i.e., terminating an existing link on the site; Bevan, Pfyl, & Barclay, 2012; Tokunaga, 2011a). Nielsen (2012) asked users what their typical feelings were after using SNSs, and 21% reported they were negative. Most commonly, users said they were "sad," "angry," "jealous," "overwhelmed," and "anxious," also feeling that they had "wasted time." Thus, several studies have indicated that there are negative consequences associated with SNS use.

One area where the dark side of SNSs may be the most prevalent is that of romantic relationships. Recent research has begun to acknowledge the role that SNSs play in the initiation, escalation, maintenance, and dissolution of romantic relationships (e.g., Fox & Warber, 2013; Fox, Warber, et al., 2013; Marshall, 2012; Papp, Danielewicz, & Cayemberg, 2012; Utz & Beukeboom, 2011). Facebook often provides substantial information about partners to each other and to the network. This flow of information allows people to accomplish significant information seeking and uncertainty reduction (Berger & Calabrese, 1975) without engaging in direct interaction with their partner (Fox, Warber, et al., 2013; Tokunaga, 2011b). However, it also introduces new sources of potential conflict into relationships, may create undesirable uncertainty, and gives other social network members much greater access to partners' information.

7.2 Affordances of SNSs

SNSs have specific affordances that enable the actions one can take within the site (Treem & Leonardi, 2012). *Connectivity* or *association* enables network members, no matter how disparate or geographically distant, to recognize each other's presence and often view each other's content through the common node or "friend." *Visibility* means that information that was not easily accessible or publicized previously is now shared among the network (Treem & Leonardi, 2012). Given that social network members often have a significant influence on an individual's romantic relationships (Hogerbrugge, Komter, & Scheepers, 2013; Sprecher, 2010), the affordances of SNSs may maximize the network's influence on—or meddling in—a romantic relationship. *Persistence*, *editability*, and *replicability* are tied to the digital nature of the text, pictures, and other content posted to an SNS. Because digital material is easily captured, saved, duplicated, and recirculated, information shared online may be accessible long after the initial post and difficult to remove permanently (Treem & Leonardi, 2012). Furthermore, several tools enable digital information to be manipulated, from simple cropping to intensive reconfiguration using programs such as Photoshop.

Given these affordances, social networking sites can initiate, promote, and exacerbate many facets of the dark side of relationships. One particular Facebook feature, the ability to go "Facebook official" or "FBO" (i.e., link to one's partner in the relationship status), affords partner-specific connectivity (Fox, Warber, et al., 2013; Fox & Warber, 2013; Papp et al., 2012). Although this opportunity may seem like a way to promote togetherness, partners often have differing perceptions of the meaning and timing of this relationship status (Fox & Warber, 2013), which can lead to conflict (Osborn, Fox, & Warber, 2012). Connectivity and visibility enable individuals to view information about romantic partners that they may not have regular access to, such as seeing pictures and posts from previous relationships, which may foster relational uncertainty, jealousy, or suspicions. Persistence and replicability can make it difficult to hide relational indiscretions or otherwise suspicious behaviors if they are posted to an SNS. Even if the offending content is removed, others may have stored it or shared it among other networks. Thus, the same SNS affordances that allow us to share experiences and memories amongst friends also have the potential to do damage in romantic relationships.

7.3 Technological Incompatibility

Perhaps one of the earliest relationship difficulties to emerge on account of SNSs is *technological incompatibility*, which is any problematic discrepancy in technology use between partners. This incompatibility may include the amount of use, the timing of the use, the type of connections maintained, or the content shared on a site (Osborn et al., 2012). For example, Britta may get frustrated with Jeff's constant Twitter use, feeling he should spend less time online and more time talking to her. Alternatively, Olivia may not be on Facebook frequently, but Elliot gets annoyed that she insists on checking her notifications throughout dinner. Olivia, on the other hand, doesn't like that Elliot is still friends with all of his ex-girlfriends on Facebook, given she unfriended all of her exes. Philip may feel uncomfortable with Terrance's insistence on posting all of their intimate honeymoon pictures publicly on Instagram, because Philip prefers to keep his social media presence professional.

Any of these discrepancies in SNS use may create conflict for romantic partners. Hand, Thomas, Buboltz, et al. (2013) found that perceptions of the romantic partner's social media use were negatively associated with relational intimacy. Rather than remaining unclear or making assumptions about the other person's preference, it may be important for romantic partners at any stage of a relationship to discuss their wishes and expectations to make sure they understand each other and avoid SNS-related conflict.

7.4 Secret Tests

When beginning a new relationship, maintaining a stable relationship, or terminating a relationship, individuals must battle the uncertainty in their minds by seeking ways to reduce or reconcile this uncertainty (Berger & Calabrese, 1975). The strategies used to reduce uncertainty may differ depending on the individual or relationship stage, but individuals often use strategies to acquire information about their romantic relational partner (Baxter & Wilmot, 1984). These strategies, or *secret tests*, allow individuals to gain insights and reduce uncertainty (Baxter & Wilmot, 1984).

SNSs are optimal places to conduct secret tests and even provide new ways of testing relationships. Although an individual may initiate some of these tests with positive or hopeful intent, such as trying to determine the seriousness of a relationship, other tests can be detrimental or designed to catch the partner engaging in an inappropriate behavior. Fox, Peterson, and Warber (2013) found both positive and negative ways secret tests were executed via SNSs. Partners often took advantage of the affordances of SNSs (e.g., the visibility of a categorical relationship status that can be linked to the partner; the ability to make comments to one's partner visible to the network; the visibility of one's connections and communication with other network members) to test the definition and boundaries of their relationship and the intentions, commitment, and fidelity of their partners.

In this study, individuals reported implementing separation tests, in which they would attempt to separate themselves from the partner (Fox, Peterson, et al., 2013). They would deliberately ignore SNS messages, tags, and posts from their partner to see how he or she would react. Perhaps the most common negative test was using an SNS to try to invoke jealousy. For example, Kris may attempt to make Jeff jealous by flirting openly with another attractive male on Facebook. Dante could "like" several of his ex-girlfriend's pictures on Instagram, knowing his current girlfriend will see them. Although not as common, some individuals reported using triangle tests (Fox, Peterson, et al., 2013). For example, if Sarah doesn't trust her girlfriend Laura, she may ask another friend to post something flirtatious on Laura's page to see if Laura flirts back. Although rare, some individuals also reported creating fake social media accounts for this purpose (Fox, Peterson, et al., 2013). After finding pictures of an attractive model online, Maria could set up a fake account and propositioned her boyfriend, Andre, to see if he would cheat on her. Although secret tests may be used to benefit relationships, in these instances, partners were often using SNSs to create relational turmoil or tempt their partners with opportunities for infidelity.

7.5 Jealousy

Because SNSs provide a lot of information about an individual's social network, former romantic relationships, and current activities, they may provide fodder for a partner's jealousy. Previous studies have found that higher levels of Facebook use or involvement with Facebook predict higher levels of relational jealousy (Elphinston & Noller, 2011; Muise, Christofedes, & Desmarais, 2009) and dissatisfaction (Elphinston & Noller, 2011). Other studies have shown that certain content on a partner's SNS profile can trigger jealous or angry reactions (Muise, Christofedes, & Desmarais, in press; Muscanell, Guadagno, Rice, et al., 2013). Marshall, Bejanyan, Di Castro, et al. (2013) found that users with higher levels of attachment anxiety were more likely to experience Facebook-related jealousy.

As several scholars note (e.g., Fox & Warber, in press; Muise et al., 2009), experiences of jealousy and uncertainty in relationships may be a vicious cycle when both partners use SNSs. Individuals may seek out their partner's profile to alleviate relational concerns, but the content they find may trigger greater uncertainty or jealousy—thus leading to ongoing surveillance or monitoring, which may lead to more discontent.

7.6 Interpersonal Electronic Surveillance

Social networking sites provide a novel way for partners to gather information about each other. Indeed, monitoring another person is one of the most common uses for SNSs (Joinson, 2008). Tokunaga (2011b) identifies four characteristics of SNSs that promote *interpersonal electronic surveillance* (IES) of one's romantic partner. First, information is readily accessible through these sites. It is easy to join an SNS and only requires a simple click to access the profiles of your connections or your connections' connections. Second, information on SNSs is often comprised of various media. Users can post textual messages, photographs, links, and audio or video clips. Given that pictures are considered more credible than words on SNS profiles (Van Der Heide, D'Angelo, & Schumaker, 2012), this capability may be particularly relevant to partners with suspicions. Third, SNSs allow the archiving of profile information (i.e., they afford persistence; Treem & Leonardi, 2012). Partners may conduct IES of the target's past posts, photos, or interactions with others to gather more data. Fourth, given that neither geographical proximity nor social interaction is necessary to obtain this information, data may be gathered more surreptitiously. Many SNSs, including Facebook and Twitter, afford covert surveillance and do not provide feedback on who has accessed one's profile. Thus, the target may never know that s/he is under surveillance by the partner. Thus, the affordances of social networking sites enable partners to gather information via IES, which may answer questions about the relationship or, conversely, lead to more.

In addition to Tokunaga's characteristics, a fifth characteristic also make SNSs optimal for partner surveillance: the multiplicity of sources available in an SNS. It is not only the target who is contributing to their profile page, but also other network members. According to warranting theory, information that comes from sources other than the self is seen as more credible (Walther & Parks, 2002; Walther, Van Der Heide, Hamel, et al., 2009). Also, information that comes from multiple sources (e.g., several network members, or both comments and pictures) would also be perceived as more credible (Flanigan & Metzger, 2007). Facebook in particular makes this "friendsourcing" easy: not only can friends mention the target or upload media about the target, but they can make that information more easily accessible by tagging the target in posts, check-ins, or photos and having that information show up on the target's page as well. Thus, Facebook's affordances enable partners to gather information about each other via IES.

Several studies have shown that Facebook is commonly used to monitor one's partner or ex-partner (Darvell, Walsh, & White, 2011; Elphinston & Noller, 2011; Fox & Warber, in press; Lyndon, Bonds-Raacke, & Cratty, 2011; Marshall, 2012; Marshall et al., 2013; Tokunaga, 2011b). Part of its prolific use in this way may be because Facebook allows both self-generated and other-generated information to be tied to one's profile via posting, tagging, and apps. As such there are multiple sources of information conveniently amalgamated in one easily accessible location. A user may be able to track his or her partner by looking at Facebook events, posts, or location check-ins. Friends might tag the partner in posts about an event. Perhaps the greatest source of information is photographs, which may reveal considerable details about where a partner is, who the partner is with, and what the partner is doing. Thus, Facebook often serves as an indirect source for knowledge about romantic partners (Tokunaga, 2011b) and may inform feelings or decisions about the relationship at every stage, even after dissolution.

Research indicates that potential relationship threats often arise on Facebook pages: attractive new friends may emerge, questionable photographs from a weekend event may be shared, or flirty comments from an enviable other may appear on the partner's page (Fox, Warber, et al., 2013; Marshall et al., 2013). Without Facebook, many of these behaviors would still occur, but they would remain hidden from the partner. Even if the partner was aware, if the evidence of this behavior was not shared online, these instances would more likely be downplayed or ignored by the partner offline. It is the expression enabled through Facebook, as well as the act of distributing this information online versus offline, that creates distress that may have otherwise been avoided. Interestingly, although users are aware that Facebook's additional information may cause unnecessary tension or exacerbate existing problems in the relationship, many still acknowledge that they "creep" (i.e., inspect a person's page without their knowledge in order to gain information) on their partner's and others' profiles to obtain information the partner might otherwise try to conceal (Fox, Warber, et al., 2013; Muise et al., in press).

7.7 Cyberstalking and Obsessive Relational Intrusion

Although the term "creeping" and "Facebook stalking" already indicates that there is something discomforting about having someone surreptitiously monitoring one's SNS profile, this monitoring can ascend to a problematic or even dangerous level. Continuous surveillance and unwanted pursuit of a romantic interest is known as obsessive relational intrusion (ORI; Spitzberg & Cupach, 2003). Chaulk and Jones (2011) note that SNSs facilitate ORI because 1) targets often share personal information on these sites, including opinions, preferences, hobbies, acquaintances, future plans, and daily activities; 2) offenders can monitor this information easily, privately, and as frequently as they like; and 3) SNSs provide many different ways the offender can interact with the target. Some ORI behaviors on SNSs include sending unwanted private messages; posting unwanted material to the target's profile; tagging the target in posts or pictures; "friending," following, or otherwise linking to the target's network members, such as friends and family; intruding into the target's interactions on the pages of shared network members; or posting information about the target on others' pages.

Recent research suggests that cyberstalking via SNSs is not uncommon, although the more rigorously one chooses to define it, the less prevalent it appears to be (Dreßing, Bailer, Anders, et al., in press). In a recent study of users of a German SNS, Dreßing and colleagues found over 40% had been cyberstalked at some point and that 6.3% experienced problematic cyberstalking. Similar to offline stalking, most perpetrators were male (69.4%) and most victims were female (80.5%). Most often, the victim and perpetrator were ex-romantic partners. Despite the fact that these interactions were taking place virtually, there were still significant negative outcomes for victims. More than half reported feelings of helplessness and anger, and 68.2% reported diminished trust in other people. Approximately two-thirds reported sleep disturbances, one-third reported depression, and 16% sought counseling or therapy to deal with the consequences of cyberstalking. Thus, although SNSs may help us maintain relationships with friends and family, they may also enable unwanted attention, interference, or stalking from former partners as well.

7.8 Relationship Dissolution on SNSs

Although limited at this time, emerging research is beginning to investigate the dark side of SNSs in the wake of relationship dissolution. The end of a romantic relationship has been identified as one of the most stressful events in a person's life characterized by many emotional and relational fluctuations (Cochrane & Robertson, 1973; Koenig Kellas, Bean, Cunningham, et al., 2008). The experience of relational dissolution can lead to negative mood states, emotional volatility, physical illness, and even suicide or homicide (Gottman, 1994).

Relationship dissolution in the age of social media is a particularly messy process. If couples have been in a lengthy relationship, it is likely that they have developed a conjoined presence on the sites that they both use. Their social networks have likely become integrated online. Evidence of their bond has often been posted, shared, or tagged. Given both the public nature of the relationship and the integration of the couple's digital presence, the process of extraction may be complicated and perhaps made more painful by the use of SNSs in the relationship. This may explain why individuals often use SNSs as a communication channel after the breakup. Lyndon and colleagues (2011) identified three manners in which individuals use Facebook negatively in the wake of a breakup: *venting* (e.g., directly making negative comments about the ex-partner or the relationship), *covert provocation* (e.g., passive aggressive posting on the wall to make the ex- jealous or angry), and *public harassment* (e.g., spreading rumors about or posting embarrassing photos of the ex-partner). Each of these behaviors is likely to prolong negative emotions and experiences associated with dissolution.

Another recent study explored the different ways in which individuals react to a breakup on Facebook (Fox, Jones, & Lookadoo, 2013). Most commonly, people felt pressured by their SNS presence to pretend that they were unaffected by the breakup. Often, users exaggerated their activities after a breakup, trying to prove to their network (and often the ex- as well) that they were doing better than ever after the relationship. The process of maintaining face and trying to hide one's true emotional state may cause even greater distress. Another way people reacted to a breakup was to use Facebook to publicly bash the ex-partner—or to allow friends to bash the ex-partner on one's page (Fox, Jones, et al., 2013). In these cases, Facebook is weaponized in a battle to "win" the breakup publicly, either by hurting the ex's reputation or getting shared network members to take sides. Often, this created more animosity between ex-partners and often with other network members as well.

Another added stressor in the wake of a breakup that an individual is often faced with is constant reminders when they visit their SNS profile. An individual may be linked to the partner via a relationship status or a profile picture featuring the couple. If the couple used the SNS to communicate, old posts and pictures may populate the profile. Shared network members may have tagged the partners in shared pictures or statuses. Thus, it is unsurprising that individuals typically report cleaning up their SNS profile, deleting, hiding, or untagging pictures and posts to remove the digital detritus of the relationship (Fox, Jones, et al., 2013). Although this may be a painful process, this purging may also serve as a coping ritual for users.

After a breakup, uncertainty about the relationship's future may remain. In the wake of termination, it is not uncommon for ex-partners to remain friends on Facebook (Fox & Warber, in press; Marshall, 2012; Marshall et al., 2013; Tokunaga, 2011b). Although the current state of the relationship may be in good or bad shape, certain or uncertain, the exes still remain "friends" in name on Facebook. This lingering connection—as well as access to the ex-partner's post-breakup experiences via Facebook posts and pictures—may foster feelings of uncertainty about the relationship after dissolution (Fox, Jones, et al., 2013). Thus, it is unsurprising that individuals often monitor their exes on SNSs after breakups (Fox & Warber, in press; Marshall, 2012; Marshall et al., 2013).

Post-breakup SNS monitoring is not without consequence. Marshall (2012) found that individuals who monitor their ex-partner's Facebook page after a breakup reported greater levels of distress and negative feelings, greater longing for the ex-partner, and less emotional recovery from the breakup. Thus, even when the individual is not using an SNS for negative expression or self-disclosure about the breakup, SNSs may still have negative consequences for individuals post-dissolution.

7.9 Conclusion

As Stafford and Hillyer (2012) note, our understanding of the role of technologies in personal relationships is nascent. Although SNSs may have many benefits for relationships, the potential downsides must also be acknowledged alongside these benefits. Whereas SNSs have often been shown to have positive effects in relationships, there is great potential for the dark side to emerge in romantic relationships.

References

Baxter, L. A., & Wilmot, W. W. (1984). "Secret tests": Social strategies for acquiring information about the state of the relationship. *Human Communication Research, 11*,171-201. doi: 10.1111/j.1468-2958.1984.tb00044.x

Berger, C. R., & Calabrese, R. J. (1975). Some explorations in initial interaction and beyond: Toward a developmental theory of interpersonal communication. *Human Communication Research, 1*, 99-112. doi: 10.1111/j.1468-2958.1975.tb00258.x

Bevan, J. L., Pfyl, J., & Barclay, B. (2012). Negative emotional and cognitive responses to being unfriended on Facebook: An exploratory study. *Computers in Human Behavior, 28*, 1458-1464. doi: 10.1016/j.chb.2012.03.008

Chaulk, K., & Jones, T. (2011). Online obsessive relational intrusion: Further concerns about Facebook. *Journal of Family Violence, 26*, 245-254. doi: 10.1007/s10896-011-9360-x

Cochrane, R., & Robertson, A. (1973). The Life Events Inventory: A measure of the relative severity of psycho-social stressors. *Journal of Psychosomatic Research, 17*, 135-139. doi: 10.1016/0022-3999(73)90014-7

Darvell, M. J., Walsh, S. P., & White, K. M. (2011). Facebook tells me so: applying the theory of planned behavior to understand partner-monitoring behavior on Facebook. *Cyberpsychology, Behavior, & Social Networking, 14*, 717-722. doi: 10.1089/cyber.2011.0035

DeAndrea, D. C., Tong, S. T., & Walther, J. B. (2011). Dark sides of computer-mediated communication. In W. R. Cupach & B. H. Spitzberg (Eds.), *The dark side of close relationships II* (pp. 95-118). New York: Routledge.

Dreßing, H., Bailer, J., Anders, A., Wagner, H., & Gallas, C. (in press). Cyberstalking in a large sample of social network users: Prevalence, characteristics, and impact upon victims. *Cyberpsychology, Behavior, & Social Networking*. doi: 10.1089/cyber.2012.0231

Elphinston, R. A., & Noller, P. (2011). Time to face it! Facebook intrusion and the implications for romantic jealousy and relationship satisfaction. *Cyberpsychology, Behavior, & Social Networking, 14*, 631-635. doi: 10.1089/cyber.2010.0318

Flanagin, A. J., & Metzger, M. J. (2007). The role of site features, user attributes, and information verification behaviors on the perceived credibility of web-based information. *New Media & Society, 9*, 319-342. doi: 10.1177/1461444807075015

Fox, J., Jones, E. B., & Lookadoo, K. (2013, June). Romantic relationship dissolution on social networking sites: Social support, coping, and rituals on Facebook. Paper presented at the 63rd Annual Conference of the International Communication Association, London, UK.

Fox, J., Peterson, A., & Warber, K. M. (2013, October). Attachment style, sex, and the use of secret tests via social networking sites in romantic relationships. Paper presented at the Multi-Level Motivations in Close Relationship Dynamics Conference of the International Association for Relationship Research, Louisville, KY.

Fox, J., & Warber, K. M. (2013). Romantic relationship development in the age of Facebook: An exploratory study of emerging adults' perceptions, motives, and behaviors. *CyberPsychology, Behavior, & Social Networking, 16*, 3-7. doi:10.1089/cyber.2012.0288

Fox, J., & Warber, K. M. (in press). Social networking sites in romantic relationships: Attachment, uncertainty, and partner surveillance on Facebook. To appear in *CyberPsychology, Behavior, & Social Networking*. doi: 10.1089/cyber.2012.0667

Fox, J., Warber, K. M., & Makstaller, D. C. (2013). The role of Facebook in romantic relationship development: An exploration of Knapp's relational stage model. *Journal of Social & Personal Relationships, 30*, 772-795. doi:10.1177/026540751246837

Gottman, J. M. (1994). *What predicts divorce? The relationship between marital processes and marital outcomes*. Hillsdale, NJ: Erlbaum.

Hand, M. M., Thomas, D., Buboltz, W. C., Deemer, E. D., & Buyanjargal, M. (2013). Facebook and romantic relationships: Intimacy and couple satisfaction associated with online social network use. *Cyberpsychology, Behavior, & Social Networking, 16*, 8-13. doi: 10.1089/cyber.2012.0038

Hogerbrugge, M. J., Komter, A. E., & Scheepers, P. (2013). Dissolving long-term romantic relationships Assessing the role of the social context. *Journal of Social & Personal Relationships, 30*, 320-342. doi: 10.1177/0265407512462167

Joinson, A. N. (2008, April). Looking at, looking up, or keeping up with people? Motives and use of Facebook. In *Proceedings of the SIGCHI conference on Human Factors in Computing Systems* (pp. 1027-1036). ACM.

Koenig Kellas, J., Bean, D., Cunningham, C., & Cheng, K. Y. (2008). The ex-files: Trajectories, turning points, and adjustment in the development of post-dissolutional relationships. *Journal of Social & Personal Relationships, 25*, 23-50. doi: 10.1177/0265407507086804

Lyndon, A., Bonds-Raacke, J., & Cratty, A. D. (2011). College students' Facebook stalking of ex-partners. *Cyberpsychology, Behavior, & Social Networking, 14*, 711-716. doi: 10.1089/cyber.2010.0588

Marshall, T. C. (2012). Facebook surveillance of former romantic partners: Associations with postbreakup recovery and personal growth. *Cyberpsychology, Behavior, & Social Networking, 15*, 521-526. doi: 10.1089/cyber.2012.0125

Marshall, T. C., Bejanyan, K., Di Castro, G., & Lee, R. A. (2013). Attachment styles as predictors of Facebook-related jealousy and surveillance in romantic relationships. *Personal Relationships, 20*, 1-22. doi: 10.1111/j.1475-6811.2011.01393.x

McEwan, B. (2013). Sharing, caring, and surveilling: An actor–partner interdependence model examination of Facebook relational maintenance strategies. *Cyberpsychology, Behavior, & Social Networking*, *16*, 863-869. doi: 10.1089/cyber.2012.0717

Muise, A., Christofides, E., & Desmarais, S. (2009). More information than you ever wanted: does Facebook bring out the green-eyed monster of jealousy? *CyberPsychology & Behavior*, *12*, 441-444. doi: 10.1089/cpb.2008.0263

Muise, A., Christofedes, E., & Desmaris, S. (in press). "Creeping" or just information seeking? Gender differences in partner monitoring in response to jealousy on Facebook. *Personal Relationships*. doi: 10.1111/pere.12014

Muscanell, N. L., Guadagno, R. E., Rice, L., & Murphy, S. (2013). Don't it make my brown eyes green? An analysis of Facebook use and romantic jealousy. *Cyberpsychology, Behavior, & Social Networking*, *16*, 237-242. doi: 10.1089/cyber.2012.0411

Osborn, J., Fox, J., & Warber, K. M. (2012, November). Balancing the benefits and drawbacks of social networks: A dialectical analysis of the role of Facebook in romantic relationships. Paper presented at the 98th Annual Conference of the National Communication Association, Orlando, FL.

Papp, L. M., Danielewicz, J., & Cayemberg, C. (2012). "Are we Facebook official?" Implications of dating partners' Facebook use and profiles for intimate relationship satisfaction. *Cyberpsychology, Behavior, & Social Networking*, *15*, 85-90. doi: 10.1089/cyber.2011.0291

Smith, C. (2013, November 29). The planet's 24 largest social media sites and where their next wave of growth will come from. Retrieved from: http://www.businessinsider.com/a-global-social-media-census-2013-10

Spitzberg, B. H., & Cupach, W. R. (2003). What mad pursuit?: Obsessive relational intrusion and stalking related phenomena. *Aggression & Violent Behavior*, *8*, 345-375. doi: 10.1016/S1359-1789(02)00068-X

Stafford, L., & Hillyer, J. D. (2012). Information and communication technologies in personal relationships. *Review of Communication*, *12*, 290-312. doi: 10.1080/15358593.2012.685951

Tokunaga, R. S. (2011a). Friend me or you'll strain us: understanding negative events that occur over social networking sites. *Cyberpsychology, Behavior, & Social Networking*, *14*, 425-432. doi: 10.1089/cyber.2010.0140

Tokunaga, R. S. (2011b). Social networking site or social surveillance site? Understanding the use of interpersonal electronic surveillance in romantic relationships. *Computers in Human Behavior*, *27*, 705-13. doi: 10.1016/j/chb.2010.08.014

Treem, J., & Leonardi, P. (2012). Social media use in organizations: Exploring the affordances of visibility, editability, persistence, and association. *Communication Yearbook*, *36*, 143-189.

Utz, S., & Beukeboom, C. J. (2011). The role of social network sites in romantic relationships: Effects on jealousy and relationship happiness. *Journal of Computer-Mediated Communication*, *16*, 511-527. doi: 10.1111/j.1083-6101.2011.01552.x

Valenzuela, S., Park, N., & Kee, K. F. (2009). Is there social capital in a social network site? Facebook use and college students' life satisfaction, trust, and participation. *Journal of Computer-Mediated Communication*, *14*, 875-901. doi: 10.1111/j.1083-6101.2009.01474.x

Valkenburg, P. M., Peter, J., & Schouten, A. P. (2006). Friend networking sites and their relationship to adolescents' well-being and social self-esteem. *CyberPsychology & Behavior*, *9*, 584-590. doi: 10.1089/cpb.2006.9.584

Van Der Heide, B., D'Angelo, J. D., & Schumaker, E. M. (2012). The effects of verbal versus photographic self-presentation on impression formation in Facebook. *Journal of Communication*, *62*, 98-116. doi: 10.1111/j.1460-2466.2011.01617.x

Walther, J. B., & Parks, M. R. (2002). Cues filtered out, cues filtered in: Computer-mediated communication and relationships. In M. L. Knapp & J. A. Daly (Eds.), *Handbook of interpersonal communication* (3rd ed., pp. 529-563). Thousand Oaks, CA: Sage.

Walther, J. B., Van Der Heide, B., Hamel, L. M., & Shulman, H. C. (2009). Self-generated versus other-generated statements and impressions in computer-mediated communication: A test of warranting theory using Facebook. *Communication Research*, *36*, 229-253. doi: 10.1177/0093650208330251

Leanne M. Casey, Bonnie A. Clough

8 Making and Keeping the Connection: Improving Consumer Attitudes and Engagement in E-Mental Health Interventions

Abstract: E-mental health services are internet-based treatment options for mental illness. Potential benefits of e-mental health interventions include increased cost effectiveness, enhanced dissemination of evidence based treatments, and decreased burden on existing healthcare systems (Griffiths, Farrer, & Christensen, 2007). E-mental health services may also overcome various barriers to care such as stigma, accessibility, and socioeconomic status. Despite these benefits, consumer uptake and engagement in e-mental health services remains less than optimal. Available research indicates that consumer attitudes toward e-mental health services are problematic (Klein & Cook, 2010) but may be improved by the provision of information about the services (Casey, Joy & Clough, 2013). Research also suggests that the medium by which this information is delivered may have a significant influence on the efficacy of such interventions (Casey et al., 2013). Similarly, client engagement in e-mental health services is less than optimal, with a weighted average of 31% of clients prematurely ceasing involvement in psychological interventions delivered via the internet (Melville, Casey & Kavanagh, 2010). The current chapter will provide a review and discussion of consumer attitudes toward e-mental health services, as well as the efficacy and use of strategies to improve attitudes and enhance engagement. Recommendations for future research and clinical practice are also provided.

E-mental health refers to mental health interventions which are delivered via the internet and encompasses a broad range of service types, including those with and without human interaction (Klein & Cook, 2010; Griffiths, Farrer, & Christensen, 2007). Potential benefits of e-mental health interventions include increased cost effectiveness, enhanced dissemination of evidence based treatments, and decreased burden on existing healthcare systems (Barak, Hen, Boniel-Nissim, & Shapira, 2008)). Within the broad category of e-mental health, there are several types of treatment available.

Information websites provide content regarding diagnosis, symptoms, causes, and treatments for mental health problems (Barak, Klein, & Proudfoot, 2009). These websites are predominantly text based, although interactive elements and multimedia are often included (Barak et al., 2009). For example, Griffiths and colleagues (Griffiths, Christensen, Jorm, Evans &Groves, 2004) developed an information website on depression (*BluePages*) and found that participants accessing this site reduced their level of personal stigma experienced in regard to depression.

Interventions can also be delivered through internet programs without therapist assistance. Internet programs without therapist assistance are usually presented in a range of self-guided modules, and usually based upon a particular psychological approach (Rickwood, 2010). For example, Casey and colleagues developed an Internet-based treatment program for pathological gambling (Casey, Oei & Raylu, 2010). Known as *Improving the Odds*, this program provided a fully automated version of Internet-based Cognitive Behaviour Therapy (I-CBT) for pathological gambling which was delivered in six modules. When compared to both active treatment and waitlist control conditions, I-CBT was associated with stronger reductions in gambling related behaviour and achieved similar effect sizes to those observed in therapist-administered face to face treatment of pathological gambling.

Another form of e-mental health service is internet programs with therapist assistance, which provide structured psychological programs with the support of a health professional. This support can take many forms, including reminders and personalised feedback (Barak et al., 2009). For example, Berger, Hohl, and Caspar (2009) reported that combining I-CBT with therapist contact via email resulted in significant reductions in social anxiety, which was maintained six months after the intervention. Online counselling is also an effective treatment option, as King et al. (2009) demonstrated in their examination of online counselling to treat substance abuse.. Participants in this study were outpatients at an addiction treatment centre (N = 37) who were randomly assigned to receive counselling via internet video conferencing, or face-to-face sessions. After the six-week intervention, there were no significant differences between the groups in terms of program adherence or drug use.

In summary, e-mental health services appear to be a promising medium to administer treatment. In an extensive meta-analysis, Barak, et al., (2008) analysed 92 studies utilising e-mental health interventions. Overall, e-mental health services were found to effectively reduce symptoms across a range of conditions, with an effect size of 0.53. Notably, in the 14 studies directly comparing e-mental services with face-to-face treatments, there were no significant differences in treatment efficacy. Despite this evidence that e-mental health services can be effective, there has been relatively little examination of how well consumers engage with these services (Hordern, Georgiou, Whetton, & Progmet, 2011). Client engagement forms part of the broader concept of adherence to the therapeutic process (Clough & Casey, 2011). Two key issues in client engagement associated with e-mental health services are the rates of uptake (i.e., clients entering the service) and dropout (i.e., people ceasing the service).

8.1 Uptake of E-mental Health Services

A number of studies indicate that uptake rates of e-mental health services can be relatively low. In one study, participants were recruited to a guided online CBT program for depression from 11 participating general practitioners, who first identified eligible patients from his or her personal files, then sent out the study information packs (Woodford, Farrand, Bessant, & Williams, 2011). Only seven participants were recruited over eight months from 1,606 study packages sent out. In another study on the evaluation of the effectiveness of an online treatment program for depression, out of 12,051 study packages sent out to eligible depressed and non-depressed individuals only 255 people were recruited (Clarke et al., 2005). However, there are a number of limitations in the studies finding low-uptake of computer and online treatment programs for mental health conditions. A number of studies in this area have neglected to publish their recruitment methods and treatment uptake rates as well as there being insufficient trials conducted in routine settings (Bennett & Glasgow, 2009). Reported studies vary considerably on recruitment methods: participants are either self-selected, or specifically selected by health-care practitioners, and it is possible that the reluctance to take up treatment could be related to reluctance to be involved in a clinical trial and not the medium of treatment itself (Kaltenthaler et al., 2008). Despite these limitations, there is a growing consensus that participation in online treatment program is less than optimal.

8.2 Consumer Satisfaction with E-mental Health Services

Paradoxically, e-mental health services are well accepted by consumers who have actually participated in e-mental health treatments. Research has shown high satisfaction rates amongst users who have completed, or are participating in, an online treatment program. Titov and colleagues investigated therapist assisted internet-based treatment for depression (Titov, Andrews, Johnston, Schwencke, & Choi, 2009). Treatment involved an eight to ten week program consisting of online lessons, homework, an online discussion forum, and email communication with a therapist. Immediately following the completion of treatment, the participants completed measures which assessed their opinions about the face-to-face and e-mental health treatment options. These measures included rating e-mental health treatment on several dimensions. In terms of preference and efficacy, no significant differences were found between endorsements for e-mental health and face-to-face services. Immediately after participation, the treatment was rated as logical (9/10) and effective (8/10), and participants reported that they would be confident recommending the treatment to others (9/10). At six months follow up, there was no change in the rating of treatment efficacy, and only slight reductions in ratings of logic (8/10) and confidence in recommending the treatment (8/10). In a study that directly compared behavioural treatment delivered via an internet-based program with therapist assistance to or face-to-face therapy Kiropoulos and colleagues reported that after 12 weeks of treatment for panic disorder, both treatment conditions were rated as equally satisfying and credible at the conclusion of treatment and achieved significant improvements in panic frequency, depression, and stress (Kiropoulos et al., 2008). Although the face-to-face group reported more enjoyment during therapist interactions, there was no significant difference in the degree of therapeutic alliance achieved.

8.3 Attitudes to E-mental Health Services

Attitudes of potential consumers of e-mental health services generally remain problematic. A consistent finding across the literature is that face-to-face services are preferred in comparison to e-mental health services. Tsan & Day (2007) analysed attitudes towards counselling delivered via face-to-face treatment, online instant messaging, internet microphone, email or internet video conferencing in a sample of college students (N = 176). Eighty-seven per cent of the sample reported a preference for face-to-face treatment. Similarly, Horgan and Sweeney (2010) reported that in a sample of university students aged between 18 and 24 years (N = 922), e-mental health services were the preferred treatment format for only 20.6 per cent of the sample. Opinions and experiences with e-mental health services have also been assessed by Neal, Campbell, Williams, Liu, & Nussbaumer (2011) who conducted an online study of Canadians aged between 18 and 25 years of age (*N* = 1308). In this study, participants were asked about their opinions and experience in regards to online-mental health treatment. Sixty-eight per cent of the sample indicated that they would not consider contacting a psychologist online, and only 17 per cent reported that they would use a self-directed online program if they needed help.

Attitudes regarding the helpfulness of mental health services have also been examined by Leach and colleagues in a study that assessed the perceived helpfulness of treatments delivered via a website, book or health educator (Leach, Christensen, Griffiths, Jorm, & Mackinnon, 2007). Although over half of the sample (*N* = 3998) stated that a website would be useful, it was rated as the least helpful treatment option. In a study of university students (N = 330) in the United Kingdom, participants were provided with a description of a traumatic event, resulting post traumatic stress disorder symptoms, and 14 potential treatment options (Tarrier, Liversidge, & Gregg, 2006). Participants rated the treatments on several dimensions, and ranked them according to their suitability for treating post traumatic stress disorder. Information was also gathered about prior knowledge of the services, and whether the prior knowledge was positive or negative. Notably, only 8.2 per cent of the sample were familiar with computer-based therapy, and 6.6 per cent with e-therapy. These findings contrasted with knowledge of face-to-face treatments such as cognitive therapy (43.5

per cent), group therapy (63.8 per cent), and family therapy (47 per cent). Additionally, the e-mental health services were amongst the least endorsed treatments, ranking 12th and 13th out of the 14 services. Carper, McHugh and Barlow (2011) gave information about various forms of computer based psychological treatment (e.g., email-based psychotherapy) to patients seeking treatment for an anxiety or a related disorder. These patients were asked to rank the various forms of computer based psychological treatment and to answer a questionnaire about their perceptions of computerized therapy. Overall, the patients' perceptions of computer based psychological therapy were found to be neutral to slightly negative and they reported low intentions of utilising computer based psychological therapy in the future. Analysis of individual items revealed that participants did, however, report that computer-based treatment had advantages such as reduced cost, being easier to access, and flexibility in meeting individual needs. This finding is similar to other studies in which participants reported perceiving advantages to internet-based treatment but expressed an overall preference for face-to-face treatment (Mohr et al., 2010).

One explanation for the lack of interest in internet-based treatment is the general lack of information that potential consumers may have about this treatment modality. There is certainly evidence that knowledge about treatment is associated with treatment preferences. For instance, primary care patients ($N = 1187$) with depressive symptoms responded to a telephone survey regarding their preferences for treatment and their knowledge about treatment (Dwight-Johnson, Sherbourne, Liao & Wells, 2000). The survey revealed that patients with greater knowledge about antidepressant medication were more likely than those without knowledge to desire active treatment for depression (medication, individual counselling or group counselling). Counselling was the most preferred treatment among participants who reported preferring active treatment over no treatment. Patients reporting a preference for counselling also reported having a greater knowledge about counselling than patients who did not prefer counselling.

The provision of information regarding treatment outcomes has also been shown to have a positive impact on hopefulness about treatment outcomes and psychotherapy treatment uptake rates (Woodhead, Ivan & Emery, 2012). In this study, participants ($N = 50$) aged over 60 years with depressive symptoms, who were recommended to receive psychotherapy were also given information about the outcomes achieved by older adults in psychotherapy, (i.e., 80% remained depression free 3 years after psychotherapy). Participants then rated how important they perceived the information to be and were given the opportunity to receive psychotherapy. Weak, but significant, positive correlations were found between participants who elected to initiate treatment and the participants' ratings of how important they perceived the information to be (Spearman's $r = 0.30$, $p = 0.04$). That is, participants who elected to initiate treatment reported that they perceived the information regarding treatment outcomes to be important.

Unfortunately, potential consumers of e-mental health services appear to have relatively little information about these services. Carper et al. (2011) found that the observability of computer based psychological treatment was rated as very low, with potential consumers reporting that they did not often see treatment being used in this format and were unfamiliar with it. This finding may indicate that there is a need to better understand an internet-based treatment in order to feel confident accessing treatment in this modality. Thus, it is possible that the provision of more detailed information may enhance the likelihood of engaging in internet-based treatment.

The possibility that additional information regarding internet-based treatment may increase utilisation of this treatment medium is supported by an Australian online survey (Klein and Cook, 2010). Participants (N = 218) were asked whether they would prefer to use face-to-face treatment or internet-based treatment if they were experiencing a mental health problem. In line with previous research, the majority of participants (77.1%) reported a preference for face-to-face treatment. However, only 9.6% of participants reported that they would not use e-mental health services. So, while the majority of participants indicated a preference for face-to-face treatment, only a small number of participants indicated that they would not use internet-based treatment. In attempting to clarify this finding, the researchers examined the concerns raised by participants in regard to internet-based health services. Fifty-four percent of participants indicated a need to know more about internet-based health services, suggesting a lack of information about these type of services may underlie the reluctance to access treatment offered through this medium.

8.4 Providing Information to Improve Attitudes

Despite a lack of awareness about e-mental health services, research indicates that individuals are receptive to gaining more information about these treatment options. Furthermore, there is preliminary evidence that knowledge and familiarity may enhance attitudes towards services. A number of studies have investigated the impact of providing information to improve attitudes towards mental health services, although most of this has been conducted with regard to services provided face to face. The American Psychological Association conducted a national media campaign to increase usage of psychological services (Farberman, 1997). This campaign provided consumers with information about psychological services and their potential benefits. It resulted in a marked increase in enquiries from states in which the campaign had been implemented. Esters, Cooker, and Ittenbach (1988) delivered a school based intervention to adolescents between 13 and 17 years of age ($N = 40$). The treatment group in this study viewed a video presentation about mental illness, local help sources, and the qualifications of mental health professionals. The control group attended their normal classes, and did not watch the video presentation. In comparison to the control group, participants in the intervention group reported a significant increase in mental health knowledge as well as significantly attitudes towards help seeking. These findings were maintained at a 12 week follow up, and indicate that education can influence attitudes about mental illness.

Sharp, Hargrove, Johnson, & Deal (2006) examined the impact of an informational intervention upon the help seeking attitudes of American university students (*N* = 123). All participants watched a 40 minute lecture and slide show presentation. In the intervention group, the topics addressed in the presentation were psychological disorders, the therapeutic process, and the role of mental health professionals. Participants in the control group watched a presentation on astronomy. Participants were also provided with the contact details of their local mental health services. Attitudes towards help seeking and opinions about mental illness were significantly more improved for participants in the intervention group and were maintained at four weeks following the study. Sawamura, Ito, Koyama, Tajima and Higuchi (2010) provided 122 psychiatric clinic outpatients who met criteria for a depressive disorder with either treatment as usual or treatment with the provision of an additional educational leaflet. The educational leaflet included information about depressive disorders, available treatments, and strategies for coping with stress. Participants were asked to indicate their attitudes and beliefs about depression and antidepressants at their first and third visit. Participants who received the educational leaflet demonstrated significantly improved attitudes and beliefs about depression and antidepressant treatment at their third visit, whereas the attitudes and beliefs of participants who did not receive the leaflet did not change.

Nicholas, Oliver, Lee, and O'Brien (2004) examined the impact of informational intervention about e-mental health services in secondary schools with participants aged 13 to 18 years (*N* = 243). The topic of the intervention was 'Reach Out', an e-mental health service for young people in Australia. Interactive presentations were used to promote Reach Out as a place where young people could seek help for a variety of personal problems. Following the presentation, 70% of participants reported that the intervention had taught them where they could seek help if they were experiencing difficulties and 45% of participants visited the Reach Out website following the presentation. Notably, six months after the presentation, 63 per cent of participants reported that they would use the Reach Out website in the future if they needed help. Although the interpretation of these findings is constrained by the absence of a control group, this study suggests that information may enhance help seeking intentions and awareness of e-mental health services.

An important issue to consider is the type of information that may improve the attitudes of potential utilisers of these treatments (Sawamura et al, 2010). Young (2005) asked clients (N =48) taking part in an online treatment program for internet addiction about their decision to access online counselling. Of these clients 71% reported that the convenience and flexibility offered by online treatment was an important factor and 52% reported that understanding the credentials of the counsellor was also an important factor. Bradley (2010) explored what features of an internet-based self-help program for psychological distress would encourage adolescents to seek help. Adolescents reported an online treatment program that was credible, offered privacy, convenience, and accessibility was the most appealing.

Providing information about issues of privacy and confidentiality may be particularly important to users of e-mental health services. A survey of internet users (N = 7014) in America compared the internet usage patterns of participants who reported experiencing a stigmatised illness, such as depression, to those who reported other health related conditions, such as back pain (Berger, Wagner & Baker, 2005). The survey revealed that participants who reported a stigmatised illness were significantly more likely to access the internet for health information and to communicate with clinicians on the internet about their condition than participants who did not report having a stigmatised illness

Providing information about the efficacy of treatment programs may also be important, although again much of this evidence comes from research into improving attitudes toward face to face psychological interventions. Interviews with employees of a manufacturing plant (N =984) revealed that the likelihood of accessing an employee assistance program providing psychological treatment for drinking problems was directly increased by their belief in the efficacy of the program (Delaney, Grube & Ames, 1998). Ahmed & Westra (2009) provided participants demonstrating a high fear of negative evaluation with a rationale about CBT for the treatment of social anxiety. Participants' expectancies for improvements in their anxiety and their perceived helpfulness of exposure to information about treatment efficacy were measured before and after being exposed to the information. Participants' perceptions of the helpfulness of treatment and their expectations for anxiety change significantly improved following the presentation of a rationale for therapy. Mitchell and Gordon (2007) found that a sample of university students rated a computerised CBT treatment for depression as less credible, unlikely to help improve depression, and also reported that they were unlikely to use it. However, after their participants were exposed to a sample demonstration of the treatment, increases were found in credibility, expectation for improvement, and perceived likelihood of using the treatment in the future.

It is evident that an association exists between treatment preferences and consumers knowledge or understanding of available treatments. Therefore, providing information regarding the outcomes and process of e-mental health services may increase their perceived likelihood of uptake. Casey, Joy & Clough (2013) directly tested this possibility in a randomised control study by investigating the relationship between knowledge of e-mental health services and attitudes toward e-mental health services. The attitudes examined were the perceived helpfulness of e-mental health services and the likelihood of using the services. Participants ($N = 217$) were randomly assigned to one of three conditions: provision of e-mental health information by means of film; provision of e-mental health information by text; or provision of no e-mental health information. Main effects were found for type of e-mental health service and for both perceived helpfulness and likelihood of future use. Participants perceived online programs without therapist assistance as being significantly less helpful, and reported reduced likelihood of engaging these programs when compared to other e-mental health services. There was also a main effect for type of information intervention, in that the text group reported higher likelihood of e-mental health use in the future, whereas there were no effects for the film group. Results indicated that participants perceive important differences between types of e-mental health services, and that a brief text intervention can improve attitudes toward these services.

Finally, provision of information may also be important for clinicians, with research suggesting that particularly in rural areas health professionals play an important role in the referral of clients to treatment pathways (Griffiths & Christensen, 2007). However, research suggests that professional opinions of e-mental health programs remain largely unfavourable (Tarrier et al., 2006), although more research is needed in this area.

8.5 Adherence and Dropout from E-mental Health services

Researchers vary considerably in their use of the terms to describe clients ceasing treatment. "Premature termination", "attrition" and "dropout" are used interchangeably in the literature to indicate clients who terminate before the completion of treatment. High attrition rates are common for e-mental health services and are thought to be due to the low intensity and unstructured nature of many online treatment programs (Bennett & Glasgow, 2009). However, attrition rates are found to be similar to traditional face-to-face therapy when online treatment programs are combined with therapist support (Kaltenthaler et al, 2008; Melville, Casey, & Kavanagh, 2010; Proudfoot, 2004). In a comprehensive review of the literature (1990 to 2009) on the extent of dropout from internet-based treatment programs for psychological disorders, a weighted mean of 31% was found for dropout rates (Melville et al., 2010). Within e-mental health, client engagement includes not only initial uptake of services but also participation in therapeutic modules and activities (i.e., adherence), and completion of a therapeutic program. Research investigating strategies to minimize client dropout in e-mental health services is currently limited, as is research investigating ways of enhancing client adherence to these programs.

8.6 Adherence

Client adherence during a psychological program is an important predictor of treatment outcome. This relationship is particularly true when considering self help or unguided programs (Rapee, Abbott, Baillie, & Gaston, 2007). Nordgreen and colleagues (2012) examined patient adherence in guided and unguided e-mental health treatment for social phobia. Results indicated greater adherence for guided compared to unguided treatment. For the unguided self-help group, higher participant ratings of treatment credibility were associated with greater treatment adherence. This effect was not found for the guided group, suggesting that client perceptions of treatment credibility may be of particular importance for programs with reduced or no therapist contact.

The efficacy of internet delivered therapy with therapist telephone support was examined by Carlbring et al (2007). Participants in the treatment group were found to have high adherence to the social anxiety program, with 93% of participants completing all modules of the program. However, as the study did not contain a comparison treatment group, a direct comparison of the unique contribution of the telephone support was not possible. Although patient adherence was found to be significantly greater (93% vs. 62%) when compared to participants from a previous study (Andersson et al., 2006) that completed the same e-therapy program without telephone support. These results indicate that client engagement during e-mental health programs may be increased by the addition of minimal therapist support and contact during the program.

8.7 Dropout

Although Melville et al (2010) failed to find consistent associations between the various client, contextual, and treatment related variables among participants who dropped out of e-mental health programs, there is some evidence that dropout may be lower among those clients with more favourable treatment expectations and perceptions of credibility prior to treatment commencing (Cavanagh et al., 2009). This finding further supports the importance of interventions providing information not only to increase uptake but also to potentially reduce dropout once clients have started programs. Similarly, minimal therapist contact either by phone or email may be an important strategy for increasing client adherence to treatment modules, and promoting greater program completion (Andersson et al., 2006; Carlbring et al., 2007). Such therapist contact might also be beneficial for the recovery of participants who dropout of treatment prematurely.

Alternatively, it may be worth considering how this form of contact can be built into e-mental health services. Melville, Casey, and Kavanagh (in preparation) randomised those participants who dropped out of an online treatment program for pathological gambling to receive either an automated treatment recovery intervention or no intervention. Those in the treatment recovery group were automatically emailed following dropout from the program, with the email inviting them to a return to treatment intervention. The return to treatment intervention was an online program, which explored participant reasons for discontinuing treatment, and provided problem solving and motivational strategies for continuing treatment. At the end of the return to treatment intervention, participants were then asked if they would like to resume their work in the original e-therapy program. Participants in the control condition also received an email upon dropout from the e-therapy program. This email acknowledged their withdrawal from the program and offered participants the option to return to treatment, but did not offer the recovery intervention. Results indicated significant support for this approach to reducing dropout, with 32% of those participants in the treatment recovery condition returning to treatment compared to 9% in the control condition. Interventions such as this, which require minimal or no therapist input, could substantially improve client engagement and reduce dropout in e-mental health programs.

8.8 Summary

The effectiveness of e-mental health therapies is dependent on client engagement with these services. These engagement behaviours can include initial uptake of services, engagement with activities and modules, and completion of programs. A range of efficacious e-mental health programs now exist, however ongoing difficulties with client engagement in these services remain. Recent research suggests that uptake of services can be improved through educational interventions, which may be important for both health professionals and consumers.

These educational interventions may also be beneficial in improving client perceptions of credibility and effectiveness of e-mental health interventions, particularly for those programs with minimal or no therapist contact. Improving client attitudes and understanding of e-mental health programs has been found to have beneficial effects for engagement with therapeutic content, as well as reducing dropout. Client engagement with e-mental health programs would also likely improve with the integration of dropout recovery programs, such as those used by Melville et al. (in preparation).

Despite the ongoing difficulties with client engagement currently observed in e-mental health programs, the difficulties reported are similar to those observed in face-to-face treatment programs. Ongoing difficulties exist in traditional therapy modalities with regards to help seeking behaviours and uptake of services, engagement during therapy and homework adherence, as well as the completion of treatment programs. A considerable amount of research has been conducted in these areas with various therapeutic strategies (e.g., motivational, session contracting, dropout recovery) found to enhance client engagement in these areas. As of yet, research in the use of these engagement interventions is limited with regards to e-mental health interventions. Future research should explore the integration of these strategies with the aim of increasing client engagement and thereby the effectiveness of e-mental health programs.

References

Ahmed, M., & Westra, H. A. (2009). Impact of a treatment rationale on expectancy and engagement in cognitive behavioural therapy for social anxiety. Cognitive Therapy and Research, 33, 314-322.

Andersson, G., Carlbring, P., Holmstrom, A., Sparthan, E., Furmark, T., Nilsson-Ihrfelt, E., . . . Ekselius, L. (2006). Internet-based self-help with therapist feedback and in vivo group exposure for social phobia: A randomized controlled trial. [Article]. Journal of Consulting and Clinical Psychology, 74(4), 677-686. doi: 10.1037/0022-006x.74.4.677

Barak, A., Hen, L., Boniel-Nissim, M., & Shapira, N. a. (2008). A comprehensive review and a meta-analysis of the effectiveness of Internet-based psychotherapeutic interventions. Journal of Technology in Human Services, 26(2-4), 109-160. doi: http://dx.doi.org/10.1080/15228830802094429

Barak, A., Klein, B., & Proudfoot, J. G. (2009). Defining Internet-supported therapeutic interventions. Annals of Behavioral Medicine, 38(1), 4-17.

Bennett, G. G., & Glasgow, R. E. (2009). The delivery of public health interventions via the Internet: actualizing their potential. Annu Rev Public Health, 30, 273-292.

Berger, M., Wagner, T. H., & Baker, L. C. (2005). Internet use and stigmatized illness. Social Science & Medicine, 61(8), 1821-1827. doi: DOI: 10.1016/j.socscimed.2005.03.025

Carlbring, P., Gunnarsdottir, M., Hedensjo, L., Andersson, G., Ekselius, L., & Furmark, T. (2007). Treatment of social phobia: randomised trial of internet-delivered cognitive-behavioural therapy with telephone support. [Article]. British Journal of Psychiatry, 190, 123-128. doi: 10.1192/bjp.bp.105.020107

Carper, M., McHugh, R., & Barlow, D. (2011). The Dissemination of Computer-Based Psychological Treatment: A Preliminary Analysis of Patient and Clinician Perceptions. Administration and Policy in Mental Health and Mental Health Services Research., doi: 10.1007/s10488-011-0377-5.

Casey, L. M., Joy, A., & Clough, B. A. (2013). The impact of information on attitudes toward E-mental health services. Cyberpsychology, Behavior, and Social Networking, 16(8), 593-598.

Cavanagh, K., Shapiro, D. A., Van Den Berg, S., Swain, S., Barkham, M., & Proudfoot, J. (2009). The acceptability of computer-aided cognitive behavioural therapy: a pragmatic study. [; Research Support, Non-U.S. Gov't]. Cognitive behaviour therapy, 38(4), 235-246. doi: 10.1080/16506070802561256

Clarke, G., Eubanks, D., Reid, E., Kelleher, C., O'Connor, E., DeBar, L. L., . . . Gullion, C. (2005). Overcoming depression on the Internet (ODIN) (2): A randomized trial of a self-help depression skills program with reminders. [Article]. Journal of Medical Internet Research, 7(2). doi: e16 10.2196/jmir.7.2.e16

Clough, B. A., & Casey, L. M. (2011). Technological Adjuncts to Increase Adherence to Therapy: A Review. Clinical Psychology Review, 31, 697-710.

Delaney, W., Grube, J. W., & Ames, G. M. (1998). Predicting likelihood of seeking help through the employee assistance program among salaried and union hourly employees. Addiction, 93(3), 399-410.

Dwight-Johnson, M., Sherbourne, C. D., Liao, D., & Wells, K. B. (2000). Treatment preferences among depressed primary care patients. Journal of General Internal Medicine, 15(8), 527-534.

Esters, I. G., Cooker, P. G., & Ittenbach, R. F. (1998). Effects of a unit of instruction in mental health on rural adolescents' conceptions of mental illness and attitudes about seeking help. Adolescence, 33(130), 469-469-476.

Farberman, R. K. (1997). Public attitudes about psychologists and mental health care: Research to guide the American Psychological Association public education campaign. Professional Psychology: Research and Practice, 28(2), 128-136. doi: 10.1037/0735-7028.28.2.128

Griffiths, K., Farrer, L., & Christensen, H. (2007). Clickety-click: E-mental health train on track. Australasian Psychiatry, 15(2), 100-108.

Griffiths, K. M., & Christensen, H. (2007). Internet-based mental health programs: A powerful tool in the rural medical kit. Australian Journal of Rural Health, 15(2), 81-87. doi: 10.1111/j.1440-1584.2007.00859.x

Hordern, A., Georgiou, A., Whetton, S., & Progmet, M. (2011). Consumer eHealth-an overview of the research evidence and the implications for future policy. Health Information Management Journal, 40(2), 6-14.

Horgan, Á., & Sweeney, J. (2010). Young students' use of the Internet for mental health information and support. Journal of Psychiatric and Mental Health Nursing, 17(2), 117-123. doi: 10.1111/j.1365-2850.2009.01497.x

Kaltenthaler, E., Sutcliffe, P., Parry, G., Beverley, C., Rees, A., & Ferriter, M. (2008). The acceptability to patients of computerized cognitive behaviour therapy for depression: a systematic review. Psychological Medicine, 38, 1521-1530.

King, V. L., Stoller, K. B., Kidorf, M., Kindbom, K., Hursh, S., Brady, T., & Bronner, R. K. (2009). Assessing the effectiveness of an Internet-based videoconferencing platform for delivering intensified substance abuse counseling Journal of Substance Abuse Treatment, 36, 331-338.

Kiropoulos, L. A., Klein, B., Austin, D. W., Gilson, K., Pier, C., Mitchell, J., & Ciechomski, L. (2008). Is internet-based CBT for panic disorder and agoraphobia as effective as face-to-face CBT? Journal of Anxiety Disorders, 22, 1273-1284.

Klein, B., & Cook, S. (2010). Preferences for e-mental health services amongst an online Australian sample. Electronic Journal of Applied Psychology, 6, 28-39.

Leach, L. S., Christensen, H., Griffiths, K. M., Jorm, A. F., & Mackinnon, A. J. (2007). Websites as a mode of delivering mental health information: Perceptions from the Australian public. Social Psychiatry and Psychiatric Epidemiology, 42, 167-172.

Melville, K. M., Casey, L. M., & Kavanagh, D. J. (2010). Dropout from Internet-based treatment for psychological disorders. British Journal of Clinical Psychology, 49, 455-471. doi: 10.1348/014466509x472138

Melville, K. M., Casey, L. M., & Kavanagh, D. J. (in preparation). Evaluation of a Program to Recover Dropouts from Internet-based Psychological Treatment

Mitchell, N., & Gordon, P. K. (2007). Attitudes towards computerized CBT for depression amongst a student population. [Article]. Behavioural and Cognitive Psychotherapy, 35(4), 421-430. doi: 10.1017/s1352465807003700

Mohr, D. C., Ho, J., Duffecy, J., Baron, K. G., Lehman, K. A., Jin, L., & Reifler, D. (2010). Perceived barriers to psychological treatments and their relationship to depression. Journal of Clinical Psychology, 66(4), 394-409. doi: 10.1002/jclp.20659

Neal, D. M., Campbell, A. J., Williams, L. Y., Liu, Y., & Nussbaumer, D. (2011). "I did not realize so many options are available": Cognitive authority, emerging adults, and e-mental health. Library & Information Science Research, 33(1), 25-33. doi: DOI: 10.1016/j.lisr.2010.07.015

Nicholas, J., Oliver, K., Lee, K., & O'Brien, M. (2004). Help-seeking behaviour and the Internet: An investigation among Australian adolescents Australian e-Journal for the Advancement of Mental Health, 3, 1-7.

Nordgreen, T., Havik, O. E., Öst, L. G., Furmark, T., Carlbring, P., & Andersson, G. (2012). Outcome predictors in guided and unguided self-help for social anxiety disorder. Behaviour Research and Therapy, 50(1), 13-21. doi: http://dx.doi.org/10.1016/j.brat.2011.10.009

Proudfoot, J. G. (2004). Computer-based treatment for anxiety and depression: is it feasible? Is it effective? Neuroscience & Biobehavioral Reviews, 28(3), 353-363. doi: 10.1016/j.neubiorev.2004.03.008

Rapee, R. M., Abbott, M. J., Baillie, A. J., & Gaston, J. E. (2007). Treatment of social phobia through pure self-help and therapist-augmented self-help. British Journal of Psychiatry, 191(3), 246-252.

Rickwood, D. (2010). Promoting youth mental health through computer-mediated communication. International Journal of Mental Health Promotion 12(3), 32-44.
Sawamura, K., Ito, H., Koyama, A., Tajima, M., & Higuchi, T. (2010). The effect of an educational leaflet on depressive patients' attitudes toward treatment. Psychiatry Research, 177(1), 184-187.
Sharp, W., Hargrove, D. S., Johnson, L., & Deal, W. P. (2006). Mental Health Education: An Evaluation of a Classroom Based Strategy to Modify Help Seeking for Mental Health Problems. Journal of College Student Development, 47(4), 419-438.
Tarrier, N., Liversidge, T., & Gregg, L. (2006). The acceptability and preference for the psychological treatment of PTSD. Behaviour Research and Therapy, 44(11), 1643-1656.
Titov, N., Andrews, G., Johnston, L., Schwencke, G., & Choi, I. (2009). Shyness programme: Longer term benefits, cost-effectiveness, and acceptability. Australian and New Zealand Journal of Psychiatry, 43(1), 36-44.
Tsan, J. Y., & Day, S. X. (2007). Personality and gender as predictors of online counseling use. Journal of Technology in Human Services, 25(3), 39-55.
Woodhead, E. L., Ivan, L. I., & Emery, E. E. (2012). An exploratory study of inducing positive expectancies for psychotherapy. Aging and Mental Health, 16(2), 162-166.

Lise Haddouk

9 Intersubjectivity in Video Interview

Abstract: The emergence of cyberculture with the development of the internet has led to achanges in the social link, in which communication never stops. In this context, computer-mediated intersubjective relationships represent a main line of thinking and research.

New practices in psychology emerge with ICT usage, both in the fields of research and for therapeutic purposes. Some fields like medicine already use remote health platforms that have proven useful in certain situations.

In the field of remote clinical psychology, different media are used that contribute to the framework of the remote clinical interview. Videoconferencing enables the introduction of an important element from the point of view of "sensoriality": the body image, which engages the subjects' interaction in a different way than in a written or verbal exchange. But is the use of videoconferencing sufficient to establish a clinical framework comparable to the traditional one? How can the computer-mediated relationship enable and establish a potential object relation, rather than a mirrored one?

Thinking through an online adaptation of the clinical interview framework led to the elaboration of a specific tool dedicated to this purpose, the iPSY site, and to research into the access to intersubjectivity in clinical video interviews. This study's encouraging results have fostered the a platform dedicated to the conduct of clinical interviews through videoconferencing for many psychotherapists and patients. A methodological analysis accompanies this research, in order to continuously observe this specific clinical practice.

9.1 Introduction

In today's post-modern society ICT has a variety of uses, leading to the cyberculture context in which we now live. Different comments emerge from the observations of these uses in human sciences. Some observations are questioning the notion of social link, which has drastically since remote communication was made possible by the internet in the end of the 90's [1], [2], [3].

Considering these changes, even the notion of relationship could be re-defined. Almost all friendships, from work to love, are nowadays influenced by the availability of new medias. They also represent an exchange of information and interactions involving emotional and affective factors, which may influence physical factors.

However, it is probable that the type of media used to communicate influences the quality of the relation, particularly the influence of the body image during communication. In a written chat communication, no facial or body expressions can be taken into consideration, contrarily to a video communication [4].

In the health field, the use of ICT has produced changes in the therapeutic relationship between patients and medical staff and has proven to be sometimes as much or even more efficient than classical care. In the field of psychology, research and therapeutic protocols already include uses of ICT.

Our initial approach was to consider how we could adapt the clinical interview framework online, defined in a psychodynamic pattern [5]. This question led us to create a specific tool, dedicated to videoconference interviews and facilitating access to the intersubjective dimension [6].

9.2 ICT uses in Cyberculture

9.2.1 Cyberculture Values

In the context of the Cyberculture there is a communicational paradox: in the age of mass communication, individuals are becoming increasingly isolated.

At the roots of the "cult of the Internet" [1] also lies the cult of information created by cybernetics. This term, coined by Wiener [7] later gave the root "cyber" to different words, such as cyberculture, cyberspace, cyberpsychology, etc. The new world vision supported by Wiener, although he never directly stated it, appears as an "anti-metaphysical" approach: it postulates that, somehow, there isn't anything behind the real, which is reduced to the constant and visible exchange of the information that constitutes it. According to Breton [1]: "*The new paradigm is a vision of the relation, that confines the real in the relational, and the relational in the informational*".

In our research framework using video interview, the notion of relation holds a central place: our point is to consider the principal elements of a clinical interview with a psychotherapeutic purpose, and to adapt them to an online medium. In "videocounseling", the computer-mediated relation between two human beings cannot be reduced only to an informational exchange, since the affective, emotional and intersubjective factors are essential components.

This leads us to address the notion of relation, which might be redefined by the emergence of ICT in our post-modern societies.

9.2.2 New Definition of the Social Link, of the Relation?

Different aspects seem to emerge in computer-mediated relations. We can first recall that in post-modern societies, according to Lasch [8]: "*The social conditions that predominate tend to conjure up the narcissistic traits that are present, to varying degrees, in each of us*". He describes societies of images and screens, in which a reliable world made of objects has been replaced by a world of blurred images, and in which it becomes increasingly difficult to distinguish reality from fantasy.

According to Breton [1], the "taboo of the encounter" questions the management of violence in this same encounter. Thus: "*The price for peace is a double separation, on one hand between the body and the mind, and on the other, between the bodies themselves*".

This is true in many ICT uses, from video games to psychotherapeutic care. We then talk of "virtual reality" to designate the phenomena linked to the subject's feeling of immersion in digital worlds.

While there is much talk about "virtual reality" on the internet, in the context of psychotherapeutic counseling, we are on the contrary talking about mental reality. While on the internet some uses tend to blur the traditional barrier between private life and public life, the psychotherapeutic session has its own temporality and implies a level of confidentiality that respects the private sphere. Considering the current uses of ICT in the fields of care and psychology, how can the framework of the psychotherapeutic session be adapted online?

9.2.3 ICT and Tele-health

As in the health field, a lot of research and therapeutic protocols in psychology already includeuse of ICT. Among these applications of ICT, there is « digital psychotherapeutic mediations ». In this situation technology can be used to put the subject into a situation of immersion within a digital environment. Since 1995 [9], research in this area has developed, introducing both interesting methods and results, for example in the treatment of anxiety disorders such as phobias [10, 11]. Much of this research has shown that the exposition to the "virtual" is as efficient as classical cognitive-behavioral therapies. This success could be partially explained by the phenomena of presence and the fact that the same motor regions within the brain are activated when an action is executed in reality as when the same action is mentally simulated [12].

Another type of digital mediation in psychotherapy concerns the use of videoconferencing. According to Bouchard [13], this kind of therapy allows for the development of a good therapeutic relationship for subjects with anxiety disorders, and would have comparable effectiveness to traditional face-to-face psychotherapy. Thus, the contribution of the psychodynamic approach can be interesting considering the ICT uses and the notion of relation, which is central in a psychotherapeutic interview.

The specific question we posed was how can we consider a psychodynamics-inspired clinical use of ICT through videoconferencing?

9.3 Video interview specificities

Even if the use of clinical video interviews already exist in many professional practices, a particular methodological framework, considering this new way of working, needs to be developed. It is obvious for many psychologists today that videoconferencing can be useful in situations in which they are separated from patients. Many professionals already use existing videoconferencing software such as Skype, employing it as a work tool adapted to their purpose.

However, videoconference might not be sufficient to define a clinical interview framework. « Wild » psychotherapy on the internet can present some risks for users and bring about ethical dilemmas such as data confidentiality.

A thorough analysis of the specificities of this new type of practice will lead us to describe the conception and the use of an online tool adapted and dedicated to the clinical interview.

9.3.1 Body image

Compared to a written exchange (chat) or a verbal one (phone), videoconferencing brings more « bodiness» to the communication. Thus, from a sensorial perspective, while only the voice is used on the telephone, videoconferencing also brings the visual perception of the bodies interacting during the session.We suppose that this « bodiness »-reinforced interaction can « re-humanize » the communication at a distance compared to other medias, and help both patient and psychotherapist to find an interview framework similar to a regular one.

It is also important to note that the body and the sensoriality aspects will be increasingly involved, as technology constantly improves.As such, an object relationship development might thus be preferred to a mirror relationship.

9.3.2 Object Relation vs. Mirrored One

In the context of cyberculture and post-modern societies, some ICT uses display regressive aspects and valorize the object at the expense of the values that define humanity. Are we still involved in relations one with the other, or are we alone in front of our screens?

The iPSY platform has been developed to introduce a symbolic third party, and not to favor the capture in the screen mirror. The objective is to see subjectivity emerge through the use that the subject makes of the image, of the mirror option, of the sound surroundings, of the therapist's look in the transference.

Many options included in the website result from thinking through the online adaptation of the psychotherapeutic framework; this has led to favor a transitional aspect rather than a specular one for the design and utilization of iPSY.

9.3.3 Three Levels of Interaction According to Lebovici

According to Lebovici [14], the interactive schemas derived from mother-baby observations illustrate different levels of interaction.

The behavioral interaction is visible on three main levels: bodily, visual and vocal. The bodily level refers to the physical and mental *holding* of Winnicott [15] as well as to the *handling*. The visual level corresponds to eye-to-eye dialogue, or to eyes meeting, and refers to what Winnicott [16] describes in reference to the mother's look as the mirror for the mental subject constitution through the first object relation. The affective interaction [14] derives from the emotional climate.

Finally, the fantasy interaction relates to the reciprocal influence of the mother's life development and of her baby's, both through their imaginary, conscious aspects, and their fantasized, unconscious ones. It gives meaning to the behavioral interaction.

In videocounseling, we have used these references to analyze the interviews and observe the various levels of interaction. The data collected have provided convincing results that interactions in a classical framework and in a "videocounseling" framework are similar.

9.4 The iPSY site

9.4.1 Method

Our study sample comprised of 30 patients, who all registered on our internet site and volunteered to participate. The sole screening of the study was to exclude children from the sample, to enable greater homogeneity. Also, none of the volunteering patients were over 60 years of age.

Prior to conducting the first "videocounseling" sessions, we introduced a preliminary step on iPSY to ensure that each patient was apt to follow this online therapy.

Among the 30 registered patients, several sessions were conducted with 8 of them, aged from 18 to 40. These 8 individuals were split into 2 groups: the first group members had previously followed a therapy in a standard practice run by the iPSY therapist, whereas there had been no previous interaction between iPSY and the members of the second group. The subjects read and signed informed authorization forms in both digital and paper format, after having accepted the terms of use of the site. All of these subjects were followed by the same therapist, in order to evaluate the transference and counter-transference dimension.

The first group was composed of four women, from 18 to 40 years of age, all living in the greater Paris area. Their demands were either linked to the fact they were away for significant periods of time, or that they had difficulties reaching the practice. The second group was composed of three men and one woman, from 20 to 39 years of age, living in the greater Paris area or abroad. Their demands were linked to different motives, notably the geographic distance or their isolation.

Over a two-year period, 139 session video recordings were made with this sample.

30 SADS questionnaires were also filled: this quantitative tool was included on the web site as a last registration step; it makes it possible to identify behaviors linked to social avoidance, and includes a rather simple transfer and quote protocol. It can assist in spotting tendencies that would make it difficult to establish social relations, people scoring high at SADS are supposed to feel uncomfortable socially and would rather stay alone. Indeed, the mere idea of forthcoming social interactions can generate anxiety for them.

The use of the SADS questionnaire came in addition to the qualitative data obtained through videoconferencing and was incorporated to shed an additional light on the findings.

9.4.2 Video interviews

The iPSY platform design is inspired by the face-to-face clinical interview model [5]. The particular objective of this study was to design an online tool that is as close as possible to the clinical framework and respects its rules. It has then become possible to evaluate the access to the different levels of discourse and to grasp the mental reality in videocounseling.

Several fundamental principles have been adapted online, such as the rules relative to time and money. Thus, the use of an agenda to set up an appointment on iPSY implies a delay and not an immediacy to meet the therapist. The regularity of the sessions' frequency and length has also been adapted online. "*The payment corrective influence*" [17] is another aspect included in the implementation, bringing an additional element of reality to the framework and transfer set up.

The principles of benevolent neutrality and of free association have been applied to the listening via videoconferencing.

Ethical rules were particular critical with the data security issue. Thus, it was critical to use a dedicated private server and not software such as Skype, which do not offer sufficient security features in regards to data storage and exchange.

Differentiated spaces are employed on the site, such as the waiting room and the videocounseling practice room, to help the therapist stay in control of the framework by guiding the patient through these spaces. This laying out, in the context of a remote appointment with a professional, has facilitated the implication of participants in a manner similar to a classical practice session.

We used a 12-item grid to analyze the videocounseling recordings.

Some items relate to aesthetics of the interaction and to sensorial interactions, involving the analyst's and the patient's bodies, for example through the "mirror option". This option, available in all videoconferencing software, is proposed on iPSY to give the patient the possibility to see his own image during the interview, the psychotherapist being notified by the system.

The patient elects whether or not to activate this option when he/she is in the waiting room. He/she won't be able to modify his/her choice during the session, in order not to favor the mirror dimension in the use of this option during the interview, but rather the intersubjective dimension. The choice that the patient makes can thus shed light on their personal mental problem.

Examples of other items that were part of the grid, such as the specific phenomenon of the "eye lag" in videoconferencing, which means that the interacting subjects are not looking directly into each other's eyes because of the webcam position; whereas another was the picture framing choice made by the participants. Furthermore the three interaction levels were also included in the analysis grid.

These various elements assisted in the analysis of the transference and countertransference within this online framework. This was a pre-requisite to first evaluate the system, before using it for clinical and therapeutic purposes.

9.4.3 Results

9.4.3.1 Quantitative results

SADS results showed that the overall cohort population had very high scores (15.3 on average). This could mean that the people who registered on iPSY, but did not go further into videocounseling, had more drastic social avoidance disorders than the persons we met. This could also confirm the hypothesis that the tool enables a face-to-face encounter, which is comparable but not identical to a traditional practice situation, with sensorial interactions involving the body of the therapist and the patient.

The overall cohort scores are slightly higher than those of the first group (14.75) and much higher than those of the second group (3).

This could mean that the people who solely followed our framework to meet a therapist, and never went to a therapist's practice, are actually less prone to social avoidance than those we had previously met in a traditional framework. This would thus mean that our system didn't particularly attract subjects with social avoidance disorders, while we initially believed that body encounter avoidance could contribute to this choice of therapy.

However, these results do not permit a conclusive outcome given the small size and weak representativeness of our sample.

9.4.3.2 Qualitative results

The theme-based grid analysis results for these two groups validate the assumption that a clinical session is possible through videoconferencing, and comparable to the practice framework, although without being totally identical. Depending on the issues of each of the subjects, videocounseling has enabled continuity in the follow-up in different circumstances. A short presentation of the results through clinical elements relating to one subject in each group will illustrate singular uses in videocounseling.

Anne (group 1) is 39 years old, a painter, single and childless, having been married and divorced twice. The move from the traditional framework to videocounseling is linked to two factors: a somatic pathology of the hip makes her moving about difficult, and the death of her mother, which occurred a few days before the first videocounseling session.

Observing the interactive schemas during the remote sessions with Anne reveals that the silences, which are relatively few, sometimes happen when she mentions the maternal object: “It’s her I could tell: “I’m cold” and...[*silence*] I had no one else”. These rare pauses in the associative chain evoke the ongoing mourning process. Confronted by my silence, Anne sometimes reacts by fearing she can no longer hear me, which seems to upset her. She then expresses in both verbal and non-verbal ways a separation anxiety in this specific interview framework. Anne smiles broadly when she sees me on the screen, although she laughed only little during our sessions. In regards to the verbal aspects of the discourse, Anne talks very loudly, which forces me to put the volume on minimum when I review the interviews. After my interventions, her speech rate calms down, and she speaks softly again, as if the therapist’s voice could have a containing function, even remotely.

The analysis of the effects linked to the presence of the camera and to the screen frame enabled us to evaluate the dimension of the look either as a specular mirror or leading to intersubjectivity. Anne turns on the mirror option from the first session. She makes a comment about her appearance and states that she does not find herself pretty on the screen whereas, in front of her mirror, she “ain’t that bad”. This underlines the manner in which she perceives the eye of the camera, sending her back an altered image of herself as an “alias” of the therapist’s eye and maybe evoking the maternal eye in a persecution-related dimension. She displays her face close-up, with her shoulders and hands remaining invisible, unless they move and sway in front of the camera while punctuating her discourse, a sign of restlessness previously observed during our sessions in my practice. Is her proximity with the camera lens a sign of the relational distance Anne establishes in her relationships to others?

On the transference / counter-transference front, elements emerge in the use she makes of the system. As sessions go by, Anne is attempting to fit a space for the interviews but she also puts the framework to test, for example through technical questions. The recurrence of a "technical failure" (during which she no longer hears while everything seems to be working fine technically) might reveal her pain as to the more general feeling of not being heard, through some form of persecution-related transferential projection specific to the system. A number of parapraxia also mark our encounters, notably her absence at our appointments. Afterwards, I realize that her absenteeism has had the same frequency in both frameworks.

After several videoconferencing sessions, an evolution in her mental state was notable. Following a span with a depressive connotation in the pursuit of her mourning process, she can, in this space, make the transition from the living mother to the dead mother with a transitional calling. The system thus allowed continuity in our exchanges at a particular moment of her life, while pursuing a mental construction process.

The manner in which Anne took control of the tool revealed elements of her mental problems, notably her fear of a sound failure, largely linked to a more general fear of not being heard.

Frederic (group 2) is 32 years old, single and in search of a job in computer graphic design. He states a demand centered on a symptom he refers to as "water phobia" and indicates he'd rather use videocounseling because it's difficult for him to go out of his home.

Observation of the interactive schemas reveals that Frederic's silences are often associated with the same expression on his face: a tightening of the mouth, as if he were preventing the words from coming out. Frederic also places his hands in a peculiar way: he often places them in front of his mouth, an inhibition sign in reaction to certain topics raised during our sessions. This position of the hands is very visible during the first sessions, but a lot less thereafter. At other times, his hands loosen and move, notably when he manages to talk about himself or about his representation of his mental functioning. On the verbal front, he has a deep-toned voice, rather monotonous. This evolves over time, as a sign of progressive lifting of the defensive mechanisms, which can be observed on the language front.

The analysis of the impact of the camera presence and of the screen frame reveals that Frederic has chosen the mirror option not to see himself. Maybe his face disturbs him; but he could have also made this choice to be as close as possible to a traditional practice conditions. The screen frame he chose was always the same, showing his face and the top of his body. The light in the room in which he sat always placed his face against the light, which evokes a certain escape from the other's look, perceived as threatening. During our last sessions, the backdrop changed, as he sat in another room of his apartment, a lot brighter. The evolution of his "image staging" may underline a certain mental and transferential dynamic, which can be observed through the different ways in which he has taken control of the tool when using it.

Relating to this subject's initial demand which represented an issue linked to inhibition, it is possible that the distance between the bodies induced by videocounseling reassured him, enabling him to avoid a feeling of intrusion, while accessing a listening space. He said that he chose to start online because he felt comfortable and he was familiar with the computer tool. After using it for a while, Frederic came to traditional practice sessions a few times, using the tool as a mental development transitional space.

The method we used to collect data in videocounseling enabled a detailed analysis of the notable relational modalities during remote interviews. The importance of the behavioral interactions was notable through the body movements that were observed as well as through the language used. The look, solicited in a peculiar way through videocounseling, was analyzed through specifics such as the use of the picture frame or of the mirror option by the subjects. The affective interactions were observed through the subjects' verbal or non-verbal language while in interaction. Thus, in videocounseling, the access to the interactions fantasy level has brought light onto the emergence of the patient's subjectivity and onto the transference / counter-transference expressions during the sessions. Through these clinical elements, it thus appears that videocounseling on our platform seems to correspond to the creation of a third space, which facilitates the passage towards intersubjectivity.

The platform has been designed to implement the best practices of a traditional psychotherapeutic framework on an online medium, with an example of these specific practices being the patient follow-up by a single therapist, through a formal appointment and the development of a clinical transferential relationship. The body image is also very important, particularly in the context of the transference and counter-transference relationship between the patient and the therapist, which can be clearly observed on the platform.

Compared to other videoconferencing tools, that can have many different purposes, iPSY was specifically designed and developed to be used by psychotherapists. The website navigation, for both patients and therapists, follows a path leading to the clinical video interview. No other options have been included, other than these necessary to achieve this objective (registration, choice of therapist, patients management, calendar and appointment management, payment, technical support, and optional evaluation tools such as questionnaires). iPSY is also used today as an ongoing research platform, enabling a group of professional therapists who use the system to share information and contribute to research and further developments.

9.5 Conclusion

Our experience of the videocounseling practice confirms the idea that the "virtual" doesn't oppose the real, but that they similarly enable the emergence of the mental reality, and can also reach to the level of the symbolic as it is understood in psychoanalysis.

Adapting the clinical session framework with iPSY has thus allowed us to find that the intersubjective dimension is similar in the context of exchanges with subjects, whether online or in a traditional context, by placing emphasis on the body position in the remote relation and by suggesting a time-space framework that permits remote clinical work. Videocounseling practice also enlightens us about the specificities of a distance online relationship. These promising results led us to redesign the system used for the initial research to extend its usage to multiple professionals, while pursuing the research work on a larger scale. Different approaches are envisaged today on the clinical front, both with independent professionals and with institutions working on domains such as trauma, expatriation or adolescence.

In numerous situations, iPSY can bring an interesting addition to standard care and thus represents an advance in health care through technology.

References

[1] Breton, P. (2000). Le culte de l'Internet, une menace pour le lien social ? Paris : Éditions La Découverte.

[2] Breton, P. ; PROULX, S. (2002). L'explosion de la communication à l'aube du XXIème siècle. Paris : Éditions La Découverte.

[3] Turkle, S. (2011). Alone Together: Why We Expect More from Technology and Less from Each Other. New-York : Basic Books.

[4] Haddouk, L. (2013). La place du corps dans les rites numériques. Illustration : la visioconsultation. Les Cahiers du Numérique, 9(3-4), 83-110.

[5] Chiland, C. (1983). L'entretien clinique, Paris : PUF.

[6] Haddouk, L., Govindama, Y., Marty, F. (2013). A Video Interview Experience. Cyberpsychology, Behavior and Social Networking, 16(5), 402-405.

[7] Wiener, N. (1954). The Human Use of Human Beings: Cybernetics and Society. Boston : Houghton Mifflin.

[8] Lasch, C. (1979). The Culture of narcissism. NY : Paperback.

[9] Rothbaum, B.O. et Hodges, L.F., (1995). Effectiveness of Virtual Reality Graded Exposure in the Treatment of Acrophobia. American Journal of Psychiatry, 152, 626-628.

[10] Bouchard, S., St-Jacques, J., Robillard, G., & Renaud, P. (2007). Efficacité d'un traitement d'exposition en réalité virtuelle pour le traitement de l'arachnophobie chez l'enfant : Une étude pilote. Journal de Thérapie Comportementale et Cognitive, 17(3), 101-108.

[11] Bouchard, S., St-Jacques, J., Robillard, G., Côté, S., et Renaud, P. (2003). Efficacité de l'exposition en réalité virtuelle pour l'acrophobie : Une étude préliminaire. Journal de Thérapie Comportementale et Cognitive, 13(3), 107-112.

[12] Fuchs, P. (dir.), Arnaldi, B., Bourdot, P., et Burkhardt, J.M. (2006). Le Traité de la réalité virtuelle, t. IV, Les Applications de la réalité virtuelle. Paris : Presses de l'École des mines.

[13] Bouchard, S., Germain, V., Marchand, A., Guay, S., et Drouin, M.-S. (2010). Assessment of the Therapeutic Alliance in Face-to-Face or Videoconference Treatment for Posttraumatic Stress Disorder. CyberPsychology and Behavior, 13(1), 29-35.

[14] Lebovici, S. (1994). Les interactions fantasmatiques. Revue de Medecine Psychosomatique, 37/38, 39-50.

[15] Winnicott, D.W. (1956). Primary maternal preoccupation. In Through Pediatrics to Psychoanalysis. London : Routledge.

[16] Winnicott, D.W. (1971). Mirror-role of Mother and Family in Child Development. In Playing and reality. London : Tavistock Publications.
[17] Freud, S. (1913). Further recommendations on the technique of Psycho-Analysis. In La technique psychanalytique, Collected papers of..., NY : Basic Books.

Megan Moreno, Natalie Goniu, Peter Moreno, Doug Diekema

10 Ethical and Regulatory Considerations For Social Media Research

Abstract: Social media websites (SMWs) are increasingly popular research tools. These sites provide new opportunities for researchers, but raise new challenges for Institutional Review Boards (IRBs) that review these research protocols. To date, there is little guidance regarding how an Institutional Review Board (IRB) should review studies involving SMWs. The purpose of this paper was to review common risks inherent in social media research and consider how researchers can consider these risks when writing research protocols. This chapter focuses on three common research approaches: 1) observational research such as observing content created and posted on SMW, 2) interactive research including studies in which a researchers wishes to access SMW content that requires permission from the user, and 3) survey/interview research in which SMWs may be used to recruit participants. Concomitant with these research approaches we gave particular attention to issues pertinent to SMW research including privacy, consent and confidentiality. After considering these challenges, we outline key considerations for both researchers and reviewers when creating or reviewing SMW IRB protocols. Our goal in this chapter is to provide a detailed examination of relevant IRB and regulatory issues for both researchers and those who review their protocols.

SMWs provide opportunities for user participation in the creation and display of multimedia data. These popular websites are increasingly emerging as valuable research tools across a variety of fields including psychology, communication, sociology and public health.

10.1 Use of Social Media in Research

10.1.1 Benefits of Social Media Research Methods

There are several aspects of SMWs that provide unique advantages to researchers. First, SMWs present innovative opportunities to examine displayed online behaviors and beliefs in a context that is naturalistic, as it is part of the participants' daily lives. Second, SMWs allow a researcher to reach out and conduct studies within populations that may be hard to reach in traditional research, such as underserved populations. Finally, in many cases, this research may be feasible and low cost as it can be conducted from the researcher's office using a SMW.

10.1.2 Challenges of Social Media Research Methods

SMWs present many new opportunities for research, but also raise new challenges for IRBs that review these research protocols and assess ethical and regulatory issues. It remains difficult to determine what risks and privacy expectations are unique to the SMW realm, and what challenges can be addressed by modifications of known and understood risks inherent in research. To date, there is little guidance from federal regulations or institutions, and very little existing literature, on how an IRB should review research protocols involving SMWs (M. A. Moreno, Fost, & Christakis, 2008; M. A. Moreno, Goniu, Moreno, & Diekema, 2013; Zimmer, 2010).

10.1.3 Purpose of This Chapter

Given these challenges, the purpose of this chapter is to review common risks inherent in social media research and discuss whether these risks represent concerns unique to social media, or modifications to our current understanding of research risks generally. We focused this chapter on three common research approaches: observational research, interactive research and survey/interview research. Concomitant with these research approaches we gave particular attention to issues regarding privacy, consent and confidentiality. After considering these challenges, we conclude this chapter with key considerations for researchers and reviewers when creating or reviewing SMW IRB protocols. Our goal is to provide perspectives on key issues related to social media research towards fostering an open discussion for both researchers and those who review their protocols. Throughout this paper, we have framed our discussion around four SMWs that are currently popular: Twitter, YouTube, LinkedIn and Facebook. Studies of these SMWs illustrate both similarities and differences in social media research techniques and concomitant potential IRB concerns.

10.2 Common Regulatory Concerns with Social Media Research

Like all research, studies that use SMWs pose potential risks to participants. The nature of these risks, however, is not unique to SMWs, and can best be understood within current regulatory frameworks that apply to all research. Research using SMWs fall into three basic categories, all of which are addressed by current federal regulations and institutional guidelines: observational, interactive and survey/interview. We will begin our discussion with observational research because it primarily raises privacy concerns that also apply to the other two research categories.

10.2.1 Observational Research

Observational research in the context of social media usually involves observing content created and posted on SMWs. On Twitter, this may include observing individual "tweets" or a Twitter "feed." On YouTube, this may include observing or coding videos, data about those videos, or comments posted by viewers in response to videos. On LinkedIn or Facebook, data may include evaluating an individual profile, a group, or posted content such as advertisements.

A common first question to ask regarding social media observational research is whether the research is exempt. In the United States, the federal regulations found at 45 CFR 46 govern human subjects research. These regulations identify several types of research that are exempt from the federal requirements for human subjects research, and thus would not require IRB review. These include research that does not involve human subjects and research identified as exempt from the federal regulations. However, an important caveat here is that although the regulations at 45 CFR 46 no longer apply if an activity does not fall under the definition of human subjects research or falls into one of the exempt categories, other federal regulating and funding agencies may nonetheless require IRB review. Furthermore, state and local laws and institutional policy may dictate IRB review in some situations where federal regulation does not. Because the multiple layers of regulation can be quite complicated, research using SMWs should be submitted for IRB review, even if the project does not appear to be human subjects research or even if it appears to fall into an exempt category. The local IRB should have sufficient expertise to determine whether the project can proceed without further review (as non-human subjects research or as exempt) or whether it requires a more extensive IRB review. The discussion that follows reflects the requirements of 45 CFR 46 in order to guide IRBs in navigating the kinds of projects that involve SMWs.

A key issue in considering observational research using social media is whether the proposed project qualifies as human subjects research under existing federal regulations and if so, what type of review is needed. The federal regulations define a human subject as a living individual about whom an investigator conducting research obtains data through intervention or interaction with the individual or obtains identifiable private information. According to 45 CFR 46.102(f) "*Private information*" includes information about behavior that occurs in a context in which an individual can reasonably expect that no observation or recording is taking place, and information which has been provided for specific purposes by an individual and which the individual can reasonably expect will not be made public (for example, a medical record). Private information must be individually identifiable (i.e., the identity of the subject is or may readily be ascertained by the investigator or associated with the information) in order for obtaining the information to constitute research involving human subjects. Based on that definition, if access to a SMW is publicly accessible, information on that website is not private, and information gathering requires no intervention or interaction with the person who posted it online, then the proposed project does not constitute human subjects research, and as such, is not regulated under 45 CFR 46. For example, an observational study of YouTube videos involves a review of content that was posted for unrestricted viewing by any internet user. In this case, the research activity would not meet the definition of human subjects research because the information being reviewed cannot be considered private (it can be viewed by anyone), and it does not require any interaction with the subject to access it. As such, the federal regulations governing human subjects research at 45 CFR 46, including the requirement for IRB review, would not apply to this particular study, and barring state, local, or institutional requirements to the contrary, local IRBs should be comfortable making a determination that such a project represents non-human subjects research.

In addition to the question of whether an observational project constitutes human subjects research, the federal regulations specifically identify observational research as exempt from the requirements of 45CFR 46 if the study involves observation of public behavior, except when information obtained is: a) recorded in such a manner that subjects can be identified either directly or through identifiers linked to the subjects, *and* b) any disclosure of subjects' responses outside the published research that could reasonably place subjects at risk of criminal or civic liability, or be damaging to the subjects' financial standing, employability or reputation. Although public behavior is not defined, one can assume that this category of research would likely apply to an investigator observing websites such as Facebook or LinkedIn, provided that only publicly available profiles were evaluated in order to make collective observations. Presumably, the kind of information made available only to members of more selective networks via "friending" and other mechanisms, would not be considered public behavior and therefore not eligible for exempt status. It is also important to note that this category does not apply to minors if the investigator participates in the activities being observed. Any contact to establish connections with profiles that require authorization of the subject (e.g. "friending") would be considered participation, and would clearly not qualify as exempt when attempting to observe the SMWs of minors.

Changes in SMW policies and controversies related to particular studies have raised new issues regarding whether observation of public behavior via SMWs should continue to receive IRB approval (Lewis, Kaufman, Gonzalez, Wimmer, & Christakis, 2008). In an early SMW study, researchers collected publicly available information from Facebook, but reported it in such a way that participants were individually identifiable (Zimmer, 2010). In 2011, one university IRB's review and interpretation of the Facebook Rights and Responsibilities statement led to controversy over whether a SMW-based study could be approved. At that time, this Facebook policy stated: "*If you collect information from users, you will: obtain their consent, make it clear you (and not Facebook) are the one collecting their information, and post a privacy policy explaining what information you collect and how you will use it.*" In 2013, Facebook changed its privacy policies towards younger adolescents to allow them to make some of their content publicly available, which would allow marketers and potentially researchers to access this data (Kelly, 2013). These debates regarding privacy concerns in observational research, and SMW research generally, involves three major topics: user involvement in privacy protection, website privacy guidelines, and legal considerations.

10.2.1.1 User Involvement in Privacy Settings snd Website Access

Some SMWs allow users to choose their own privacy settings. On Facebook and LinkedIn for example, profile owners have the choice to protect their displayed information through profile security settings (Jackson-Newsom & Shelton; Schulenberg et al., 2005). Profile security settings can be "private" (i.e. limiting some or all profile information access to online friends approved by the profile owner), or "public" (i.e. allowing any user access to the profile). However, on Facebook, some information, such as the profile owner's name, profile picture, friends, "likes", and gender, is considered publicly available and thus is always publicly available. Privacy settings can limit access to the profile as a whole, or settings can be customized to limit access to certain profile viewers or to particular sections of the profile. Similar settings are available on LinkedIn and Twitter. Thus, participants decide whether or not their posted content is publicly available, which may in turn affect whether an IRB views observation of this content as exempt or otherwise permissible research.

In the past, some IRBs have considered whether or not the website itself requires a username and password log-in to determine if the site is of a public or private nature. If a username and password were required, the site was not considered public, thus consent could be required to view content. Newer SMWs raise concerns about whether that policy can still guide these decisions, because many SMWs require usernames and passwords for only particular purposes or only under certain circumstances. YouTube, for example, requires a username and password to verify one is over the age of 18 to post videos and view videos of adult content. Anyone may view general YouTube videos, with or without a username or password. One would therefore not expect that consent would be required to conduct observational study of general YouTube videos. Other SMWs such as Facebook require a username and password to ensure that only the profile owner posts information to his or her page, and to provide tailored advertisements to users and data to marketing companies. The availability of the information posted, however, is determined by the profile owner, who can expressly make the information available to the public. Thus, old paradigms of IRB rules related to internet research may need reconsideration.

10.2.1.2 Website Purpose and Privacy Statements

A reasonable expectation of privacy for a SMW user is comprised of a combination of the intent of the website as well as the website's explicit statement of privacy rules.

The most consistency between website intent and Privacy Policy is that of Twitter, which explicitly stated: *"Twitter instantly connects people everywhere to what's most meaningful to them. Any registered user can send a Tweet...that is public by default. What you say on Twitter may be viewed all around the world instantly."*

Similarly, YouTube's statement of intent of being a forum of sharing videos publicly is consistent with their Privacy Policy, which is now identical to that of Google. At the time of this paper, this policy stated that one *"when you share information publicly, it may be indexable by search engines...Our services provide you with different options on sharing and removing your content."*

The statement of intent for LinkedIn is "connecting the world's professionals." This statement has consistency with the site's Privacy Policy, which stated that: *"The information you provide to LinkedIn may reveal, or allow others to identify, your nationality, ethnic origin, religion, gender, age, geography, or other aspects of your private life."* These synergistic statements present a clear expectation that the responsibility of the content of displayed information and its protection lies with the profile owner.

The described intention of the Facebook site was "to share information with people." This intent was reflected in the first part of their Privacy Policy, which states: *"When you publish content or information using the 'everyone' setting, it means that you are allowing everyone, including people off of Facebook, to access and use that information, and to associate it with you (i.e., your name and profile picture)."* Further in the Privacy Policy, a statement indicated: *"Information set to 'everyone' is publicly available information....Such information may, for example, be accessed by everyone on the Internet (including people not logged into Facebook), be indexed by third-party search engines and be imported, exported, distributed and re-distributed by us and others without privacy limitations."* These statements demonstrated clear wording and were directed at the user. Thus, Facebook informed the user that if profile security settings are publicly available, profile owners should not have a reasonable expectation of privacy.

Facebook also discussed access to information by third parties through these statements: *"We generally limit search engines' access to our site. We may allow them to access information set to the 'everyone' setting (along with your name and profile picture) and your profile information that is visible to everyone."* Facebook then explained how this access to information by third parties can be avoided: *"You can change the visibility of some of your profile information using the customize section of your privacy settings."*

Separate from the Privacy Policy was a "Rights and Responsibilities" hyperlink. This section explained, *"If you collect information from users, you will: obtain their consent, make it clear you (and not Facebook) are the one collecting their information, and post a privacy policy explaining what information you collect and how you will use it."* This statement appeared to be directed at a third party, such as a researcher, who aimed to collect information from Facebook profiles. Thus, a contradiction exists between statements in the Privacy Policy compared to the Rights and Responsibilities sections regarding their intended audience as well as their direction.

10.2.1.3 Legal Considerations

Many IRBs seek guidance from court cases involving the invasion of privacy to determine what would constitute a privacy violation in the research context. Under the Fourth Amendment to the United States Constitution, individuals are protected from governmental searches when and where they have a "reasonable expectation of privacy." This expectation is limited by what society recognizes as reasonable, given the circumstances of the individual at the time of the search. Courts have held, for example, that an individual generally has a reasonable expectation of privacy within his or her own home, but does not have a reasonable expectation of privacy in things the individual knowingly exposes to the public ("Katz v. United States," 1967). The right to privacy is similarly recognized in civil cases between nongovernmental parties. A defendant can be liable, for example, when he or she makes public disclosures of private facts about the plaintiff. Courts deciding such cases often apply a "reasonable expectation of privacy" analysis to the alleged disclosure, typically finding that a fact is private when a reasonable person in the plaintiff's position would expect the fact to be private.

Federal and state courts have examined Facebook's privacy policy and determined that individuals do not have a reasonable expectation of privacy in information they post on their Facebook pages. In Romano v. Steelcase (2010), the plaintiff Romano sued the Steelcase company for damages, claiming their actions had caused her permanent injury and suffering. Steelcase sought information from Romano's current and historical Facebook accounts, including deleted pages, to rebut these claims. The court granted Steelcase's request to access the information on these pages, holding that Romano did not have a reasonable expectation of privacy in information that she published on social networking websites. The court noted that Facebook privacy policies plainly state that information users post may be shared with others, notwithstanding the users' privacy settings, and that information-sharing is the "very nature and purpose of these social networking sites else they would cease to exist." Other courts have similarly concluded that a person has no reasonable expectation of privacy in writings that the person makes available to the public on a social networking site ("Moreno v. Hanford Sentinel Inc.," 2009), or more generally in materials intended for publication or public posting ("Guest v. Leis," 2001). At least one court has held that a user's privacy settings could create a reasonable expectation of privacy in certain circumstances, but the majority view is that privacy settings do not give rise to such an expectation even when the user restricts access to his or her postings (88 A.L.R. 6th 319, II.A.).

10.3 Interactive Research

Interactive research takes place when a researcher wishes to assess SMW content that is not publicly available. To access this information, the researcher needs to contact the participant for permission to view the content. On Facebook, this interaction may include a “friend request.” Some have argued that a “friend request” may lead to a misrepresentation of the researcher’s intentions for the relationship. Similarly, on Twitter, access to “protected” Tweets means that the researcher must become a “follower” of that participant, also potentially implying a closeness of relationship. It is important to recognize that the terms “friending” and “following” have very different meanings for those inhabiting today’s social media world. Previous studies have determined that Facebook “friending” implies a loose tie relationship, often including associates or acquaintances (M.A. Moreno, Brockman, Rogers, & Christakis, 2010). Further, the absolute number of Facebook “friends” is often considered a marker of positive social capital (M.A. Moreno, et al., 2010; Trull & Ebner-Priemer, 2009). On Twitter, users can be “followers” of people they have never personally met, such as celebrities and politicians. Thus, both “friending” and “following” in and of itself are unlikely to trigger unreasonable expectations for a close or prolonged relationship on the part of participants.

However, “friending” and “following” participants may be a double-edged sword for researchers. On the one hand, it may instill a sense of trust in participants. If participants see the research is friends with or follows someone they know, they may be more willing to divulge more about themselves in their responses or participate in future studies with that researcher. On the other hand though, “friending” and “following” participants opens up the door for the research to be negatively judged by participants. If participants do not agree with something on the researcher’s SMW, it may lead to the participant being less willing to participate. This does not mean researchers should post fake or untrue content about themselves, as that would be unethical; researchers should instead make sure the content on their SMWs accurately reflects how they want to be portrayed (Cote, 2013).

Research projects that require access to protected levels of SMWs, such as those requiring that a “friend” or “follower” request be accepted, involve interaction with the subject of the research and thus would constitute human subjects research. In order to be considered exempt (under 45 CFR 46.101(b)(4)), one would have to argue that the data being accessed through a “friend” request was publically available, a difficult argument to make for data to which the owner has restricted access. In this kind of research, it is likely that an IRB would require some kind of disclosure of the investigator’s intentions and the informed consent of the subjects. If the researcher conducts a study involving minors from whom “friend” or “follower” requests are made, the requirement for parental consent may pose a nearly insurmountable barrier to the research. In such cases, an investigator may wish to ask the IRB to consider a waiver of parental consent. The IRB is allowed to grant such waivers if they determine that a research protocol is designed for conditions or for a subject population for which parental or guardian permission is not a reasonable requirement to protect the subjects. In these cases, an IRB may be willing to approve a consent procedure which does not include parental consent, and would be allowed to do so if the project involves no more than minimal risk to the participants, the waiver will not adversely affect the rights and welfare of the subjects, the research could not be practically carried out without the waiver, and the subjects will be provided with additional pertinent information after participation when appropriate (McCarty, Vander Stoep, & McCauley, 2007). In addition, the IRB must assure that an appropriate mechanism for protecting the children who will participate as subjects in the research is substituted, and that the waiver is not inconsistent with federal, state, or local law. According to the federal regulations at 45 CFR 46.408(c), "the choice of an appropriate mechanism would depend upon the nature and purpose of the activities described in the protocol, the risk and anticipated benefit to the research subjects, and their age, maturity, status, and condition." It should also be noted that the Children's Online Privacy and Protection Act (COPPA) mandates parental permission if subjects under the age of 13 are being recruited and they provide identifiable information.

10.4 Survey/Interview Research

Researchers conducting surveys or interviews may potentially use SMWs to recruit subjects. This kind of research clearly qualifies as human subjects research, but is potentially exempt when only adults are recruited, and when either the information obtained is recorded in such a manner that human subjects cannot be identified, directly or through identifiers linked to the subjects *or* any disclosure of the human subjects' responses outside the research could not reasonably place the subjects at risk of criminal or civil liability or be damaging to the subjects' financial standing, employability, or reputation (45 CFR 46.101(b)(2)). Survey and interview research that involves minors cannot be considered exempt.

10.5 Risks Regarding Consent in the SMW Arena

Research that involves interaction with participants via a SMW, or uses a SMW to recruit participants, may also involve seeking informed consent online. Two potential concerns exist when obtaining informed consent online. A first concern is the lack of face-to-face contact with participants. When approaching participants on social media websites, or collecting data from the online representations of participants, there are often situations in which the researcher has no direct face-to-face contact with the participant. Thus, there may be reduced opportunities for the researcher to observe participant reactions to the consent process. Concerns regarding the lack of physical interaction during the consent process are more salient when the study collects information that is potentially illegal or stigmatizing, or when the study participant will be from an at-risk population such as minors or people who are cognitively impaired. Further, there are concerns that a participant will not read the consent form before signing. These are valid concerns, but not ones that are unique to SMWs. Many research studies employ mailed surveys and consent forms, situations that do not provide opportunities to interact face-to-face with participants. In these situations, the survey is frequently accompanied by a cover letter that contains the required elements of informed consent, with return of the survey considered to be an implicit consent to participate. Many IRBs will not require a signed consent form in these cases, and the federal regulations allow an IRB to grant a waiver of documentation of consent if the research presents no more than minimal risk of harm to subjects and involves no procedures for which written consent is normally required outside of the research context. Since surveys are generally minimal risk and use procedures that are commonly performed without consent in non-research settings, it is reasonable for IRBs to waive the requirement for documentation of consent for online surveys. In such situations, an investigator may provide a phone number for participants to call if they have questions about the survey.

It is even possible that online recruitment and consent processes may increase the likelihood that a researcher will hear from participants if questions or concerns arise when compared to mailed surveys. Given that people may be more likely to lash out inappropriately or "flame" online, there is the implication of a heightened sense of security and safety when conversing over the internet. Hence, this may increase the likelihood that the participant will contact the researcher online with questions arising from an online consent form compared to the participant taking the effort to call in order to address concerns about a mailed consent form. Further, lack of direct contact with the participant may eliminate interviewer bias, such as age or ethnicity, which could influence the participant's responses (McKee, 2013; Walker, 2013).

A second concern is how to obtain parental consent. Surveys for research purposes are not exempt under the federal regulations, and these regulations state that minors under the age of 18 years must have parental consent in addition to the assent of the minor prior to participation in most research trials, unless the study receives a waiver of parental consent (the conditions that must be met for a waiver of parental consent are described above). Obtaining parental consent in a study that involves recruitment through SMWs provides new challenges as a minor may be able to complete the parental consent process posing online as the parent. Adolescents are typically more internet savvy than their parents and may find this process quite simple. However, this risk is not unique to SMW research. Minors can and have easily forged their parent's signature using traditional paper consent forms. Although representing a parent's consent online by checking a box may be easier than forging a parent's signature, both methods are possible and easily achieved by a modern adolescent. In any case, a requirement for parental consent for surveys of adolescents using SMWs poses significant barriers, and IRBs should consider granting waivers of parental permission when the criteria can be met.

10.6 Confidentiality: A Key to Any Social Media Research Approach

An important area of concern with SMW research is the protection of confidentiality. Similar to other types of research involving survey or interview data, protection of participant identities is critical. Website research may initially be perceived as lower risk because participant information can be collected in absence of some HIPAA Protected Information such as an address or phone number. However, online data can present increased risks; studies that publish direct text quotes from a SMW may directly identify participants. Entering a direct quote from a SMW into a Google search engine can lead to a specific web link, such as a link to that person's LinkedIn profile, and thus identify the participant.

Presenting unique combinations of data that are linked to individuals may also identify participants. These concerns were clearly demonstrated through controversy surrounding the "Tastes, Ties and Time" project (Lewis, et al., 2008). In this project, researchers downloaded a large dataset of Facebook information from a single university. The identities of some participants were eventually determined based on the uniqueness of the information presented. The university was identified through the list of college majors represented in the study population. Further, some participants were identified by being a member of an underrepresented minority group. This project stirred ongoing controversy regarding confidentiality within Facebook research (Zimmer, 2010).

10.7 Recommendations for Researchers and IRBs

To conclude, SMWs are immensely popular and present new opportunities for research as well as new challenges for IRBs to evaluate these proposals' risks and benefits. In considering risks of SMW research, researchers and IRBs should balance consideration of unique risks with those consistent with traditional research methods.

Thus, specific recommendations for researchers and IRBs include:

10.7.1 Observational Research

- IRBs should consider whether the proposed study meets criteria as human subjects research. For example, an analysis of YouTube videos depicting physical therapy techniques is a study involving video clips, not human subjects. As another example, a researcher proposes to study how many college students'

Facebook pages depict images of junk food without collecting any profile owner identifiers on the page such as age, gender or location. In this case the unit of analysis is the page rather than the profile owner.

- IRBs should give consideration to risk level and content of the study. For example, a project that evaluates how many times a 15-year-old tweets the word "Justin Bieber" has a low risk level. In contrast, a project that observes an online group discussion of ALS patients to see which ones report decreased symptoms with a new medication (O'Connor, 2013) has a higher risk level. Increased attention should be devoted to higher risk studies, concomitant with a higher threshold to grant waiver of participant consent. IRB proposals that include collection of illegal or stigmatizing information from SMWs, or involve data collection from minor's SMW profiles, should be considered carefully.

10.7.2 Interactive Research

- Researchers should present an accurate portrayal of their identity on SMWs, but undue concern regarding participants' investment in the relationship defined by "friending" or "following" is likely unnecessary.

10.7.3 Survey/Interview Research

- Researchers should provide contact information for questions during the consent process, including contact information online and via SMW that can be monitored and responded to quickly.
- In the future, SMW researchers should consider using SMWs to obtain parental consent for adolescents' participation in research studies, as parents are increasingly becoming members of SMW sites such as Facebook (Lenhart, 2009).

10.7.4 Overall Recommendations

- To protect confidentiality, researchers should understand the risks of and avoid direct text quotes in presenting SMW text quotations from research subjects. Researchers should avoid presenting participants' personal information in ways that they could be identified within their schools or communities. If direct quotes are used, researches should consider acquiring informed consent from the participant (Lawsone, 2004). Past research has shown that participants generally reacted positively upon learning research had been done on their SMW profile (Megan A. Moreno, Grant, Kacvinsky, Moreno, & Fleming, 2012), so obtaining informed consent is a feasible task. Researchers should also avoid presenting participants' personal information in ways that they could be identified within their schools or communities.

- One Facebook section, "Applicable to Developers/Operators of Applications and Websites," included the following statement at the time of this chapter: "you will only request data you need to operate your application." This section also instructed outside parties: "*you will have a privacy policy that tells users what user data you are going to use and how you will use, display, share, or transfer that data.*" Researchers should consider applying these principles by only collecting the essential data needed to answer the research question, and presenting that data carefully to avoid participant identification. Researchers should consider listing a privacy policy on their lab web pages, as well as developing a lab SMW page, that describes what data they use and how it is used. One possible strategy is to develop a Facebook page as a "professional identity" for the principal investigator or staff, separate from a personal Facebook page. In this way, participants can friend the researcher in a professional rather than personal context.
- A little recognized but challenging issue is that each state has its own law regarding informed consent. This includes how consent should be documented and the age at which consent can be obtained for various health topics. How, or whether, this process applies to SMW is unclear. If the researcher is located in Illinois and conducting a multistate survey of Twitter users, what level regulation should take precedence? This issue merits further discussion and consideration as researchers move towards more fully harnessing the global research opportunities provided by SMWs.
- For additional reading to understand the broader scope of internet research ethics from the perspective of the US federal government, see this report from the Department of Health and Human Services: http://www.hhs.gov/ohrp/sachrp/mtgings/2013%20March%20Mtg/internet_research.pdf

References

Cote, I. (2013). Fieldwork in the Era of Social Media: Opportunities and Challenges. Ps-Political Science & Politics, 46(3), 615-619. doi: 10.1017/s1049096513000565 Guest v. Leis (6th Cir. 2001).

Jackson-Newsom, J., & Shelton, T. L. Psychobiological models of adolescent risk: Implications for prevention and intervention. Dev Psychobiol, 52(3), 295-297. doi: 10.1002/dev.20458

Katz v. United States (US 1967).

Kelly, H. (2013). Facebook changes privacy settings for teens, CNN. Retrieved from http://www.cnn.com/TECH/social.media/archive/

Lawsone, D. (2004). Blurring the boundaries: ethical considerations for online research using synchronous CMC forums. Readings in virtual research ethics: issues and controversies.

Lenhart, A. (2009). Adults on Social Network Sites: Pew Internet and American Life Project.

Lewis, K., Kaufman, J., Gonzalez, M., Wimmer, A., & Christakis, N. (2008). Tastes, ties, and time: A new social network dataset using Facebook.com. Social Networks, 30(4), 330-342. doi: 10.1016/j.socnet.2008.07.002

McCarty, C. A., Vander Stoep, A., & McCauley, E. (2007). Cognitive features associated with depressive symptoms in adolescence: directionality and specificity. J Clin Child Adolesc Psychol, 36(2), 147-158. doi: 10.1080/15374410701274926

McKee, R. (2013). Ethical issues in using social media for health and health care research. Health Policy, 110(2-3), 298-301. doi: 10.1016/j.healthpol.2013.02.006

Moreno, M. A., Brockman, L. N., Rogers, C. B., & Christakis, D. A. (2010). An Evaluation of The Distribution of Sexual References Among "Top 8" MySpace Friends. J Adolesc Health, 47(4), 418-420.

Moreno, M. A., Fost, N. C., & Christakis, D. A. (2008). Research ethics in the MySpace era. Pediatrics, 121(1), 157-161. doi: 121/1/157 [pii] 10.1542/peds.2007-3015

Moreno, M. A., Goniu, N., Moreno, P. S., & Diekema, D. (2013). Ethics of Social Media Research: Common Concerns and Practical Considerations. Cyberpsychol Behav Soc Netw. doi: 10.1089/cyber.2012.0334

Moreno, M. A., Grant, A., Kacvinsky, L., Moreno, P., & Fleming, M. (2012). Older Adolescents' Views Regarding Participation in Facebook Research. Journal of Adolescent Health, 51(5), 439-444. doi: 10.1016/j.jadohealth.2012.02.001

Moreno v. Hanford Sentinel Inc. (Ct App. 2009 2009).

O'Connor, D. (2013). The Apomediated World: Regulating Research When Social Media Has Changed Research. Journal of Law Medicine & Ethics, 41(2), 470-483. doi: 10.1111/jlme.12056

Schulenberg, J. E., Merline, A. C., Johnston, L. D., O'Malley, P. M., Bachman, J. G., & Laetz, V. B. (2005). Trajectories of Marijuana Use During the Transition to Adulthood: The Big Picture Based on National Panel Data. J Drug Issues, 35(2), 255-279.

Trull, T., & Ebner-Priemer, U. (2009). Using experience sampling methods/ecological momentary assessment (ESM/EMA) in clinical assessment and clinical research: Introduction to the special section. Psychological Assessment, 21(4), 457-462.

Walker, D.-M. (2013). The internet as a medium for health services research. Part 2. Nurse researcher, 20(5), 33-37.

Zimmer, M. (2010). "But the data is already public": on the ethics of research in Facebook. Ethics and Information Technology, 12(4), 313-325. doi: 10.1007/s10676-010-9227-5

Megan A Moreno, Rosalind Koff

11 Media Theories and the Facebook Influence Model

Abstract: Social media are immensely popular among, and influential upon today's youth. Previous media theories including Uses and Gratifications, Cultivation Analysis, and Media Ecology Theory have proposed ways in which media are used and can be influential. The rise of social media presents new challenges to existing behavioral and media theories. Recently, a new concept map called the Facebook Influence Model was developed to provide a conceptual approach to Facebook using primary data. This mixed-methods study applied concept mapping methodology, a validated five-step method to visually represent complex topics. The five steps include preparation, brainstorming, sort and rank, analysis, and interpretation. College student participants were identified using purposeful sampling. A total of 169 statements were generated during brainstorming and sorted into between 6 and 22 groups. The final concept map included 13 clusters. Interpretation of the data led to grouping of clusters into four final domains including: connection, comparison, identification, and Facebook as an experience. The Facebook Influence Concept Map illustrates key constructs that contribute to influence, incorporating perspectives of older adolescent Facebook users. While Facebook provides a novel lens through which to consider behavioral influence, it can best be considered in the context of existing behavioral theory. The concept map may be used towards development of potential future intervention efforts.

11.1 Media Theories and the Facebook Influence Model

Over the past decade, media has undergone a fundamental shift. Traditional media such as television and radio provided content in a one-directional manner, disseminating content created by a company or corporation to be consumed by passive viewers. Alternatively, new media - often called social media or interactive media - provide endless opportunities for users to act as both consumers and creators of media. Examples of interactivity on social media may include posting a new photo to Instagram, commenting on a YouTube video, or "downvoting" content on Reddit. New media are digital, and often have the characteristics of being manipulatable, networkable, dense, compressible, and interactive (Flew & Smith, 2011). The emergence of new, digital technologies "signals a potentially radical shift of who is in control of information, experience and resources" (Shapiro, 1999). In this setting of dramatic change and rapid advancement, this chapter will consider social media and health behavior theory.

11.2 Previous Media Theory

Media scholars have long debated the idea of *audience agency* in media consumption. While the study of film and television lend themselves to the concept of an audience of 'viewers' or 'consumers', new media content leans towards the idea of an audience of 'users' (Livingston, 2004). Historically, media has been created and supplied by a small number of media producers and content was highly controlled through exclusive and often political professional industries (Cha, Kwak, Rodriguez, Ahn, & Moon, 2007). With the shift into Web 2.0 applications, the media industry experienced a large paradigm shift in both media production and circulation: "Audiences, empowered by these new technologies, occupying a space at the intersection between new and old media, are demanding the right to participate within culture" (Jenkins, 2006). The outcome of this desire for involvement is room for regular people to create and distribute media content themselves, opening the door for diverse opinions and perspectives, or user-generated content (Deuze, 2007).

In order to understand the dynamics of online participation today, we must conceptualize areas where traditional media theory aligns with new media practices. The ability to apply traditional media theory to the new media landscape is best understood by the observation that there is an "underlying consistency of the content of the messages we consume and the nature of the symbolic environment in which we live" even if the delivery technology of the media chances (Shanahan & Morgan, 1999). This idea suggests that even though the media we consume may change, the inherent content and intentions behind our media use are somewhat consistent over time and through different media. This occurred historically as films took message content from literature and again when television did the same by repackaging radio programming. Previous scholars have suggested that a change in media is merely "new bottles for old wine" (McLuhan, 1964).

11.2.1 Uses and Gratifications

Uses and Gratifications Theory (UGT) discusses how people actively seek out specific media content for particular purposes and intentional goals (Katz, Blumler, & Gurevitch, 1974). UGT establishes an active, rather than passive, audience member who has the ability to consciously examine and evaluate media in order to accomplish specific outcomes (Wang, Fine, & Cai, 2008). UGT embodied a functional shift of communications scholarship, from examining not what media did to people, but to what people could do with media.

UGT initially grew out of the needs and motivation theory, which suggests that people act in line with a specific personal hierarchy of needs (Maslow, 1970). Communications scholars quickly caught on to this notion and sought to determine typologies of needs for media consumption. Many versions of these typologies exist, and suggest a variety of categories of purposeful media consumption that people may engage in.

UGT "provides a framework for understanding when and how individual media consumers become more or less active and the consequences of that increased or decreased involvement" (West & Turner, 2007). The theory has five main assumptions: (1) an audience is active and goal-oriented in their media consumption, (2) media are used for gratifications, (3) media are in competition with other means of need satisfaction, (4) people understand their personal media use, interests, and motives enough to communicate with researchers about their choices, (5) the audience members are the only people who can make judgments regarding the value of the media content.

The first assumption says that people bring both their own activity and goals to media. Four goals involved have been defined as diversion, or an escape from daily routines or problems, personal relationships, or when media acts as a substitute for friendship, surveillance, or information seeking for media to assist in an end-goal, and personal identity, or the ways one can reinforce his or her individual values (McQuail, Blumler, & Brown, 1972).

The second assumption points to the agency of the audience in making a media choice. As UGT views audience members as active, they take initiative in seeking out media. The third assumption is the idea that media must compete with other sources to fulfill an audience's needs, which indicates that the audience and media do not exist in isolation but as a part of a larger society. This society influences both media, and audiences, in different ways.

A fourth assumption, that people are self-aware of their media use, discusses one of the perceived limitations of the theory. Some researchers feel that self-report data are insufficient for understanding media use and that individuals may be unable to communicate their thought processes or habits for purposes of research. However, this thought is rooted in scholarship that views audience members as inactive. Another concern is that media use is not always active so accidental exposure and influence can occur.

The fifth and final assumption of UGT requests that researchers make a concerted effort to remove their personal value judgments from the study of media content. As UGT discusses how an audience member fills his or her needs through the use of media, only an audience member should be able to evaluate the value of the given media content.

11.2.2 Cultivation Analysis

Cultivation Analysis grew as a response to the pervasive television culture that was already well established in the 1970s. As a part of a larger study, regular examinations of television programming and the "conceptions of social reality that viewing cultivates in audiences" were assessed (Gerbner & Gross, 1976). Their initial idea was that mass communication cultivates certain beliefs about reality that are shared and held in common among mass communication viewers. Later, the same investigator noted, "most of what we know, or think we know, we have never personally experienced," suggesting that we "know" things due to the stories seen and heard in the media (Gerbner, 1998).

Cultivation research in the internet era requires the consideration of cable and satellite networks, the use of digital video recording devices, and the internet. While the packaging of the content may change, the fundamental frameworks around television consumption remain. Cultivation Analysis sees media as a transmissional process in which media are sending messages across time and space, with a ritual perspective media are seen as representative of society's shared beliefs. This process is further understood through the assumptions of Cultivation Analysis.

Cultivation Analysis says that the mediated reality depicted in mass communication functions as a foundation from which consumers cultivate their own social reality. All assumptions of this theory were developed with television specifically in mind, highlighting it as a unique medium. Due to the ubiquity of the technology, a lack of literacy necessary for consumption (unlike print media), free access (unlike the movies), combined pictures and sound, no mobility required, and its ageless nature for all demographics. The three assumptions for Cultivation Analysis, based on the relationship between television and culture, are: (1) television as essentially and fundamentally different from all other forms of mass media, (2) television as shaping our society's ways of thinking and relating, (3) the effects of television is limited.

11.2.3 Media Ecology Theory

Media Ecology Theory (MET) aims to understand the social impact of technology and communication (McLuhan, 1964). MET claims that media act directly to shape and organize culture. Media ecology, or the study of how media and communication processes influence human perception, feeling, understanding, and value, is focused around communication studies (Parameswaran, 2008).

Marshall McLuhan (1964) understood the influence of technologies including clocks, radios, television, movies, and games. He focused on defining the relationship between technology and members of a specific culture. He noted that electronic media have revolutionized society, and society quickly become reliant on these communication technologies. McLuhan felt that it was almost impossible to find a society unaffected by electronic media.

As society has evolved, its technology has also evolved. From the first books published to the internet, society has both been affected by, and in turn affected, media. The rules of media set forth by MET – enhancement, obsolescence, retrieval and reversal – show how technology affects communication through the development of new technology. MET focuses on the idea that society cannot escape the influence of technology and that technology will forever remain central to almost every action in modern life.

The influence of media technology on society is the main concept of MET, upheld by three main assumptions: media is infused into every act and action in society, media fixes our perceptions and organizes our experiences, and media tie the world together, We cannot escape the media presence in our lives as it is ubiquitous in our realities of day-to-day life. Media directly influences us, as they are powerful in our view of the world. Media connects the world into a "global village," where media can tie anyone around the globe into a single social, cultural, political, and economic system (Parameswaran, 2008). As a result, we have the ability to receive information instantaneously.

11.3 Theory applied to New Media

While the aforementioned theories are rooted in traditional communication theory, it is important to understand where they fit or misalign among new media phenomenon.

Media Ecology can help us to understand why people continue to interact online, despite somewhat of a loss of control over their public and private boundaries. As noted by McLuhan (1964), society quickly became reliant on electronic media – such as social networking sites – for many reasons such as efficiency and ease. Technology has continually progressed overtime – forcing people to adapt – and social networking sites are no different.

As society becomes increasingly comfortable and reliant on new media forms for communication, researchers seek to understand how other offline elements of traditional communication theory and daily life may translate online.

Traditional communication theories have been applied to many new technologies, such as video games and internet use (Papacharissi & Rubin, 2000). One study found that while newspapers were the predominant written news source pre-internet, people now seek out news on the internet for the same reasons that they did before – the need for orientation (Dimmick, Chen, & Li, 2004). Another study evaluating early cell phone use utilized UGT for understanding how consumers utilized mobile phones and landlines differently. Although these early mobile phones were contextually different than landlines, many of the same intentions of use were found between the two (Leung & Wei, 2000).

Research shows many ties between traditional media motives and new media motives. Evidence suggests similar motives in using television or the internet for specific means (Kaye, 2004). A recent study showed that 78% of consumers trust peer recommendations online, while only 14% trust advertisements (Advertising, 2009). Social networking sites, however, provide a unique form of peer recommendation.

While UGT has been applied to show that people seek out communication online for similar reasons as offline, CA provides insight into why social networking sites are potentially influential due to the recent push towards decision-making based on online influences. As CA claims that media functions as an overarching transmitter of society's shared beliefs, peer creation, and dissemination of lifestyle choices through the use of rich, personal media are an extension of this. The reality communicated through social networking sites is no longer edited and packaged by media professionals, but by users themselves, allowing others to cultivate their own version of reality. If UGT tells us that users are going online for social comparison, or to survey and learn from their peers, CA suggests that social networking sites function as reinforcement of user perceptions of societal ideals.

11.4 Need for Theory to Extend to Health Behaviors

Against the backdrop of these theories, most of them based on the Communication field, researchers have called for theory to be more specific to understand influence or behavior change in the setting of a type of media in which users were both creators and consumers. A 2010 Rand report stated "existing theories do not easily account for the likely effects of users new roles in creating and distributing content, as well as consuming it" (Collins, Martino, & Shaw, 2011). The report called for the development of new theory that accounted for factors that were considered moderators of new media effects, such as interactivity, privatization of use, portability, and the social aspects of new media. The authors argued that existing theories of media and behavior may be able to "stretch to cover these factors under broad conceptual labels", but the development of new theory may also be warranted. However, the perspective of how social media may be perceived as influential to its users remains a gap in our understanding. Further, the representation of users' views in the development of theory was also missing. Thus, investigators sought to develop a new theory specific to social networking site platforms such as Facebook.

11.5 Concept Mapping Towards Developing New Theory

The Facebook Influence Model study utilized concept mapping methodology to develop a conceptual model of Facebook influence (Moreno, Kota, Schoohs, & Whitehill, 2013). It was anticipated that a conceptual framework to describe Facebook influence would be complex; thus investigators sought an analytical approach that would accommodate this complexity. Concept mapping methodology is frequently used towards developing conceptual frameworks to describe complex topics (Jones & Johnston; W. Trochim & Kane, 2005; W. M. K. Trochim, 1989a, 1989b; W. M. K. Trochim, Cook, & Setze, 1994). Further, this approach allows the conceptual framework to be built from the "bottom up" based entirely on the views of key stakeholders. Given that young adults are among the most avid social media users, the model was meant to be based on the views and experiences of these particular Facebook users. The concept mapping approach also provides a method to go beyond qualitative analysis to allow more complex statistical modeling to ensure that the process was systematic.

Concept mapping integrates open-ended qualitative data collection methods and quantitative analytical tools in a standardized and replicable process (W. Trochim & Kane, 2005; W. M. K. Trochim, 1989b). The outcome of this process is a concept map or a visual representation of the key concepts and their inter-relationships. While this map does not dictate cause and effect between an exposure and outcome, it can be applied to explore relationships with pertinent variables in different contexts. The final map that is created is entirely in the language of the participants and produces a visual representation of core Facebook domains that is easy to interpret. This method has been used in previous health research to provide insights into complex phenomena such as sexual behavior or mental illness (Nunnally & Bernstein, 1994; Shern, Trochim, & Lacomb, 1995; Strahan & Gerbasi, 1972; W. M. K. Trochim, et al., 1994).

Concept mapping directly involves participants and balances group consensus with individual contributions as some steps are done individually while others require group participation. Concept mapping studies generally use sample sizes typical of qualitative research. Usually between 20 and 75 participants are involved in some or all of the data collection steps. There are five steps involved with the concept map creation process: preparation, generation, structuring, representation, and interpretation (W. M. K. Trochim, 1989b). The goal of preparation is to develop a focus prompt used to generate brainstorming statements from participants in the generation step. The goal of the brainstorming step is to generate a large list of participant-generated items with sufficient breadth and depth to represent the full spectrum of ideas related to Facebook influence. The brainstorming step was conducted using a semi-structured focus group format. The goal of the structuring step is to sort and rank the statements that were generated in the brainstorming step. This process provides insights into how individual ideas are related to form overarching constructs. The goal of representation is to apply quantitative approaches to analyze the sorted and ranked statement data into a visual point map representing individual items. Analyses were conducted using the Concept Systems Core software version 4 (Concept Systems, Inc, NY) and SAS software version 9.3 (SAS, Cary, NC). The goal of these sessions was to allow participants to view, discuss and interpret the concept map. Full details on the methods involved are provided in the published paper (Moreno, et al., 2013).

11.6 The Facebook Influence Model study

11.6.1 Brainstorming

The initial focus prompt was "*What makes Facebook influential is...*" A total of 187 statements were produced during the generation step of data collection in response to this prompt. Refining the statement list led to removal of duplicate statements and merging similar statements. The final list of brainstorming statements included 169 unique aspects of Facebook that were perceived to be influential.

11.6.2 Sorting

During the sorting procedure, participants sorted the statements into between 6 and 22 groups (Mean=13, Median=12). During the rating procedure, the mean item influence rating was 3.2 (Standard Deviation=0.5). Cluster analysis indicated that the 13 cluster solution presented in Figure 1 was found to represent the best fit for the data after assessing between 6 and 20 clusters.

11.6.3 Representation

The 13 clusters depicted on the Facebook Influence Concept Map (Figure 1) included: connection to people, far reaching, fast communication, curiosity about others, business and promotion, accessible and adaptable, data and information, Facebook establishing social norms, identity expression, influence on identity, positive experiences, negative experiences, and distractions. The concept map provides a visual representation of both key constructs and their relationship in proximity to each other. These 13 clusters embody unique aspects of Facebook that represent perceived sources of influence.

11.6.4 Interpretation

After reviewing this map during the participant interpretation step and discussions with our experts, there were no recommendations to delete or add clusters to the map. Participants often commented on the sheer number of clusters within the map and that it took some time to process the clusters and their relationships to each other. Recommendations emerged to subcategorize the map by further sorting the 13 clusters into 4 domains which included: connection, comparison, identification, and Facebook as an experience. These constructs can be considered within domains based on their proximity on the map and the overlap in concepts within each cluster.

Table 2 provides the cluster groups, clusters within them, and example items from each cluster.

Participants frequently commented on the most centrally located cluster of *Facebook establishing social norms*. Many participants felt that this cluster's central location was because many of the items in this cluster were related to the surrounding clusters, but also represented unique ways in which Facebook does not only represent social norms, but has "*become* the new social norm." Participants described how Facebook has contributed new standards for online behavior and even new language terms, such as "status update," and "Facebook stalking." Participants often discussed whether or not people's Facebook behaviors were volitional attempts to influence social norms. One participant described, *"uploading photos contributes to setting the social norm. I don't think we upload photos to set social norms, we upload photos to share and connect with other people and a byproduct of that is setting social norms."*

11.7 Application of the Facebook Influence Model

Previous work has illustrated the influence of media on adolescent and young adult behavior. Facebook provides a venue for peer interaction and social networking; both are recognized as contributors to behavior (Boyd, 2007). While Facebook provides a novel lens through which to consider behavioral influence, its influence can best be considered in the context of robust behavioral theory. Thus, each of the 4 domains can be considered alongside the framework of previous supporting work. In some cases the concept map is synergistic with previous models and in others it provides expanded applications of the initial framework or entirely novel contributions.

11.7.1 Connection

The 6 clusters that comprise the "connecting" domain on the concept map illustrate ways in which Facebook provides and enhances peer communication, networking and connection. These items dovetail well with decades of previous work that emphasizes the role of peers as a major focus of adolescence, including the older adolescent/young adult years that comprise college. Further, UGT argues that a fundamental goal of media use is to develop personal relationships. Facebook expands the ability to connect with those known and new to people with great frequency and accessibility. Facebook allows this connection to take place across long distances and in real-time at any time of day or night. The influence of items in this cluster has synergy with the Homophily Model which explains that media role models are more likely to be mimicked when the media model is viewed as someone like you (Eyal & Rubin, 2003). Facebook provides an accessible platform to identify and connect with these like-minded peers without the traditional limits of geography. Via social networking, adolescents can have direct or indirect human contact, so virtual communication can occur in a way that is similar to face-to-face communication (Sher & Rutledge, 2007). This can positively impact college students who are seeking peers with similar unusual hobbies such as bagpipes, or negatively influence college students who are seeking peers to engage in risk-taking such as drug use.

11.7.2 Comparison

Comparison among peers has long been part of adolescence and young adulthood; social norms play a large role in perceptions of attitudes and behaviors that are acceptable and desirable. For example, previous studies have shown that adolescents who perceive their peers as sexually active are more likely to voice intention to become sexually active themselves (Kinsman, Romer, Furstenberg, & Schwarz, 1998). This is supported by UGT which claims that people use Facebook as a tool (use) for connection and comparison (gratification). Further, Cultivation Analysis contributes to media as a transmissional process in which messages are sent and media are seen as representative of society's shared beliefs. Facebook allows this comparison to take place using tangible "evidence" such as photos, stated behaviors, and the ability to note peer feedback via comments on this information. The concept of 'creep culture' began with Facebook, and describes how Facebook allows for passive investigation into peers' lives using the lens of Facebook.

11.7.3 Identification

This group describes the clusters regarding exploring and reflecting on one's identity using Facebook. Identity development is an essential part of older adolescent development, and Facebook provides a novel platform on which these efforts can take place (Neinstein & Anderson, 2002). The Media Practice Model explains that users choose and interact with media based on who they are, and who they want to be at that moment (Brown, 2000). Facebook allows a profile owner to develop an online identity through a profile. Profile owners can then reflect and revise that identity via feedback from peers' comments and "likes," or by personal browsing through the Facebook "timeline." The ability to develop one's identity in real-time provides a unique multimedia view of the self.

11.7.4 Immersive Eperience of Facebook

Both negative and positive experiences are described in these grouped clusters, experiences that can even alter the experience of a given day, including mood and decisions. This cluster may represent the most intriguing set up of items to consider, as it suggests that today's college students' are well aware that these sites present immersive experiences including positive, negative, distracting, and tool-based features, yet still are willing to make substantial commitments to their involvement in these online environments. This construct is supported by Media Ecology Theory, which argues that media is infused into every art and action in society, be it good or bad.

11.8 Conclusions

In considering the intersection between The Facebook Influence Model and existing media theory and behavioral models, it seems reasonable to expect that Facebook would not provide an entirely new mechanism by which behaviors are influenced. The rich set of constructs included in the Facebook Influence Model are clearly tied to previous theory. The unique combination of these constructs to represent aspects of Facebook that are influential to behavior provide a comprehensive base for theoretical consideration to inform future work and the potential for intervention development using Facebook.

The Rand report from 2010 argued that "interventions based in new media or incorporating new media components should be developed and tested." The report also recognized that these interventions must be informed by sound theory either existing or newly developed. Only by understanding the theoretical grounding can future efforts avoid the pitfalls that many mass media interventions encounter by assuming that any accurate message, broadly distributed, will be effective. The concept map may contribute to the development of future interventions using Facebook. For example, the model supports the importance of *comparison* among Facebook users. At present, Facebook provides prompts that incorporate peer comparison to try to influence user behavior, such as "22 of your friends have already switched to Timeline." Future work could consider providing such prompts to promote positive health behaviors linked to keywords present on profiles, such as "12 of your friends exercised this week." As another example, the model illustrates the role of Facebook as a place in which *identity development* takes place. Researchers could consider providing prompts as Facebook advertisements that trigger users to consider whether they want certain behaviors as part of their online identity. For example, an advertisement could be triggered by keywords related to tobacco use on a profile, and could include a message such as "Do you want your tobacco use to be part of your public online identity?" These are only a few of the myriad of ideas that future researchers may consider. Investigators interested in targeting a specific construct could also consider that construct in light of previous theory. For example, investigators interested in studying the *comparison* construct could also consider Cultivation Theory as part of their theoretical basis. Through the application of the

Facebook Influence Model and its grounding in previous media communication and health behavior theory, these models may inform both future research and clinical practice efforts to further understand and address this immersive and influential new tool.

References

Advertising, N. G. (2009). Consumers Trust Real Friends and Virtual Strangers the Most Retrieved Dec 2013, from http://www.nielsen.com/us/en/newswire/2009/global-advertising-consumers-trust-real-friends-and-virtual-strangers-the-most.html>.

Boyd, d. (2007). Why Youth (Heart) Social Networking Sites: The Role of Networked Publics in Teenage Social Life. In D. Buckingham (Ed.), MacArthur Foundation Series on Digital Learning: Youth, Identity and Media Volume (pp. 119-142). Cambridge, MA: MIT press.

Brown, J. D. (2000). Adolescents' sexual media diets. J Adolesc Health, 27(2 Suppl), 35-40. doi: S1054139X00001415 [pii]

Cha, M., Kwak, H., Rodriguez, P., Ahn, Y., & Moon, S. (2007). I Tube, You Tube, Everybody Tubes: Analyzing the World's Largest User Generated Content Video System. Paper presented at the 7th ACM SIGCOMM conference on Internet measurement

Collins, R. L., Martino, S., & Shaw, R. (2011). Influence of New Media on Adolescent Sexual Health: Evidence and Opportunities: RAND Corporation.

Deuze, M. (2007). Media Work. Cambridge: Polity.

Dimmick, J., Chen, Y., & Li, Z. (2004). Competition Between the Internet and Traditional News Media: The Gratification-Opportunities Niche Dimension. Journal of Media Economics, 17(1), 19-33.

Eyal, K., & Rubin, A. M. (2003). Viewer aggression and homophily, identification, and parasocial relationships with television characters. Journal of Broadcasting & Electronic Media, 47(1), 77-98.

Flew, T., & Smith, R. (2011). New Media: An Introduction: Oxford University Press.

Gerbner, G. (1998). Cultivation analysis: An overview. Mass communication and society, 1, 175-194.

Gerbner, G., & Gross, L. (1976). Living with Television: The Violence Profile. Journal of Communication, 26(2), 172-194.

Jenkins, H. (2006). Convergence Culture: Where old and new media collide. New York: New York University Press.

Jones, M., & Johnston, D. Understanding phenomena in the real world: the case for real time data collection in health services research. J Health Serv Res Policy. doi: jhsrp.2010.010016 [pii] 10.1258/jhsrp.2010.010016

Katz, E., Blumler, J., & Gurevitch, M. (1974). Utilization of mass communication by the individual. In J. Blumler & A. R. Katz (Eds.), The Uses of mass communications: Current perspectives on gratifications research (pp. 19-32). Beverly Hills: Sage.

Kaye, B. (2004). A web for all reasons: Uses and gratifications of internet components for political information. Telematics and informatics, 21(3), 197-223.

Kinsman, S. B., Romer, D., Furstenberg, F. F., & Schwarz, D. F. (1998). Early sexual initiation: the role of peer norms. Pediatrics, 102(5), 1185-1192.

Leung, L., & Wei, R. (2000). More than just talk on the move: Uses and Gratifications of the cellular phone. Journalism and Mass Communication Quarterly, 77, 308-320.

Livingston, A. (2004). Smartphones and other mobile devices: The Swiss Army Knives of the 21st Century. EDUCAUSE Quarterly, 27(2), 46-52.

Maslow, A. H. (1970). Motivation and personality. New York: Harper and Row.

McLuhan, M. (1964). Understanding media; the extensions of man (1st ed ed.). New York: McGraw Hill.
McQuail, D., Blumler, J. G., & Brown, J. (1972). The television audience: A revised perspective. In McQuail (Ed.), Sociology of mass communication: Selected readings (pp. 135-165). Harmondsworth: Penguin.
Moreno, M. A., Kota, R., Schoohs, S., & Whitehill, J. M. (2013). The Facebook Influence Model: A Concept Mapping Approach. Cyberpsychol Behav Soc Netw. doi: 10.1089/cyber.2013.0025
Neinstein, L., & Anderson, M. (2002). Adolescent Development. In L. Neinstein (Ed.), Adolescent Health Care: A Practical Guide (pp. 767-792). Philadelphia: Lippincott Williams and Wilkins.
Nunnally, J. C., & Bernstein, I. H. (1994). Psychometric Theory (3rd ed.). New York: McGraw-Hill.
Papacharissi, Z., & Rubin, A. M. (2000). Predictors of Internet use. Journal of Broadcasting and Electronic Media, 44, 175-196.
Parameswaran, K. (2008). Interactive Television Programmes-A study in media ecology. Language in India, 8, 16.
Shanahan, J., & Morgan, M. (1999). Television and its viewers: Cultivation theory and research. Cambridge: Cambridge University Press.
Shapiro, A. L. (1999). Media/Society: Industries, images and audiences. Thousand Oaks, CA: Pine Forge Press.
Sher, K. J., & Rutledge, P. C. (2007). Heavy drinking across the transition to college: predicting first-semester heavy drinking from precollege variables. Addict Behav, 32(4), 819-835. doi: S0306-4603(06)00204-8 [pii] 10.1016/j.addbeh.2006.06.024
Shern, D. L., Trochim, W. M. K., & Lacomb, C. A. (1995). The Use of Concept Mapping for Assessing Fidelity of Model Transfer - an Example from Psychiatric Rehabilitation. Evaluation and Program Planning, 18(2), 143-153.
Strahan, R., & Gerbasi, K. C. (1972). Short, Homogeneous Versions of Marlow-Crowne Social Desirability Scale. Journal of Clinical Psychology, 28(2), 191-&.
Trochim, W., & Kane, M. (2005). Concept mapping: an introduction to structured conceptualization in health care. International Journal for Quality in Health Care, 17(3), 187-191. doi: DOI 10.1093/intqhc/mzi038
Trochim, W. M. K. (1989a). Concept Mapping - Soft Science or Hard Art. Evaluation and Program Planning, 12(1), 87-110.
Trochim, W. M. K. (1989b). An Introduction to Concept Mapping for Planning and Evaluation. Evaluation and Program Planning, 12(1), 1-16.
Trochim, W. M. K., Cook, J. A., & Setze, R. J. (1994). Using Concept Mapping to Develop a Conceptual-Framework of Staffs Views of a Supported Employment Program for Individuals with Severe Mental-Illness. Journal of Consulting and Clinical Psychology, 62(4), 766-775.
Wang, Q., Fine, E. L., & Cai, D. A. (2008). Loneliness, gender and parasocial interaction: A users and gratifications approach. Communication Quarterly, 56, 87-109.
West, R. L., & Turner, L. H. (2007). Introducing Communication Theory: Analysis and Application. Boston: McGraw Hill.

Nicole Muscanell, Rosanna Guadagno

12 Social Networking and Romantic Relationships: A Review of Jealousy and Related Emotions

Abstract: Social networking sites (SNSs) such as Facebook are centered on interpersonal connections; providing both personal information and user generated content, along with the members of their social circles. This format facilitates relationship formation and maintenance. As a result, use of these sites can affect offline interpersonal relationships. In this chapter, we review contemporary research examining the use of SNSs and the resulting impact on jealousy and related emotions in the context of romantic relationships. Specifically, we review research on partner surveillance and monitoring, the way couples utilize their social media profiles (e.g., whether or not they share couple-specific information), individual differences, such as gender differences in the experience of jealousy, and the role of social media use on actual relationship outcomes.

12.1 Social Networking and Romantic Relationships:

12.1.1 A Review of Jealousy and Related Emotions

The following is an excerpt from the David Fincher's 2010 film, *The Social Network*:

> **Christy Lee**: Why does your status say „single" on your Facebook page?
> **Eduardo Saverin**: What?
> **Christy Lee**: Why does your relationship status say „single" on your Facebook page?!
> **Eduardo Saverin**: I was single when I set up the page.
> **Christy Lee**: And you somehow never bothered to change it?
> **Eduardo Saverin**: I –
> **Christy Lee**: *[looks at him sternly]* What?
> **Eduardo Saverin**: I don't know how.
> **Christy Lee**: Do I look stupid to you?
> **Eduardo Saverin**: No. Calm down.

Social networking sites (SNSs) such as Facebook and Twitter have become extremely popular worldwide. Through these sites, individuals can fulfill relational needs, such as forming new friendships and maintaining existing relationships, including romantic ones. While SNS use facilitates positive experiences, such as feeling connected and decreasing loneliness (Deters & Mehl, 2012) as well as the ability keep in touch with friends, family and romantic partners, it has also been associated with negative experiences, including declines in subjective well-being (Kross et al, 2013). As in the film example above, one potential consequence for couples that use SNSs is that the choices individuals make when creating and later updating their SNS profile may elicit partner jealousy resulting in turmoil within their romantic relationship. Indeed, research demonstrates that the content of one's SNS profile can cause jealousy within romantic relationships (Muise, Christofides, & Desmarais, 2009).

In this chapter, we review research focused on social networking use and the impact that partner choices have on their romantic relationships. Specifically, we demonstrate how psychological factors can explain why and how certain SNS usage patterns can lead to jealousy and other negative emotions. Further, we discuss the potential behavioral and relational consequences.

12.2 Overview of the Chapter

We discuss SNS use and romantic jealousy within three main domains: 1) SNS attributes, 2) Individual differences, and 3) Behavioral and relationship outcomes. Specifically, we demonstrate that the attributes of SNSs themselves may contribute to the experience of romantic jealousy. That is, attributes such as publicity, allow individuals access to information that they may otherwise not have had about their partner. This has implications for partner monitoring behaviors, which influence jealousy and negative emotions. Second, we discuss individual differences, or characteristics unique to individuals (e.g., personality, gender, ethnic background, age), that can influence how susceptible different people are to experiencing jealousy. We discuss individual difference characteristics such as sex, attachment style, self-esteem, and interpersonal trust levels as they relate to SNS-related jealousy. Finally, we conclude with a discussion about how SNS-related jealousy may influence subsequent behavioral outcomes such as relationship satisfaction and duration.

12.2.1 Key Definitions

The social science literature accepts the following definition of jealousy:

> "Jealousy...may be said to occur when a person either fears losing or has already lost an important relationship with another person to a rival. Jealousy may be experienced in a number of ways, but typically these are thought to include fear of loss, anger of betrayal, and insecurity (Hupka, 1984; Mathes, Adams, & Davies, 1985)" (Parrott, 1991, p. 4).

Jealousy is often confused with envy, which is characterized by a desire for the possessions, achievements, or qualities of another individual (Sagarin & Guadagno, 2004). Other related emotions typically examined in the literature on jealousy are disgust, hurt, and anger (Becker, Sagarin, Guadagno, Nicastle, & Millevoi, 2004; Sagarin, Becker, Guadagno, Wilkinson, & Nicastle, 2003). Depending on the context that invokes a jealous response, these related emotions may or may not show similar patterns of results as jealousy (Sagarin et al., 2012).

SNSs are a type of social media – broadly defined as "web-based services that allow individuals to (1) construct a public or semi-public profile within a bounded system, (2) articulate a list of other users with whom they share a connection, and (3) view and traverse their list of connections and those made by others within the system" (p. 221, boyd and Ellison, 2007). "Social media" is often used synonymously with social networking or SNS. Because much of the research on romantic jealousy has focused on sites like Facebook, we will use the term "social networking site" or "SNS" throughout the chapter. While the specifics of the various SNSs vary by time (Boyd and Ellison, 2007; Guadagno et al., 2013), culture (Kim, Sohn, & Choi, 2011), purpose (LinkedIn vs. FB), and population (Guadagno, Muscanell, & Pollio, 2013), they all have the above characteristics. Current research indicates that while 73% of all people online use social media, young adults (i.e., 18-29 years old) are the most prevalent users – 90% of this age group is online in the Western world (Pew Research Internet Project, 2013). Thus, a majority of the research we discuss next is particularly relevant to this age group.

12.3 Attributes of Social Networking Sites

We suggest that the nature of SNSs and the way individuals use them (i.e., purely for recreation, social interaction vs. purely for one's occupation) vary on two general attributes (or affordances) that are relevant to romantic jealousy: publicity and permanence. Publicity refers to the transparency of information about an individual – depending on his/her privacy settings, personal information will be accessible to a few others or potentially hundreds of others. Permanence refers to the way in which shared information and traces of online social behavior are available for long periods of time (i.e., many researchers [including us] argue that nothing on the Internet is ever deleted). Many SNSs are designed to encourage people to disclose much of their personal information to a broad audience and this information stays online indefinitely, sometimes even after a person has passed away. Thus, as a result, interpersonal relationships on SNSs such as Facebook are typically visible to many people and persist far longer than most imagine (Church, 2013). This can result in a loss of privacy within interpersonal relationships. Hence, the way SNS users interact with, or attempt to control certain attributes of their social media presence also has potential consequences for interpersonal relationships. We next discuss how these attributes and user-specific settings can lead to the experience of jealousy and also partner monitoring behaviors.

12.3.1 User Specific Settings

While publicity and permanence characterize many of the core controversies on SNSs and the Internet more broadly, it is also possible that the way in which privacy settings are configured -- specifically what types of information users choose to share (or conceal) may elicit negative emotions within romantic relationships. For instance, if an individual shares (or omits) couple-specific information (e.g., his/her relationship status, photos with his/her romantic partner), this may impact the relationship and their SNS experience.

In one such study, Muscanell, Guadagno, Rice, and Murphy (2013) examined these issues in relation to jealousy in romantic relationships[1] on Facebook. Participants were asked to imagine one of several scenarios in which they happened to view their romantic partner's Facebook profile still logged on and displaying a photograph of their partner tagged with an unknown person of the opposite sex. The number of photos of the participant with his/her romantic partner was also varied by condition as 1) none, 2) a few, 3) or many. Second, the privacy settings of the couple photo(s) were manipulated by asking participants to imagine that their partner's privacy settings were set to: completely viewable by all Facebook users, only viewable by Facebook friends, or completely private. Following the vignette, participants reported their level of jealousy, anger, disgust, and hurt in response to the passage. Results indicated that privacy settings and the availability of couple-specific photographs influenced jealousy and related emotions such that women reported more intense jealousy, anger, and hurt relative to men in response to the scenario. Further, when participants imagined their partner's profile was set to private and displayed few relationship photos, women reported the most intense jealousy. For men, this was only the case when the profile was set to private and there were many couple photos.

These results suggest that the content and privacy settings of one's romantic partner's Facebook profile affect the extent to which people experience SNS-related jealousy and related negative emotions (Muscanell et al., 2013). The researchers speculated that the gender differences found in the different levels of privacy may be related to concerns about online infidelity (see Guadagno & Sagarin, 2010). Importantly, the results provide clear evidence that SNSs are yet another context in which relationship dynamics play out for individuals. Given this, it is unsurprising to learn that "Facebook stalking" a behavior in which individuals seek out evidence to confirm or disconfirm infidelity also occurs on Facebook, particularly during relationship termination, and primarily from the partner that did not want to terminate the relationship (Tong, 2013).

1 This chapter focuses on research germane to heterosexual couples.

12.3.2 Partner Monitoring (Surveillance)

The public and permanent nature of SNSs can allow individuals in a romantic relationship access to information that they normally would not have (e.g., photographs of former romantic partners publically available). One implication then is that individuals can monitor or "Facebook stalk" their romantic partner for evidence of infidelity. The terms "partner monitoring" and "surveillance" are often used interchangeably in the subsequently discussed research. Thus, for simplicity, we will refer to it as "partner monitoring" or "partner monitoring behaviors". Muise, Christofides, and Desmarais (2009) found just that: participants who spent more time on Facebook were also exposed to more information about their romantic partner. Similar to Muscanell et al. (2013), they argue that this information can often be ambiguous (e.g., a short nondescript message to one's partner from an opposite sex SNS "friend"), and when individuals see information without context, this may result in increased feelings of jealousy given that a person may not be completely sure what the public information means. This can further fuel "stalking" or information searching behavior on Facebook, as ambiguous information may cause uncertainty, doubts about a partner's commitment, and feelings of jealousy.

More recently, Muise, Chrisofides, and Desmarais (2013) further examined partner monitoring behaviors on Facebook. Across two studies, they found that partner monitoring was related to Facebook jealousy. In their first study, Muise et al. asked participants to view a mock Facebook profile page and imagine that it belonged to their romantic partner. This profile was also linked to another profile whose ownership was manipulated. Participants believed that the linked profile belonged to an unknown other, a mutual friend (of the couple), or their romantic partner's cousin. Participants' search time on the interactive mock profile was assessed. Results revealed that women were most jealous if the linked profile belonged to an unknown woman, whereas men were more jealous if the linked page belonged to a mutual (male) friend. Further, women spent more time searching in the unknown other condition. These findings suggest that, at least for women, jealousy and information seeking were related.

In their second study, the researchers examined daily Facebook use across 14 nights (Muise et al., 2013). Participants rated their daily experiences with jealousy, and partner monitoring. Similar to Study 1, they found that for women, higher levels of jealousy were related to increased partner monitoring. Other research similarly supports the relation between partner monitoring and jealousy, such that frequent Facebook users often report increased feelings of jealousy and admit to more monitoring of their romantic partner's profile (Marshall, Bejanyan, Castro, & Lee, 2012).

Overall, research findings on the relation between jealousy and partner monitoring suggest that the attributes of SNSs, such as publicity and permanence, along with a person's ability to control what they share, can result in jealousy and negative emotions such as anger, hurt, and disgust in response to their partners' choices. When romantic couples use sites such as Facebook, they gain access to information about their partner that they might not have otherwise had access to, yet some of this information may be ambiguous (e.g., an unknown opposite-sex person leaving a nondescript public message), which may further fuel partner monitoring behaviors. However, while partner monitoring and jealousy are strongly related, it is also the case that some people are simply more prone to Facebook stalking and jealousy. Next, we explain how factors unique to an individual may make some people more susceptible to experiencing Facebook jealousy.

12.4 Individual Differences

While the attributes of SNSs play a significant role on whether or not individuals experience jealousy, personality and other individual differences should also be considered. A great number of researchers in social and personality psychology, and in psychology more generally, have demonstrated the importance of considering not only situational (context) factors, but also person-centered variables (and the interaction between the two) in regards to understanding and explaining a wide variety of behavioral outcomes (Allport, 1927; Fleeson, & Noftle, 2008; Kenrick, & Funder, 1988; Witkin, 2006). Thus, we believe it is important to consider person level characteristics and as such we highlight some of the individual difference characteristics that have been shown to influence partner monitoring behaviors and the experience of romantic jealousy on SNSs.

12.4.1 Sex Differences

Psychological research has long shown that there are sex differences in the experience of jealousy and related emotions (Buss, Larsen, Westen & Semmelrogth, 1992; Sagarin et al., 2003; Sagarin & Guadagno, 2004). Specifically, women tend to experience more intense feelings of jealousy, hurt, anger, and disgust as compared to men in response to infidelity. Sagarin and Guadagno (2004) examined sex differences in the intensity of jealousy hypothesizing that it stems from relationship maintenance orientation. In their first study, men and women were asked to provide an example of an instance when they felt extremely jealous. They found that women, relative to men, were far more likely to provide relational exemplars – primarily focused on their romantic relationships. In a second study, the researchers found that when both men and women were instructed to focus on relational jealousy by modifying the measure of jealousy to specifically indicate jealousy in a romantic relationship, men and women did not differ in their reported jealousy. Thus, this greater tendency to focus on relationship maintenance may make women more sensitive to threats of infidelity as compared to men.

Research on SNS use shows that some sex differences may generalize to the experience of jealousy on Facebook. For example, as reviewed above, Muscanell et al. (2013) demonstrated that women experienced more intense feelings of jealousy, hurt, anger, and disgust relative to men when imagining a jealousy-provoking Facebook scenario. Muise et al. (2009) also found similar evidence of gender differences in jealousy resulting from SNS use. And, in their previously discussed 2013 study, the authors found that women were more likely than men to engage in partner monitoring behaviors in addition to reporting higher amounts of Facebook jealousy. In their 2013 study, Muise et al. also found that women with high attachment anxiety (women who hold insecurities and are generally anxious about their relationships) were likely to be jealous and reported increased partner monitoring. Another potential explanation then, is that women (especially those with relationship insecurities) may be more prone to experiencing jealousy because of their insecurities and they are more likely to engage in partner monitoring behaviors on Facebook.

Finally, McAndrew and Shah (2013) also found that women reported more jealousy in response to Facebook use. Further, they assessed the extent to which participants thought their romantic partner was likely to experience jealousy resulting from Facebook use. When the researchers compared participant's own ratings of jealousy to their predictions about their partners, women did not perceive themselves as being more jealous than their male partners. However, men did perceive and anticipate that their female partners would be more jealous than themselves. The authors suggested that misunderstandings between romantic partners regarding Facebook use may result from misperceptions about how partners will react to Facebook activity.

Overall, the evidence to date suggests that men and women may differ in their susceptibility and experience of jealousy resulting from SNS use. This may be in part due to social and cultural factors such as women's greater tendency to focus on relationship maintenance, and/or misperceptions about how jealous one's partner would feel in a jealousy-provoking situation. Further, as with jealousy in response to non-mediated contexts, women generally report higher levels of jealousy in their social networking lives.

12.4.2 Attachment Styles

As Muise et al. (2013) reported, attachment style is another relevant characteristic which differs between individuals. Research demonstrates that attachment style plays a significant role in people's relationship outcomes (Feeney & Noller, 1990; Simpson, 1990). In general, individuals with more secure attachment styles (as opposed to those with high anxiety and insecurity) are not only more well adjusted, but have more positive relationship experiences, such as more commitment, trust, and relationship satisfaction (Shaver & Hazan, 1993).

Recent research has extended the examination of attachment style and its relation to romantic relationships and SNSs. For instance, Fox and Warber (2013) found that attachment style predicted partner monitoring on Facebook. Specifically, they found that individuals with a preoccupied (feeling unworthy) or fearful attachment (excessive worrying) style reported monitoring their partner's Facebook behavior more often. Both preoccupied and fearful attachment styles are qualified by high relationship anxiety and may lead to increased partner monitoring. Specifically, for preoccupied individuals, partner monitoring may allow individuals to feel more control (and attempt to reduce their anxiety). For fearful individuals, partner monitoring on Facebook might allow these individuals to monitor their partner without direct confrontation.

Marshall, Bejanyan, Castro, and Lee (2013) found that anxious attachment was positively related to Facebook jealousy and partner monitoring. Further, trust and daily jealousy partially explained this relationship such that anxiously attached individuals reported less trust and more jealousy. This in turn predicted more partner monitoring behaviors. The authors explained that anxious individuals tend to feel unworthy or unloved and distrustful of their partners, which in turn may heighten jealousy and partner monitoring behaviors. Overall, anxiously attached individuals may thus be more prone to jealousy and monitoring behaviors due to their relationship insecurities. These individuals may be more prone to partner monitoring behaviors because their insecurities about their relationship may drive them to seek out evidence on SNS that either confirms or disconfirms their worries.

12.4.3 Self-esteem, Need for Popularity, and Trait Jealousy

Other research has extended the research on individual differences and SNS-related jealousy by examining factors such as self-esteem, need for popularity, and trait jealousy (Utz and Beukeboom, 2011). Interestingly, they found that SNS users reported more SNS-related happiness relative to SNS jealousy. However, the individual difference variables did moderate the relation between SNS use and the experience of jealousy. Overall, low self-esteem individuals reported more SNS-related jealousy. In addition, for these individuals with low self-esteem, need for popularity, trait jealousy, and partner monitoring behaviors all predicted SNS-related jealousy. More simply, for low self-esteem individuals, higher need for popularity and trait jealousy, along with higher amounts of partner monitoring, predicted more SNS-related jealousy. For those with high self-esteem, only partner monitoring and self-reported use of the SNS for grooming (maintaining social contacts) positively predicted SNS-related jealousy. The authors suggested that low self-esteem individuals, especially those with a high need for populatrity, may be more sensitive to negative cues or potential threats to their romantic relationship, and thus making them more prone to SNS jealousy. In the case of individuals with high self-esteem, the authors suggest that these individuals may be exposed to more relationship threatening information given their inclination to use SNS for grooming or maintaining social contacts. That is, these individuals should look at their connections' profiles more often and may consequently be exposed to more relationship related information, and this could predict SNS jealousy. Finally, for both low and high self-esteem individuals, partner monitoring positively predicted jealousy. One implication is that frequently monitoring a partner's behavior on SNSs may lead to SNS-related jealousy more generally, regardless of one's self-confidence.

Overall, the existing evidence suggests that individual difference characteristics as well as relational factors such as intimacy and commitment play a significant role in influencing the level of jealousy experienced by SNS users. Furthermore, women and people with certain dispositions, such as those with anxious attachment styles or low self-esteem, may particularly be more sensitive to relationship threats and SNS-related jealousy.

12.5 Behavioral Responses and Relational Outcomes

As reviewed above, there is strong support for the idea that SNS usage can lead to the experience of jealousy and other related emotions for individuals in romantic relationships. But what is less clear is what the short and long term behavioral consequences of SNS-related jealousy are. For instance, while we know about self-reported partner monitoring, what do we know about how people behave (in the moment) when exposed to jealousy provoking scenarios and what are the effects on relationship outcomes?

12.5.1 Behavioral Intentions

To our knowledge, there is little to no research examining behavioral responses to jealousy-evoking SNS scenarios. However, in one recent study, we assessed open-ended responses from participants who imagined their partner's profile on Facebook displaying a photo of their partner with an unknown other that, depending on condition, varied with respect to privacy settings and quantity of partner photos (Muscanell et al., 2013). Here we present previously unreported coded descriptive data on participants' reported response to the scenario described above in which we examined the role of partner photos and privacy settings on relational jealousy. Two independent raters (93% - 100% agreement) categorized participants' written responses into several different categories including: confronting their partner, confronting the unknown person, ending the relationship, passive aggressive behavior (e.g., commenting on the photo, tagging one's partner in new photos), and asking their partner to take action (i.e., remove the offending photo or defriend the unknown person). Overall, the most frequent behavioral response reported by participants (59.4%) was that they would confront their partner about the situation. Many of these responses specifically revealed intentions to find out more about the situation and about the unknown person via discussion with their partner, and to give their partner a chance to clarify the situation. Only a small number of participants reported that they would take more extreme measures: 8.3% of participants reported that they would end the relationship, 1.3% reported that they would engage in partner monitoring behaviors, and 6.6% reported that they would engage in some form of aggressive behavior (e.g., screaming, physical confrontation, and or destruction of property). Also, 6.6% reported that they would engage in some form of passive aggressive behavior (e.g., tagging their partner in a photo with themselves). Finally, 9.6% of participants reported that they would directly ask their partner to take action (i.e., removing the photo or defriending the unknown person). In addition, individuals did not anticipate that they would directly end their relationship.[2]

These findings provide a preliminary glimpse into the behavioral implications of SNS-related jealousy and other negative emotions. In general, participants largely reported that in a scenario in which they find somewhat ambiguous information on their partner's SNS profile, they would directly confront him/her about. This suggests that ambiguous content may lead to confrontation, discussion, and/or arguments. What is less clear is how often incidents like these actually occur and whether more blatant situations would result in more severe relationship outcomes such as physical confrontations and relationship termination. Future research should longitudinally examine couples to better understand how often instances of SNS-related jealousy occur (and under what contexts), and how SNS use impacts the relationship over time.

12.5.2 Relationship Satisfaction

Other research has examined the impact of SNS-related jealousy on relationship outcomes. For example, Elphinston and Noller (2011) explored the relation between Facebook intrusion, romantic jealousy, and relationship satisfaction among Facebook users. The authors defined Facebook intrusion as being characterized by an excessive attachment to Facebook that it interferes with everyday activities. They found that jealous cognitions (suspicious thoughts about one's partner) and partner monitoring behaviors explained the relationship between Facebook intrusion ("excessive attachment to Facebook which interferes with day-to-day activities and relationship functioning", p. 631, Elphinston & Noller, 2011) and relationship satisfaction.

2 These data did not differ by sex or experimental condition.

Specifically, high levels of Facebook intrusion produced more jealous cognitions and partner monitoring behaviors, and this in turn led to lower relationship satisfaction. The authors explained that because Facebook is a means for interpersonal interaction, individuals with high Facebook intrusion are also more likely to find romantic relationships to be important. Thus, an implication of this research is that these individuals are more sensitive to relationship threats and their excessive attachment to and use of Facebook exposes them to more potentially threatening information. This in turn can increase jealous thoughts and ultimately decrease relationship satisfaction.

While the previous study suggests that SNS use can lead to jealousy and ultimately less satisfaction with a romantic relationship, there is also some research that suggests there are positive relationship outcomes. For instance, in the previously discussed study by Utz and Beukeboom (2011) the authors found that low self-esteem individuals were more prone to SNS-related jealousy. However, they also examined relationship happiness and, in general, they found that individuals were more likely to experience relationship happiness as compared to SNS jealousy. They suggested that SNS use may offer individuals the opportunity for public demonstrations of affection and commitment, which can then lead to more relationship happiness and satisfaction.

Similarly, other research indicates that posting couple-related information relates to positive relationship outcomes. For example, across three studies, Saslow, Muise, Impett, and Dubin (2012) found that people who were more satisfied with their romantic relationships were more likely to post couple photos on Facebook. Similarly, Papp, Danielewicz, and Cayemberg (2012) examined dyadic picture sharing on Facebook. They found that participants whose profile photos were with their partners and whose relationship status was also shared publicly had higher relationship satisfaction. Further, women reported more relationship satisfaction when their male partners shared their relationship status on Facebook, whereas men felt more relationship satisfaction when their female partner shared dyadic profile pictures.

Overall, the evidence suggests that while Facebook use is related to jealousy and negative outcomes, such as lower relationship satisfaction and greater confrontations within the relationship, there is also the potential for positive outcomes depending on how people utilize and share information they post to Facebook. Specifically, while more partner monitoring is linked with jealousy and relationship dissatisfaction, individuals who use SNSs to publicly and jointly share details of their relationship may experience more relationship satisfaction and happiness. It may be that for individuals who are not characterized by anxious attachment or low self-esteem, SNSs offer the potential to provide positive relationship experiences. Future research is needed in order to determine which kinds of individuals and romantic couples are more likely to benefit from SNS use.

12.5.3 Relationship Duration

To our knowledge, little research has examined the direct impact of SNS use on relationship duration and termination. However, two recent studies do suggest that SNS use can lead to increased relationship conflict and ultimately termination of the relationship (Clayton, Nagurney, & Smith, 2013; Clayton, 2014). One study explored the relation between Facebook use and cheating (Clayton, Nagurney, & Smith, 2013). They found that greater Facebook use was associated with negative relationship outcomes (cheating). Further, they found that relationship conflict – operationalized as the frequency of arguments with their partners resulting from Facebook use – explained this relationship. That is, using Facebook predicted increased conflict over Facebook activity/use, which then predicted an increased likelihood of cheating with a Facebook "friend". The authors suggest an implication of these findings is that SNS-based conflict and resulting infidelity may predict relationship termination. A more recent study more directly examined SNS use and relationship termination (Clayton, 2014). This study examined Twitter use and negative relationship outcomes. Similar to the previously described study, it was found that Twitter use predicts relationship conflicts (arguments caused by Twitter use). This in turn predicts negative relationship outcomes such as infidelity, and breakup and divorce. Thus, this initial evidence suggests that SNS use can lead to less duration of the relationship (ultimately resulting in termination). However, what is less clear is the role that jealousy plays as these studies focused on SNS relationship conflict. Future research should further examine whether jealousy (in addition to relationship conflict) is directly related to infidelity and relationship duration and termination.

12.6 Conclusion

Overall, there are a number of psychological factors that are related to SNS use and jealousy within romantic relationships. We argue that there are a combination of factors that may influence whether individuals are likely to experience SNS-related jealousy or related emotions such as anger, hurt, and disgust. These factors include SNS attributes, such as publicity and permanence, the way individuals utilize SNS specific settings, the type of content shared or observed, and individual differences. Overall, publicity and permanence, as well as the information that individuals choose to share in their SNS profiles, can affect relationship satisfaction and the experience of jealousy. In general, SNS use provides individuals with access to more information about their romantic partner's past and current relationships with others who may be perceived as a threat to the relationship. Because SNSs tend to be platforms in which information is permanently stored and at least somewhat publicly (given that a user does not delete information and has SNS friends) available. This can lead to partner monitoring behaviors, which may further increase jealousy. Further, individuals may be exposed to ambiguous pieces of information (i.e., seeing one's partner tagged with an unknown other or seeing a nondescript message from another user posted publicly on one's partner's public message center such as the Facebook Wall). Findings so far suggest that individuals may interpret ambiguous information as being more threatening or potentially negative rather than responding with confidence in their romantic relationship. Thus, increased exposure to ambiguous information may also increase jealousy.

In addition to these situational factors that affect jealous-responding, individual difference factors affect relational jealousy as well. For instance, characteristics such as attachment style, self-esteem level, and gender are also related to relational jealousy. Individuals with anxious attachment styles and/or those with low self-esteem may experience more anxiety and insecurity regarding their relationships (and their overall self-image), which may make them more sensitive to potential relationship threats. Thus, these individuals may be more prone to experience SNS related jealousy, and their insecurities may further fuel partner monitoring behaviors in an attempt to reduce or control their relational anxiety by searching for more information about their partner. Further, women for cultural and social reasons may be more relational focused. For example, according to Social Role Theory (Eagly, 1987), women have traditionally been found to be more communally oriented, meaning that they focus more on relationship formation and maintenance as compared to men who tend to be agentic (independent and task focused). These differences in orientation can be understood to be resulting from differences in traditional social and cultural expectations for the behavior of men and women (i.e., traditionally men were the breadwinners and women took care of the house/family – although this does not necessarily hold true today). One consequence is that women, who tend to be more relationship oriented, may thus be more likely to be threatened by threats of infidelity, and may be more affected by the hyper-social context created by SNSs. Overall, these results suggest that in general, those who have the tendency to be more focused on relationships, more prone to relational anxiety or insecurity, and those with lower self-image may be particularly likely to experience SNS jealousy.

Finally, it is less clear what direct effect SNS-related jealousy has on behavioral responses and long-term relationship outcomes. Evidence is currently mixed, suggesting that SNS use can lead to jealousy and decreased relationship satisfaction; however, it can also lead to increases in relationship happiness and satisfaction for couples who display dyadic or couple specific information (i.e., relationship status and photos with one's romantic partner which can be viewed publicly on the SNS profile). Future research is needed to further examine whether the positive consequences of using SNS outweigh the negative ones in the context of romantic relationships. With regard to behavioral outcomes, preliminary evidence suggests that, in the very least, SNS-related jealousy relates to direct conflict within the relationship. However, because this initial evidence relies on self-report methods, it is less clear how individuals would actually react in real time if they were to experience jealousy-provoking scenarios in real life. Thus, more research that examines real life experiences of SNS-related jealousy and relationship outcomes is needed. It is worth noting that many of these studies rely on self-report methods of jealousy and/or related emotions, which is understandable given the difficult nature of systematically examining such constructs. Yet, there is still a need for research that uses methods that are less prone to self-report biases (e.g., actual behavior, observational, and physiological methods).

To conclude, SNSs such as Facebook and Twitter seem to be a double-edged sword for romantic couples who use them. SNS use may provide opportunities for experiencing relationship satisfaction and happiness and/or it may bring out the green-eyed monster in individuals, leading to jealousy and emotions such as hurt, anger, and disgust. While SNS-related jealousy is clearly something that a significant number of SNS users experience, the factors predicting it are complex in nature and are not easy to measure objectively—SNS attributes, situational/contextual factors, and person characteristics are all important predictors of whether or not, and to what extent, individuals experience SNS-related jealousy. As SNSs continue to change with time (as they frequently do), future research will need to keep in mind the specific attributes that SNSs offer at the given time, in addition to more clearly exploring the specific types of contextual information that are likely to be particularly jealousy-provoking, and who (at the person level) will be likely to be susceptible to feeling and responding jealously to such information.

References

Allport, G. W. (1927). Concepts of trait and personality. *Psychological Bulletin, 24*(5), 284-293.

Becker, D. V., Sagarin, B. J., Guadagno, R. E., Nicastle, L. D., & Millevoi, A. (2004). When the sexes need not differ: Emotional responses to the sexual and emotional aspects of infidelity. *Personal Relationships, 11,* 529-538.

Buss, D. M., Larsen, R. J., Wesen, D., & Semmelroth, J. (1992). Sex differences in jealousy: Evolution, physiology, and psychology. *Psychological Science, 3,* 251-255.

Carpenter, C. J., & Spottswood, E. L. (2013). Exploring romantic relationships on social networking sites using the self-expansion model. *Computers in Human Behavior, 29,* 1531-1537.

Church, S. H. (2013). Digital gravescapes: Digital memorializing on Facebook. *The Information Society: An International Journal, 29,* 184-189.

Clayton, R. B. (2014). The third wheel: The impact of Twitter use on relationship infidelity and divorce. *Cyberpsychology, Behavior, and Social Networking,* Advanced online publication.

Clayton, R. B., Nagurney, A., & Smith, J. R. (2013). Cheating, breakup, and divorce: Is Facebook use to blame? *Cyberpsychology, Behavior, and Social Networking,* Advanced online publication.

Deters, F. G., & Mehl, M. R. (2012). Does posting Facebook status updates increase or deacrease loneliness? An online social networking experiment. *Social Psychological and Personality Science, 4*(5), 579-586.

Eagly, A. H. (1987). *Sex differences in social behavior: A social-role interpretation.*Hillsdale, NJ: Erlbaum.

Elphinston, R. A., & Noller, P. (2011). Time to face it! Facebook intrusion and the implications for romantic jealousy and relationship satisfaction. *Cyberpsychology, Behavior, and Social Networking, 14*(11), 631-635.

Elpinston, R. A., Feeney, J. A., Noller, P., Conner, J. P., & Fitzgerald, J. (2013). Romantic jealousy and relationship satisfaction: The costs of rumination. *Western Journal of Communication, 77*(3), 293-304.

Feeney, J. A., & Noller, P. (1990). Attachment style as a predictor of adult romantic relationships. *Journal of Personality and Social Psychology, 2*, 281-291.

Fleeson, W., & Noftle, E. (2008). The end of the person-situation debate: An emerging synthesis in the answer to the consistency question. *Social and Personality Psychology Compass, 2*(4), 1667-1684.

Fox, J., & Warber, K. M. (2013). Romantic relationship development in the age of Facebook: An exploratory study of emerging adults' perceptions, motives, and behaviors. *Cyberpsychology, Behavior, and Social Networking, 16*(1), 3-7.

Fox, J., & Warber, K. M. (2014). Social networking sites in romantic relationships: Attachment, uncertainty, and partner surveillance on Facebook. *Cyberpsychology, Behavior, and Social Networking, 17*(1), 3-7.

Guadagno, R. E., & Sagarin, B. J. (2010). Sex Differences in Response to Jealousy: An Evolutionary Perspective on Online Infidelity. *Journal of Applied Social Psychology, 40*, 2636-2655.

Guadagno, R. E., Loewald, T. A., Muscanell, N. L., Barth, J. M., *Goodwin, M. K., & Yang, Y. L. (2013). Facebook history collector: A new method for directly collecting data from Facebook. *International Journal of Interactive Communication Systems and Technologies, 3*(1), 57-67

Hand, M. M., Thomas, D., Buboltz, W. C., Deemer, E. D., & Buyanjargal, M. (2013). Facebook and romantic relationships: Intimacy and couple satisfaction associated with online social network use. *Cyberpsychology, Behavior, and Social Networking, 16*(1), 8-13.

Kenrick, D. T., & Funder, D. C. (1988). Profiting from the controversy: Lessons from the person-situation debate. *American Psychologist, 43*(1), 23-34.

Kim, Y., Sohn, D., & Choi, S. M. (2011). Cultural differences in motivations for using social network sites: A comparative study of American and Korean college students. *Computers in Human Behavior, 27*(1), 365-372.

Kross, E., Marshall, T.C., Bejanyan, K., Di Castro, G., & Lee, R. A. (2012). Attachment styles as predictors of Facebook-related jealousy and surveillance in romantic relaionships. *Personal Relationships, 20*, 1-22.

McAndrew, F. T., & Shah, S. S. (2013). Sex differences in jealousy over Facebook activity. *Computers in Human Behavior, 29*, 2603-2606.

Muise, A., Christofides, E., & Desmarais, S. (2013). "Creeping" or just information seeking? Gender differences in partner monitoring in response to jealousy on Facebook. *Personal Relationships*, Advanced online publication.

Muise, A., Christofides, E., & Desmarais, S. (2009). More information than you ever wanted: Does Facebook bring out the green-eyed monster of jealousy? *CyberPsychology & Behavior*, 12(4), 441-444.

Muscanell, N. L., Guadagno, R. E., Rice, L., & Murphy, S. (2013). Don't it make my brown eyes green? An analysis of Facebook use and romantic jealousy. *Cyberpsychology, Behavior, and Social Networking, 16*(4), 1-6.

Papp, L. M., Danielewicz, J., & Cayember, C. (2012). "Are we Facebook official?" Implications of dating partners' Facebook use and profiles for intimate relationship satisfaction. *Cyberpsychology, Behavior, and Social Networking, 15*(2), 85-90.

Pew Research Internet Project (2013). Social Networking Fact Sheet. Retrieved on June 18, 2014 from http://www.pewinternet.org/fact-sheets/social-networking-fact-sheet/

Sagarin, B. J., Becker, D. V., Guadagno, R. E., Wilkinson, W., & Nicastle, L. D. (2012). A reproductive threat-based model of evolved sex differences in jealousy. *Evolutionary Psychology, 10*, 487-503.

Sagarin, B. J., & Guadagno, R. E. (2004). Sex differences in the contexts of extreme jealousy. *Personal Relationships, 11*, 319-328.

Sagarin, B. J., Martin, A. L., Coutinho, S. A., Edlund, J. E., Patel, L., Skowronski, J. J., & Zengel, B. (2012). Sex differences in jealousy: A meta-analytic examination. *Evolution and Human Behavior, 33*, 595-614.

Saslow, L. R., Muise, A. Impett, E. A., & Dubin, M. (2013). Can you see how happy we are? Facebook images and relationship satisfaction. *Social Psychological and Personality Science, 4*, 411-418.

Simpson, J. A. (1990). Influence of attachment styles on romantic relationships. *Journal of Personality and Social Psychology, 59*(5), 971-980.

Tong, S. T. (2013). Facebook use during relationship termination: Uncertainty reduction and surveillance. *CyberPsychology, Behavior, & Social Networking, 16*, 1-6.

Utz, S., & Beukeboom, C. J. (2011). The role of social network sites in romantic relationships: Effects on jealousy and relationship happiness. *Journal of Computer-Mediated Communication, 16*(11), 511-527.

Witkin, H. A. (2006). The nature and importance of individual differences in perception. *Journal of Personality, 18*(2), 145-170.

Noella Edelmann

13 What is Lurking? A Literature Review of Research on Lurking

Abstract: There has been a massive growth in user-driven online applications such as blogs, podcasts, wikis, and social networking, as well as online users having different ways of using online and social media. Although it is known that online participation is not evenly distributed among users, research often focuses on the small core of participants that generates most of the visible online content and activity. This chapter aims to provide an understanding of the phenomenon of online lurking by providing a review of the definitions of lurking, and shows that lurkers are both active and valuable online participants.

13.1 Introduction

The internet offers ways to interact with others, access information, as well as enables and facilitates contact among individuals (Anderson, 2006; Sypher and Collins, 2001; McKenna and Bargh, 2000). Online, individuals can chat, argue, engage in intellectual discourse, exchange knowledge, share emotions and provide emotional support, plan, brainstorm, gossip, feud, fall in love, find friends or lose them, and play games. Online technologies and media make finding others who are similar or share similar interests easy, they help those who are less confident to speak out and participate, and seem to provide almost infinite choices (Anderson, 2009, 2006; Katz, 1997).

Social networking encourages activities such as forming personal networks, connecting and linking to others, participating in discussions, and creating communities. But what is particular about the "new", "social", or "web 2.0" media is that it has given online participation additional dimensions: the new "architecture of participation" not only encourages contribution by users but also helps them gain control over information, the process of production and diffusion, as well as the software itself (Governor, Hinchcliffe and Nickull, 2009, p.22). The distinction between interaction and content production has blurred as users increasingly use online sites such as YouTube, Facebook, and Digg to produce and share knowledge and information, writing blogs, creating Wikis, producing and combining services ("mash-ups"), as well as organising and engaging in discussion (Archmann, 2010; Slot and Frissen, 2007). Successful outcomes of online participation and collaboration are possible even though online participants have never met face-to-face, and benefits may include better performance and quality, more efficiency, higher productivity, and improved attendance (Brandon and Hillingshead, 2007; Abreu, 2000; Cascio,

2000). It has been suggested that the internet may be the 'glue' that helps people stay together and that it supports the collective help necessary for solving a range of social and societal problems (Cruickshank, Edelmann and Smith, 2010; Huysman and Wulf, 2005).

But research on different online environments shows that online participation is not evenly distributed among users: individuals share information and connect with others at varying levels of involvement, and often a small core of participants generates most of the conversation and content (Martin and Robinson, 2007; Joyce and Kraut, 2006; Rafaeli and Raban, 2005; Skitka and Sargis, 2005; Preece, 2000). Nielsen (2009, 2006) states that low levels of participation and online information sharing are a characteristic of the online environment, describing online participation with the 90-9-1 rule: 90% of the users read or observe (but don't contribute), 9% of the users contribute from time to time, and 1% of the users participate a lot and account for most contributions. This proportion seems to be found in several online environments, for example in open-source communities 4% of the participants provide 50% of the answers on a user-to-user help site (Lakhani and Hippel, 2003) and in Wikipedia, 2.5% of the users contribute 80% of all the content (Tapscott and Williams, 2006). Typical online social networks – that are about interactivity more than anything else – are similar: the top 10% of users account for 30% of all production, e.g. on Twitter, the top 10% of prolific Twitter users account for over 90% of tweets (Heil and Piskorski 2009). A recent study on social media by Williams, Crittenden, Keo and McCarty (2012), revealed that 80% of their research sample (college students) see themselves as spectators rather than active users on social media.

Many researchers describe this dominant group of users in mass media, web 1.0, and web 2.0 as "lurkers". Online participation is not balanced, and the most common or popular online behaviour users engage in is lurking, and users who engage in lurking are known as "lurkers". Whilst participation in online and offline environments can be quite similar, lurking is possible because of the online technology: it provides access without being visible nor having to publicly participate (Joinson, 2001). Understanding online participation requires an understanding of lurking, in particular the implications of lurking for online research, but a review of the definitions of lurkers shows a broad range of definitions, as well as definitions thatare changing. Although reaserchers tend to use more neutral terms for the largest group of users, the more negative definition of lurking and assumptions about them seem to have remained. Understanding lurkers, their activies and value in the online environment are important when studying online environments, in particular in terms of how online research is conducted and results interpreted.

13.2 Defining Lurkers

A review of the research literature shows that there is a wide range of definitions, from lurkers as "free-riders" (Smith and Kollock 1999), to being the online "scourge" (in Antin and Cheshire, 2010, p. 128) or even "lovecats" (Sanders, 2010). But defining lurkers must begin with a clear distinction: lurkers are not non-users. Lurkers do use technology, they do visit sites and they do login. Non-users on the other hand, are those who do not use any information and communication technologies for a number of reasons, such as a lack of financial resources (Martin and Robinson 2007), poor education or lack of skills (Livingstone 2004), emotional reasons (such as technophobia, van Dijk 2005), because they resent using it (Hargittai, 2007; Selwyn, 2006), or simply because they do not want to. Furthermore, lurkers do not represent the unconnected, those who "are out of the loop, socially and otherwise" (Sypher and Collins 2001, p. 101).

13.2.1 Lurking: from "Never Posting" to "Luring the Gullible"

English language dictionaries define lurking as "to lie in wait (as in an ambush), to move furtively, to sneak, to go unnoticed or to exist unobserved or unsuspected. Synonyms include hiding, sneaking, hide, sneak, crouch, prowl, snoop, lie in wait, slink, skulk, concealment, moving stealthily or furtively" (Collins English Thesaurus, 2012, no page ref.). In the context of the online environment, dictionaires define lurking as to read but not contribute to the discussion in a newsgroup, electronic network, or community (Free Online Dictionary, 2012; Oxford Dictionaries Online, 2012).

In research on online communication, lurkers are understood as those who are known to read an online group's postings regularly but rarely participate. Sometimes they are described in terms how many posts they (don't) contribute, and this varies from those who "never" post (Nonnecke, Andrews and Preece, 2006; Preece, Nonnecke and Andrews, 2004), to those who have not posted in recent months (Nonnecke and Preece, 2000), who post infrequently (Ridings, Gefen and Arinze, 2006), who have not made a contribution in the first 12 months after subscribing to a list (Stegbauer and Rausch, 2002), or who contribute less than the average number of postings (Taylor, 2002).

It is known that lurkers access and login into sites, regularly read the postings and blogs, and anonymously use the content, but remain "silent". As lurkers tend to be the majority in the online environment - over 90% of the online group – their silence leads them to be called the "silent majority" or the "non-public audience" in an electronic forum (Strout, 2011; The Jargon File, 2010; Preece and Shneiderman, 2009; Nielsen, 2006; Stegbauer and Rausch, 2002; Takahashi, Fujimoto and Yamasaki, 2002; Nonnecke and Preece, 2000).

By being silent, anonymous, and not contributing visibly, lurkers are deemed to be the inactive, passive, peripheral or non-productive participants of online communities (Leshed, 2005; Rafaeli and Raban, 2005). Researchers describe them as TV viewers (Morris and Ogan, 1996), "TV zappers" or "aimless www surfers" (Stegbauer and Rausch, 2002, p. 263), those who do not interact with other members of the online communities, are passive, hard to involve, or non-public participants (Nonnecke et al. 2006; Rafaeli and Raban, 2005; Andrews et al., 2003). They are also defined as participants who do not actively and visibly contribute (Nielsen, 2006; Nonnecke and Preece, 2001), as well as peripheral or non-productive participants of online communities (Nonnecke et al. 2006; Leshed, 2005; Nonnecke and Preece, 2003, 2001).

Other definitions see lurkers as bystanders, someone who hangs around, wants something for nothing, shows a lack of commitment to the community, or is a threat to online groups (Cher Ping and Seng Chee 2001; Nonnecke and Preece, 1999). Ostrom (1990) suggests that lurkers get the benefits of belonging to the group without giving anything back or committing themselves to the online community, and Ling et al. (2005) describe them as "social loafers", i.e., users who contribute less or exert less effort to an online collective task. Researchers also view lurkers as selfish free-riders who aim to take advantage without contributing or reciprocating (Smith & Kollock 1999), where the lurkers' behaviours "results in unbalanced contribution: some enthusiasts contribute while others enjoy those contributions without reciprocating" and "eventually enthusiasm will erode leading to the slowdown or even demise of the group or community" (Rafaeli and Raban, 2005, p. 71). Rafaeli and Raban argue that free-riding allows participants to hide and easily assume false identities, making the lurking "problem" worse. Lurking is thus seen as an inappropriate behaviour or the detrimental use of technology (Butler, Sproull, Kiesler and Kraut 2002), an obstruction, exhausting bandwidth,"the scourge that prevents successful collective efforts" (Antin & Cheshire, 2010, p. 128), or cyber-tricksters "lurking the Web and luring the gullible" (OECD, 2003, p. 145).

13.2.2 Lurking as "Normal" Online Behaviour

Lurking seems to be the most popular online behaviour: some people spend many hours lurking, and know the topics of the conversation and key players of the online community well, becoming so immersed in the community's discussions that they feel they know the participants, belong to the community, and emphasise strongly with the issues in the online community (Soroka and Rafaela, 2006; Rafaeli, Ravid and Soroka, 2004; Nonnecke and Preece, 2000, 2003; Nonnecke et al., 1999). Lukers work at knowing the group, understanding the group and they are often committed to the group. They also do have opinions, ideas and information that can be of value to the community, but may be waiting for the right moment to contribute, are trying to see whether there contributions are appropriate to the online community, or evaluating the community atmosphere. It is seen as a positive and helpful behaviour, it enables new members to learn community norms, see whether their concerns are relevant to the community, and sometimes they can receive help and support without having to disclose themselves. Lurking is useful and desirable, particularly for very busy groups; if all members participate visibly, it could cause repetition of queries and result in an overload of posting. Lurkers avoid contributing to the chaos and information overload often found in communities, and, by side-posting or contacting individuals directly instead, they are engaging in pro-social and thoughtful altruistic behaviour (Haythornthwaite, 2009). Some online groups encourage lurking because it helps potential new users get a feeling for the group, the kind of people who participate in it, and how it operates (van Uden-Kraan, Drossaert, Taal, Seydel and van de Laar, 2008).

Nonnecke and Preece (2000) believe that lurking is one style of online behaviour, and describe it as situated action that is taken for many reasons including personal and group-, work-, and tool-related factors. Different users have different needs, different motivations and will have and require different skills and tools. Although participation includes activities such as creating relevant content, participation also involves activities such as consuming content e.g. reading the material that others provide or post. The majority of lurkers (53.9%) choose not to post because "just reading/browsing is enough" (Nonnecke et al., 2006, p. 13), and they may even be learning vicariously by reading the experiences other participants report (Arnold & Paulus, 2010). This means that lurkers are not ignoring the material (Edelmann and Cruickshank 2011), they may be engaged in other activities such as reading, listening and learning. Characterising readers as free-riders is inappropriate, as reading represents a legitimate form of participation and contribution; as readers they participate rather than try to take advantage of others' efforts and "if everyone chose to free-ride, Wikipedia would not exist (Antin and Cheshire, 2010, p. 127). Muller (2012, no page ref.) describes lurkers as "social readers", participants engaged in "social reading", where reading is not as a solitary, unconnected, unproductive action, but understood as an activity everybody does, a social activity that occurs in a social context, involves other people, and contributes to the social worlds of readers, authors and organisations. Muller suggests that everybody is a lurker, as we all read before engaging in another activity such as creating or posting content.

Lurkers are listeners, a important role, especially for others, as "if everyone is talking, is anybody listening?" (Goggin & Hjorth, 2009, p. 2). Listening (by reading the posts) and acting as an audience may represent a legitimate form of participation, and can be seen as a form of contributing to the community. According to Crawford (2009), "listening" is a useful metaphor for engagement and paying attention online, and, as readers and listeners, lurkers contribute a mode of receptiveness that encourages others to make public contributions. In many contexts lurkers serve as listeners, as conventional mass media audience, making them the justification and target for certain online activities (e.g. advertising, Soroka & Rafaela, 2006).

13.2.3 Active Lurking

Blanchard and Bowles (2001 p.60) helped popularize the notion "none of us is as smart as all of us". Attributed to originally being a Japanese proverb, it means that more can be accomplished by working together than on one's own –thus highlighting the importance of participation and contribution. In line with this, Shirky (2010) emphasises that any activity and any form of participation should be encouraged, as any "banal use" of the online environment (he mentions posting YouTube videos of kittens or writing bloviating blog posts) is "still more creative and generous than watching TV. We don't really care how individuals create and share; it's enough that they exercise this kind of freedom." (quoted in Garber, 2010, no page ref.). However, are posters more active than lurkers? Is active posting really the only legitimate online activity?

The lurker is not passive reader, a failure, or a free rider, but is a positive and active participant who can have an active role without posting a message. Willett (1998) considered lurking in terms of "active lurkers" and "passive lurkers". For Willet, "active lurkers" are those who make direct contact with posters in an interactive environment, propagate information or knowledge gained, whilst "passive lurkers" read for their own use only. Lurkers should not be approached as participants who do not actively contribute to an online environment, but as the indirect contributors of the online community's influence on its outside environment, by forwarding the topics in an online community to others who are not members of it and other online communites, or use information or knowledge gained from an online community for their personal or organizational activities. Research by Nonnecke and Preece (2003) found that active posting is not the only way to be part of a community, that lurking is more than not-posting or just reading others' posts and can include activities such as editing and organising messages. They suggest that lurking is a strategic and personal activity that involves a "complex set of actions, rationales and contexts" (Nonnecke & Preece 2003, p. 116). They see lurking as an activity, driven by the individual's needs, goals, reasons, and personal background. Lurkers use different strategies that help them identify community messages from other messages, decide whether to read or not, which threads to follow, deal with the messages, keep the information manageable, and finally, to maximise return on effort. The lurking activity is carried out methodoligically and strategically, may change according to the context, and individuals are capable of explaining the choice of method and strategy they follow. Nonnecke and Preece conclude that lurkers may have never posted a message, but they are not passive, rather, they are active and goal-driven.

Based on the assumption that lurkers may have a strong and wide influence outside the online community, Takahashi et al (2003) proposes a classification of online participants that includes lurkers and the the types of actions lurkers take outside the online community, and if the online community affects their thoughts. The classification of the participants and lurkers is based on the users and their 1. expectations of purpose of an online community; 2. stance on participation; 3. personal speciality and interests; 4. attitude towards information handling; 5. awareness of the existence of others. Within this classification, the lurker becomes a useful participant, and the lurker's point of view is a means of supporting or managing online communities and innovation. Even if lurkers do not propagate or use information or knowledge gained from an online community, their thoughts can be changed by it and reveal the influence of an online community.

13.3 Some Implications for Research

Lurkers should not be disenfranchised but given more attention, and, as lurking seems to be the most popular online behaviour, not be seen as dysfunctional behaviour but as an activity that many people enjoy doing. Understanding lurking is an initial, and certainly easier, step requiring less effort than trying to reach the non-users or those who are not at all interested in participation, the "ignorers" (Edelmann and Cruickshank, 2011).

Businesses and public institutions alike want users to actively participate online as the internet seems to be able to overcome a number of difficulties found in offline situations, as well as encourages innovation and the generation of new ideas (Tapscott and Williams 2006). Yet the research by Takahashi et al. (2007) shows that not only is it is difficult to evaluate the value of participation by counting the number of posts and other activities, and trying to convert these into economic quantities, but that a clearer understanding of online participation and lurking within an online community will allow the lurkers to occupy a more important position as a resource. Understanding lurking is central to understanding online social behaviour and cognition among the less salient participants, especially as lurkers do have opinions, ideas, and information that can be of value. Research on the online environment needs to consider that the majority of participants are not "seen" and that any results obtained may represent a small number of users only. In addition, the researchers approach to the users is reflected by the choice of definitions, and will impact how research is conducted and the meaning given to the results obtained. Research needs to consider, even avoid the dichotomy between "active" and "passive", and consider the multi-dimensionality of participation, including the role and value of lurking.

13.3.1 Which Definition?

Research on lurking shows that lurking involves a complex set of behaviours, rationales, and activities in an online environment that is rich with possibilities and options (Anderson, 2009; Nonnecke et al., 1999). To empirically analyse lurking requires a clear definition, yet this literature review shows that "it is not even clear what lurking means" (Stegbauer and Rausch, 2002, p. 264). The term is often associated with users who do not participate, are sinister or annoying, want something for nothing, are unnecessary for communication, an obstruction, and, on top of that, are significantly less valuable than other online participants. Lurking tends to have pejorative connotations, although what is deemed acceptable in terms of online behaviour may depend on the purpose of the group or community, the activities and attitudes of people who belong to it, and its policies: whilst education communities may be less tolerant of heated remarks than political communities, medical communities may be even more sensitive, given the vulnerability of the participants.

Opinions about lurking and lurkers vary considerably (van Uden-Kraan et al., 2008), and the choice of definition will impact how research is conducted, its aims (including the development of strategies to reduce lurking or make active participation more interesting for participants and lurkers), and the way results are interpreted. These definitions often imply that online groups with a large proportion of lurkers may have difficulty providing the necessary services or being successful. As the goal of most online communities is discussion and interaction, may there be some justification for the negative definitions?

Active, successful online participation and engagement has been defined mainly by visible participation, and negative approaches to lurking may hamper the way online spaces are understood. Even though internet user studies now focus more on particular online behaviors rather than considering all online actions to be uniform (Howard and Jones, 2004), categorizations of online activities are still relatively broad, making it difficult to understand who does what online and why. There are several reasons for abandoning the negative attitudes and definitions. Lurkers may not be contributing visible posts, but they are not depriving other contributors of resources or depleting the community. People lurk because that is what they enjoy doing, because they have nothing to say or because they are learning, reading, listening, forwarding or engaging in some other way. Nonnecke and Preece (2003, p.110) found that lurking is a strategic activity that is more than reading posts and encourage a "re-think" of lurking, as ignoring, dismissing, or misunderstanding them will distort how we understand online life as well as leading to mistakes in the way sites and policies for online participation are organised and designed. Some authors still tend to see lurking as free-riding in negative terms, but more recently lurking is being viewed and defined in more positive terms.

13.3.2 Avoiding the Dichotomy "Active" vs. "Passive" Participation

Stegbauer and Rausch (2002, p.267) suggest that among the majority of users, lurking is a "fixed behaviour pattern" thus placing online behaviour into either/or categories. Online behaviour has often been understood in terms of a dichotomy (participating vs. lurking), and a lot of research has focused on the overt online behaviours and visible activities only. This has encouraged the notion that lurkers are not participating, and are not as valuable as the contributing or "active" members (Antin & Cheshire, 2010; Crawford, 2009). Public posting is one way the community may benefit, but it is not the only way of communicating and contributing - participation can have many meanings and is complex. Online participation needs to be understood in terms of all the users, the connections and relationships and behaviours, and including lurkers' activities may allow a more complete depiction of online participation. The many forms of online participation and contribution, such as reading, listening, and being the audience, all represent legitimate and important online behaviours (Goggin and Hjorth, 2009). Muller (2012), who describes online reading as a social activity, suggests that everybody is a lurker, as everybody needs to read before engaging in the next activity.

Crawford (2009) believes that too much emphasis has been placed on "having a voice" and ensuring that individuals use online technologies to express themselves freely, making visible posting the most important form of online participation. Lurking is an important aspect of the online environment, so research on online behaviours, online communities and online media need to acknoweldge the complexity of participation (Leshed, 2005) and go beyond lurker/poster, active/passive as they cross between online/offline, public/private, and formal/informal divisions. Crawford suggests that everyone moves between different forms of participation, such as listening and disclosing online, and that all are necessary for online engagement. Individuals have different roles in different online contexts, as the online environment is a "holistic, polycontextual communication environment comprising diverse engagement spaces – differentiated online and offline communication contexts, within a larger community ecosystem" (Cranefield et al., 2011, p. 489).

13.3.3 The Value of Lurking

Although lurkers do not contribute public posts, they do not depreive regular contributors of resources nor do they detract from the community (Lee et al 2006 in Greif, Hjorth, Lasén and Lobet-Maris, 2011). As a behaviour common to the majority of online users in information or collaborative environments, it is necessary to understand lurking in terms of how it can be beneficial, valuable, positive, and helpful, and indeed may even need to be encouraged rather than eliminated (Crawford, 2009; Muller, Freyne, Dugan, Millen, & Thom-Santelli, 2009; Takahashi,

Fujimoto, & Yamasaki, 2003, 2007). Lurking can be an activity not only valuable to the lurkers themselves, but to others too.

Some assume that lurkers not only contribute less, but that they also receive fewer benefits from passive participation than active participants (Amichai-Hamburger, 2005; Taylor, 2002). However,other researchers have shown that lurkers do derive value and receive benefits from their activities, are satisfied with their experiences of the online community and the benefits they gain, and would not engage in lurking if they did not want to (Merry and Anoush, 2012). Lurkers gain perspective, information and insight (Katz, 1998) and they use this information for their own personal or organizational activities (Takahashi et al., 2007, 2003, 2002). Other benefits from lurking include enjoyment or learning (Arnold and Paulus, 2010; Soroka and Rafaela, 2006). Work by Metzger, Wilson, Pure, and Zhao (2012) shows that lurking is an important aspect in the use of social networks, and that lurkers gain personal and social benefits by visiting other members' profiles and reading others' personal information. Lurkers scan for information that is important, inspiring, useful; they follow up on ideas they find, draw attention to broken links, seek advice and opinions, and they communicate with others using alternative channels such as email, skype, etc. (Cranefield, Yoong and Huff, 2011). Value and benefits are derived in many ways, by acting as community advocates, sharing content and influencing others, using a number of online and offline channels and networks, by choosing a single channel of (online) activity or communication digest rather than multi-channel communication technology, having access to critical information that can help save time and take better decisions, as well as learning and saving information for their job or personal life (Ogneva, 2011).

The activities of lurkers can be valuable to the online environment, they may even be a necessity for enabling communication, e.g. by helping to avoid information overload, by paying attention as listeners or as an audience, or being the justification and target for online activities (Crawford, 2009; Soroka and Rafaela, 2006). In this way lurkers may maintain the community's infrastructure and help promote it. Even Stegbauer and Rausch (2002, p.271), who describe lurkers as passive, note that lurkers have a function "connecting otherwise isolated social spaces. They possibly contribute to the passing on of contents between mailing lists and from mailing lists into Usernet". Takahashi, Fujimoto and Yamasaki (2007, 2003, 2002) also suggest that lurkers are the indirect contributors to the online community's influence beyond its boundaries. Lurkers' activities make content available beyond the members of a mailing list or social network, and are essential for the transfer of knowledge between online groups and social spaces that would otherwise be separated from each other. Lurkers extend the online group through using the information in other online groups or offline settings, thus leading to connections with other networks bringing new contacts and members, providing key activities, resources and information, as well as serving as a mass media audience and representing potential future users (Gossieaux 2010; Preece & Shneiderman 2009; Ridings et al. 2006; Soroka and Rafaeli 2006). As lurkers cross the boundaries, they transfer knowledge from one context to another, making them "boundary spanners" or "knowledge brokers", where lurkers engage in identifing context-specific knowledge needs and opportunities, promoting new ideas, facilitating knowledge and content uptake, translating, recombining and adapting knowledge, making sure it fits the new context (Cranefield et al., 2011, p. 491). Wallace (2011) suggests that there are many online member types, and even without contributing online individuals can provide value by encouraging their peers to join, understanding and discussing the issues, and by pushing community administrators to deliver content that may increase engagement and participation.

By considering the value of lurking, definitions and descriptions of lurkers have changed. Lurkers' behaviours can be understood used as a metric of online social influence, e.g. their value is understood as part of the "return on contribution" (ROC) of a resource, which is based on the number of people who read, view or consume the resource, divided by the number of people who produced this resource (Muller et al., 2009). Harquail (2010) notes that whilst comments made on blogs show that readers are engaging with the ideas presented there, there is nothing wrong with reading and not commenting: lurkers are neither "self-centered idea scavengers" nor "online introverts lacking in gumption" (no page ref.), but participants who take the information gathered in one context and use it in another. Lurking has become an "asset rather than a hindrance" (Antin and Cheshire, 2010, p. 128), either by providing information that helps complete a task or by reading or being the indicator of the value and reliability of a text. Lurkers act as an audience and motivate others to participate in more active ways. Gossieaux (2010) also subscribes to the idea that lurkers are the "hidden asset" in online communities, they are active participants who forward content and information from one community to others using a variety of different channels (e.g. telephone, in conversation, by email). Lurkers are participants able to support and innovate online communities, or, in former Yahoo! Executive Sanders' (2010, 2003) terms, they are "lovecats", people who share knowledge freely and with good intent, serving others, facilitating relationship building, and adding to group learning.

13.4 Conclusion

The web 2.0 and social networks allows individuals even more control over what they want to publish and how they want to engage online. At the same time, there is also an increasing expectation that everybody should be using online tools and be online all the time – yet people will always have different ways of engaging online, deciding how and with whom to engage and when to be available. High levels of connectivity, frequent usage, as well as the availability of and access to information, does not mean that online users will necessarily be online more, more social or more knowledgeable, or understand what they are expected to, produce through posting more content.

Understanding lurkers has been the aim of a number of researchers for a number of years, and Katz (1998, no page ref.) notes that lurkers "cruise from site to site in peaceful anonymity, picking up perspective, information and insight". He was even informed by a lurker that there is of an online list[1] where lurkers meet to discuss the sites they've lurked, and the information they gathered. So Katz argued for a more positive approach to lurkers, for example with websites which aim to "offer special welcome areas for Lurkers, newcomers and newbies, not to mention immigrants, the elderly, the technically challenged or the shy." And although attitudes towards lurkers are changing and broadening, the label remains - can a new, more suitable definition be found for the largest group of users? Recent surveys show that 85% of American adults go online (Zickuhr, 2013) and 73% of online adults use least one social network (Duggan & Smith, 2014) – it may be by redefining online users that research can better understand online behaviours, online roles, and the values associated with them.

References

Abreu, S. (2000) How to manage telecommuters. *CNN.com.technology>computing*. Retrieved January 21, 2012, from http://edition.cnn.com/2000/TECH/computing/06/19/telecommuting.idg/index.html?iref=allsearch

Amichai-Hamburger, Y. (2005). Personality and the Internet. In Y. Amichai-Hamburger (Ed.), *The social net: Human behavior in cyberspace* (pp. 27–55). New York: Oxford University Press.

Anderson, C. (2006). *The long tail : why the future of business is selling less of more*. New York, NY: Hyperion.

Anderson, C. (2009). *The longer long tail : how endless choice is creating unlimited demand*. London: Random House Business Books.

Andrews, D., Nonnecke, B., & Preece, J. (2003). Electronic survey methodology: A case study in reaching hard-to-involve Internet users. *International Journal of Human-Computer Interaction, 16*(2), 185–210.

Antin, J., & Cheshire, C. (2010). Readers are not free-riders: Reading as a form of participation on Wikipedia. In *Proceedings of the 2010 ACM conference on Computer supported cooperative work* (pp. 127–130). Savannah, Georgia: ACM.

Archmann, S. (2010, November 16). *Web 2.0: Involving citizens for better public value*. Presented at the ePractice workshop: Public Services 2.0, European Commission, Brussels, Belgium. Retrieved 10. February 2011 from http://www.epractice.eu/files/Public_services_2%200_EIPA_final%20ppt.pdf

Arnold, N., & Paulus, T. (2010). Using a social networking site for experiential learning: Appropriating, lurking, modeling and community building. *The Internet and Higher Education, 13*(4), 188–196.

author not known. (2010). The Jargon File. Retrieved December 10, 2010, from http://catb.org/esr/jargon/html/L/lurker.html

Blanchard, K. H., & Bowles, S. M. (2001). *High five!: the magic of working together*. London: HarperCollins.

1 The instant messaging service ICQ.

Brandon, D. P., & Hillingshead, A. B. (2007). Characterizing online groups. In A. N. Joinson, K. McKenna, T. Postmes, & U.-D. Reips (Eds.), *The Oxford Handbook of Internet psychology* (pp. 105–120). Oxford: Oxford University Press.

Butler, B., Sproull, L., Kiesler, S., & Kraut, R. (2002). Community effort in online groups: Who does the work and why? *Leadership at a Distance*, 346–362.

Cascio, W. (2000). Managing a virtual workplace. *Academy of Management Executive*, *14*(3), 81–90.

Cher Ping, L., & Seng Chee, T. (2001). Online discussion boards for focus group interviews: an exploratory study. *Journal of Educational Enquiry*, *2*(1).

Cheshire, C., & Antin, J. (2010). None of Us Is as Lazy as All of Us. *Information, Communication & Society*, *13*(4), 537–555.

Collins English Thesaurus. (2012). Synonyms for lurk Collins English Thesaurus. *English Thesaurus*. Retrieved September 24, 2012, from http://www.collinsdictionary.com/dictionary/english-thesaurus/lurk?showCookiePolicy=true

Cranefield, J., Yoong, P., & Huff, S. (2011). Beyond Lurking: the Invisible Follower-Feeder in an Online Community Ecosystem. In *PACIS2011 Proceedings* (pp. 487–518 Paper 40). Brisbane, Australia.

Crawford, K. (2009). Following you: Disciplines of listening in social media. *Continuum*, *23*(4), 525–535.

Cruickshank, P., Edelmann, N., & Smith, C. (2010). Signing an E-Petition as a transition from Lurking to Participation. In J. Chappellet, O. Glassey, M. Janssen, A. Macintosh, J. Scholl, E. Tambouris, & M. Wimmer (Eds.), *Electronic Government and Electronic Participation (2010)* (pp. 275–282). Lausanne, Switzerland: Trauner Druck.

Duggan, M., & Smith, A. (2014). *"Social Media Update 2013."* Pew Research Center. Retrieved 11. January 2014 from http://pewinternet.org/Reports/2013/ Social - Media - Update .aspx

Edelmann, N., & Cruickshank, P. (2011). Giving Psychology a Role in eParticipation Research. In A. Manohoran & M. Holzer (Eds.), *E-Governance and Civic Engagement: Factors and Determinants* (pp. 338–361). IGI GLobal.

Free Online Dictionary. (2012). lurk - definition of lurk by the Free Online Dictionary, Thesaurus and Encyclopedia. *The Free Dictionary*. Retrieved September 24, 2012, from http://www.thefreedictionary.com/lurk

Garber, M. (2010). Clay Shirky's "Cognitive Surplus": Is creating and sharing always a more moral choice than consuming? *Nieman Journalism Lab*. Retrieved August 26, 2010, from http://www.niemanlab.org/2010/06/clay-shirkys-cognitive-surplus-is-creating-and-sharing-always-a-more-moral-choice-than-consuming/

Goggin, G., & Hjorth, L. (2009). Waiting to Participate Introduction. *Communication, Politics & Culture*, *42*(2), 1–5.

Gossieaux, F. (2010). Active lurkers – the hidden asset in online communities. *Energence Marketing*. Retrieved August 26, 2010, from http://www.emergencemarketing.com/2010/02/18/active-lurkers-the-hidden-asset-in-online-communities/

Governor, J., Hinchcliffe, D., & Nickull, D. (2009). *Web 2.0 Architectures* (1st ed.). Sebastopol, CA: O'Reilly Media, Inc.

Greif, H., Hjorth, L., Lasén, A., & Lobet-Maris, C. (Eds.). (2011). *Cultures of participation: media practices, politics and literacy*. Frankfurt am Main: P. Lang.

Hargittai, E. (2007). Whose Space? Differences Among Users and Non-Users of Social Network Sites. *Journal of Computer-Mediated Communication*, *13*(1), article 14.

Harquail, C. V. (2010). Active Lurkers: How Idea Lovecats Demonstrate Engagement with Your Blog. Retrieved June 13, 2012, from http://authenticorganizations.com/harquail/2010/03/18/active-lurkers-how-idea-lovecats-demonstrate-engagement/

Haythornthwaite, C. (2009). Online Knowledge Crowds and Communities (pp. 1–16). Presented at the International Conference on Knowledge Communities, Reno, USA: Center for Basque Studies, University of Nevada, Reno. Retrieved 15. December 2010 from https://www.ideals.

illinois.edu/bitstream/handle/2142/14198/Online%20Knowledge%20Crowds%20and%20 Communities_Reno_2009.pdf?sequence=2

Heil, B., & Piskorski, M. (2009, June 1). New Twitter Research: Men Follow Men and Nobody Tweets. *The Conversation - Harvard Business Review*. Retrieved 25. October 2010 from http://blogs.hbr.org/cs/2009/06/new_twitter_research_men_follo.html

Howard, P., & Jones, S. (Eds.). (2004). *Society online : the Internet in context*. Thousand Oaks CA: Sage.

Huysman, M., & Wulf, V. (2005). The Role of Information Technology in Building and Sustaining the Relational Base of Communities. *The Information Society*, *21*(2), 81–89.

Joinson, A. N. (2001). Self-disclosure in computer-mediated communication: The role of self-awareness and visual anonymity. *European Journal of Social Psychology*, *31*(2), 177–192.

Joyce, E., & Kraut, R. (2006). Predicting Continued Participation in Newsgroups. *Journal of Computer-Mediated Communication*, *11*(3), article 3.

Katz, J. (1997). The Digital Citizen. *Wired*, (December), 68–82, 274–275.

Katz, J. (1998). Luring the Lurkers. *Slashdot*. Retrieved 25. August 2010, from http://news.slashdot.org/story/98/12/28/1745252/Luring-the-Lurkers

Lakhani, K., & Hippel, E. (2003). How open source software works: "free" user-to-user assistance. *Research Policy*, *32*(6), 923–943.

Leshed, G. (2005). Posters, Lurkers, and In Between: A multidimensional Model of Online Community Particiaption Patterns. Presented at the HCI International, Las Vegas.

Ling, K., Beenen, G., Ludford, P., Wang, X., Chang, K., Li, X., ... Kraut, R. (2005). Using Social Psychology to Motivate Contributions to Online Communities. *Journal of Computer-Mediated Communication*, *10*(4), article 10.

Livingstone, S. (2004). Media Literacy and the Challenge of New Information and Communication Technologies. *The Communication Review*, *7*(1), 3–14.

Martin, S. P., & Robinson, J. P. (2007). The Income Digital Divide: Trends and Predictions for Levels of Internet Use. *Social Problems*, *54*(1), 1–22.

McKenna, K. Y. A., & Bargh, J. A. (2000). Plan 9 From Cyberspace: The Implications of the Internet for Personality and Social Psychology. *Personality and Social Psychology Review*, *4*(1), 57–75.

Merry, K. M., & Anoush, S. (2012). Living and lurking on LiveJournal: The benefits of active and non-active membership. *Aslib Proceedings*, *64*(3), 241–261.

Metzger, M. J., Wilson, C., Pure, R. A., & Zhao, B. (2012). Invisible Interactions: What Latent Social Interaction Can Tell Us about Social Relationships in Social Network Sites. In F. Comunello (Ed.), *Networked Sociability and Individualism: Technology for Personal and Professional Relationships* (pp. 79–102). IGI Global.

Morris, M., & Ogan, C. (1996). The Internet as Mass Medium. *Journal of Communication*, *46*(1), 39–50.

Muller, M. (2012). SociallyYours: Social Readers and Social Reading -- rehabilitating the concepts of "lurkers" and "lurking." Retrieved 13. June 2012, from http://michael-muller.blogspot.co.at/2011/08/social-readers-and-social-reading.html

Muller, M., Freyne, J., Dugan, C., Millen, D., & Thom-Santelli, J. (2009). Return on Contribution (ROC): A Metric for Enterprise Social Software. In *Proc Europ Conf on ComputerSupported Cooperative Work* (pp. 143–150). Vienna, Austria: Springer.

Nielsen, J. (2006, updated 2009). "90-9-1" Rule for Participation Inequality: Lurkers vs. Contributors in Internet Communities. *Jakob Nielsen's Alertbox*. Retrieved 25. August 2010, from http://www.useit.com/alertbox/participation_inequality.html

Nielsen, J. (2009). Participation Inequality: Lurkers vs. Contributors in Internet Communities (Jakob Nielsen's Alertbox). Retrieved 13. March 2010 from http://www.useit.com/alertbox/participation_inequality.html

Nonnecke, B., Andrews, D., & Preece, J. (2006). Non-public and public online community participation: Needs, attitudes and behavior. *Electronic Commerce Research*, *6*(1), 7–20.
Nonnecke, B., & Preece, J. (2000). Lurker Demographics: Counting the Silent. In *Proceedings of CHI 2000*. The Hague: ACM.
Nonnecke, B., & Preece, J. (2001). Why Lurkers Lurk. In *Seventh Americas Conference on Information Systems 2001* (pp. 1521–1530).
Nonnecke, B., & Preece, J. (2003). Silent Participants: Getting to Know Lurkers Better. In *From Usenet to CoWebs - Interacting with Social Information Spaces* (pp. 110–132). London: Springer.
Nonnecke, B., Preece, J., & Bruckner, K. (1999). Shedding light on lurkers in online communities. Presented at the Ethnographic Studies in Real and Virtual Environments: Inhabited Information Spaces and Connected Communities, Edinburgh, GB. Retrieved 25. Auggust 2010 from http://folders.nottingham.edu.cn/staff/zlizrb/2009_IC_NMW/Nonnecke_1999.pdf
OECD. (2003). *Promises and Probelms of E-Democracy: Challenges of Online Citizen Engagement*. Paris, France: OECD. Retrieved from http://www.oecd.org/dataoecd/9/11/35176328.pdf
Ogneva, M. (2011). Your Community's Gem Is Lurking Right Over There. *Yammer the blog*. blog. Retrieved May 18, 2012, from http://blog.yammer.com/blog/2011/07/your-community-hidden-treasure-lurking.html
Ostrom, E. (1990). *Governing the Commons: The Evolution of Institutions for Collective Action*. Cambridge: Cambridge University Press.
Oxford Dictionaries Online. (2012). Definition of lurk. *Oxford Dictionaries*. Retrieved September 24, 2012, from http://oxforddictionaries.com/definition/english/lurk?q=lurking
Preece, J. (2000). *Online communities: designing usability, supporting sociability*. New York: John Wiley.
Preece, J., Nonnecke, B., & Andrews, D. (2004). The Top 5 Reasons For Lurking: Improving Community Experiences For Everyone. *Computers in Human Behavior*, *2*(1), 201–223.
Preece, J., & Shneiderman, B. (2009). The Reader-to-Leader Framework: Motivating technology-mediated social participation. *AIS Transactions on Human-Computer Interaction*, *1*(1), 13–32.
Rafaeli, S., & Raban, D. (2005). Information sharing online: a research challenge. *Int. J. Knowledge and Learning,*, *1*(1/2), 62–79.
Rafaeli, S., Ravid, G., & Soroka, V. (2004). De-lurking in virtual communities: a social communication network approach to measuring the effects of social and cultural capital. In *Proceedings of the 37th Annual Hawaii International Conference on System Sciences, 2004* (p. 10 pp.). Hawaii.
Ridings, C., Gefen, D., & Arinze, B. (2006). Psychological Barriers: Lurker and Poster Motivation and Behavior in Online Communities. *Communications of the Association for Information Systems:*, *18*(Article 16), 329–354.
Sanders, T. (2003). *Love Is the killer App : how to win business and Influence friends*. New York: Random House Inc.
Sanders, T. (2010). What is a "Love Cat"? Retrieved 28. November 2012, from http://www.youtube.com/watch?v=ylb9mgcTF44
Selwyn, N. (2006). Digital division or digital decision? A study of non-users and low-users of computers. *Poetics*, *34*(4-5), 273–292.
Shirky, C. (2010). *Cognitive surplus: creativity and generosity in a connected age*. London: Allen Lane.
Skitka, L., & Sargis, E. (2005). Social psychological research and the Internet: the promise and peril of a new methodological frontier. In Y. Amichai-Hamburger (Ed.), *The Social Net. Understanding human behavior in cyberspace* (pp. 1–26). Oxford: OUP.
Slot, M., & Frissen, V. (2007). Users In The "Golden" Age Of The Information Society. *Observatorio (OBS*) Journal*, *3*, 201–224.
Smith, M. A., & Kollock, P. (1999). *Communities in Cyberspace*. London: Routledge.

Soroka, V., & Rafaela, S. (2006). Invisible participants: how cultural capital relates to lurking behavior. In *Proceedings of the 15th international conference on World Wide Web* (pp. 163–172). New York: ACM.

Stegbauer, C., & Rausch, A. (2002). Lurkers in Mailing Lists. In B. Batinic, U.-D. Reips, & M. Bosnjak (Eds.), *Online Social Sciences* (pp. 263–274). WA: Hogrefe &Huber. Retrieved from http://user.uni-frankfurt.de/~chris/Lurkers.pdf

Strout, H. (2011). Why Lurkers Are Valuable To Your Online Community. *Farland Group*. Blog. Retrieved May 18, 2012, from http://www.farlandgroup.com/2011/03/why-lurkers-are-valuable-to-your-online-community/

Sypher, H., & Collins, B. (2001). Virtual-online communities: How might new technologies be related to community? In G. J. Sheperd & E. W. Rothenbuhler (Eds.), *Communication and Community.* (pp. 191–200). Mahwah: LEA, Inc.

Takahashi, M., Fujimoto, M., & Yamasaki, N. (2002). The active lurker: a new viewpoint for evaluating the influence of an in-house online community. *ACM SIGGROUP Bulletin*, *23*(3), 29–33.

Takahashi, M., Fujimoto, M., & Yamasaki, N. (2003). The active lurker: influence of an in-house online community on its outside environment. In *Proceedings of the 2003 international ACM SIGGROUP conference on Supporting group work* (pp. 1–10). Sanibel Island, Florida, USA: ACM.

Takahashi, M., Fujimoto, M., & Yamasaki, N. (2007). Active Lurking: Enhancing the Value of In-House Online Communities Through the Related Practices Around the Online Communities. *MIT Sloan School of Management Working Paper 4646-07*, *CCIWorking Paper 2007-006*, 1–11.

Tapscott, D., & Williams, A. (2006). *Wikinomics: how mass collaboration changes everything*. New York: Portfolio.

Taylor, J. C. (2002). Taylor, J. C. (2002). Teaching and learning online: the workers, the lurkers and the shirkers,. In *Keynote speech*. Retrieved from http://www.ouhk.edu.hk/CRIDAL/cridala2002/speeches/taylor.pdf

Van Dijk, J. (2005). *The deepening divide: inequality in the information society*. Thousand Oaks Calif.: Sage Pub.

Van Uden-Kraan, C. F., Drossaert, C. H., Taal, E., Seydel, E. R., & van de Laar, M. A. (2008). Self-Reported Differences in Empowerment Between Lurkers and Posters in Online Patient Support Groups. *Journal of Medical Internet Research*, *10*(2), e18.

Wallace, M. (2011). Social Media Lurkers - Are They the Most Important Community Members. *commonground*. Blog. Retrieved May 18, 2012, from http://commonground.edrnet.com/posts/0490906d9a

Willett, J. (1998). VECO - an Online Community Making a Difference, an Evaluation of the Project. Presented at the Australian Student Traineeship Foundation and Dusseldorp Skills Forum, Sydney.

Williams, D. L., Crittenden, V. L., Keo, T., & McCarty, P. (2012). The use of social media: an exploratory study of usage among digital natives: The use of social media. *Journal of Public Affairs*, *12*(2), 127–136.

Zickuhr, K. (2013). Who's not online and why. *Pew Internet & American Life Project*. Retrieved 15. January 2014 from http://pewinternet.org/~/media/Files/Reports/2013/PIP_Offline%20adults_092513_PDF.pdf

Sean D. Young, Alexander H. Jordan

14 Can Social Media Photos Influence College Students' Sexual Health Behaviors?

Abstract: Beth, a 20-year-old transfer student to South Oregon University, logs on to Facebook on a Friday afternoon in the second week of classes. Her previous school, Chesapearo Community College, was well-known for its wild parties. Chesapearo students' Facebook photos, teeming with alcohol and sexually suggestive poses, reflected the school's stereotypes and reputation as a hotbed for sexual promiscuity and unintended pregnancy. However, while browsing the South Oregon University Facebook network, Beth notices that students at her new campus don't showcase photos of themselves drunk and provocatively posed. Instead, most of the pictures show students sitting in dorm rooms talking with friends, or spending time with their families. This makes Beth rethink her plans for the party she's attending in the evening. Maybe instead of donning a short skirt and "pre-partying" with several shots of liquor, she'd fit in better at her new campus if she arrived at the party sober and wore more conservative clothing. She decides that she won't make sexual conquest a goal for the evening. She puts on her jeans to hang out with her new girlfriends and grabs a condom so that just in case something does happen with a boy, she'll be ready for it.

Can social media sites such as Facebook affect college students' sexual health behaviors? Could Facebook photos, for example, make a person reconsider his or her intention to have sex or use a condom? In this chapter we address this question empirically and test the prediction that viewing Facebook photos can act as an intervention that increases college students' intentions to use condoms—at least at schools where the actual prevalence of sexual promiscuity is not as high as students might imagine.

14.1 Sexual Health Behaviors: The Influence of Perceived Norms

Reducing risky sexual health behaviors among American college students is an extremely important but difficult goal to achieve. Despite the fact that using condoms during sexual intercourse can reduce the risk of contracting a sexually transmitted infection by 70-100% (Roper, Peterson, & Curran, 1993), only about 40% of sexually active college students report using condoms (Strader & Beaman, 1991; DiClemente, Forrest, & Mickler, 1990; Eisenberg, 2001). According to one study, for example, 36% of college students did not use a condom during their initial sexual experience with a new partner, and more than 50% failed to use a condom during their most recent sexual involvement (Freimuth, Hammond, Edgar, McDonald, & Fink, 1992). These alarmingly high rates of unprotected sex among college students not only contribute to unplanned pregnancies, but also appear to contribute to the current HIV epidemic in the United States (Centers for Disease Control and Prevention, 2003). Designing effective interventions to increase condom use is therefore critical to redressing these social problems.

Psychological research may provide useful insights into creating successful interventions to reduce risky behavior. According to work within social psychology on the perception of norms, people's behaviors—including their sexual health behaviors—are strongly influenced by their estimates of whether their peers are engaging in these same behaviors. If a person thinks that the majority of his or her peer group is frequently having unprotected sexual intercourse, then that person may be more likely to engage in such behavior. In one study of 725 college students, for example, students' overestimations of the peer-prevalence of sexual behavior led them to increase their own sexual behavior to conform to the perceived norm (Page, Hammermeister, & Scanian, 2000; see also Lambert, Kahn, & Apple, 2003). Drawing on the same insight, that perceived norms may influence students' health behaviors, researchers in another study attempted an intervention in which students were provided with information aimed to curb their prevalence overestimates. In this study, male college students were told that risky sexual behavior was relatively rare among college students (Chernoff & Davison, 2005). These students reported being more likely to use condoms than males who read general information about AIDS. College students' overestimations of risky sexual behavior may therefore increase their rates of engaging in risky sexual behaviors, whereas interventions that highlight low normative rates of sexual behavior may decrease their likelihood of engaging in these behaviors.

14.2 Facebook Photos and Condom Use: A Pilot Study

As college students increasingly turn to Facebook to learn about and interact with their peers, we predict that Facebook use may influence students' sexual health behaviors by providing information about peer-group norms. Specifically, we predict that user-uploaded photos on Facebook convey information to students about sexual norms, and that these perceived norms may affect their own sexual health behaviors in turn. Photos that suggest sexual responsibility or restraint, or that focus on alternative forms of entertainment other than sexually suggestive experiences, might be used as an intervention to increase sexual health and responsibility.

In an attempt to test this hypothesis, we ran a pilot study assessing the influence of Facebook photos on Stanford University undergraduates' perceptions of peer sexual behavior and their own intentions to engage in sexual behavior. Compared to UCLA and UC Berkeley networks, random samples of photos from student profiles at Stanford University revealed dramatically less sexually suggestive content, suggesting that Facebook use among Stanford students may *decrease* rather than increase students' perceptions of the peer-prevalence of sexual behavior.

Seventeen students in our experimental group were asked to look at 15 Facebook photos of their Stanford peers. After examining these photos and completing some filler questions, the students were asked, among other things, to estimate the percentage of their peers who have sex without condoms, as well as their own likelihood of using a condom when having sex with a person of unknown HIV status. A control group of 21 students answered the same questions without first looking at Facebook photos.

What we discovered was fascinating and served to demonstrate the power of Facebook in forming college students' decisions. Consistent with our hypothesis, students who first looked at Facebook photos made significantly lower estimates of the peer-prevalence of unprotected intercourse (14%, vs. 26% in the control group). Similarly, students who looked at Facebook photos reported a significantly greater intention (a 10% increase compared to the control group) to use condoms when having sex with a person of unknown HIV status.

14.3 Discussion and Future Directions for Research

In this study, we found that having college students look at peers' Facebook photos led them to perceive a lower peer-prevalence of unprotected sex and to state a greater intention to use condoms themselves in future sexual encounters. We attribute these results to the infrequent representation of sexuality in Stanford undergraduates' Facebook photos. Although students might overestimate base rates of sexual risk behaviors in the absence of prevalent information, the reality represented in Facebook photo albums may serve as a corrective against exaggerated perceptions of student debauchery. Of course, it is also possible that students in the control condition actually estimated the prevalence of unprotected sex more accurately than students in the experimental condition, and the low frequency of sexuality in Facebook photos was due to campus cultural norms against appearing promiscuous.

No matter the interpretation, this study provides evidence that Facebook use—in particular viewing peer photos—may influence college students' perceptions of sexual health behavior norms among their peers, which may in turn influence students' own sexual health behaviors. At schools where students' Facebook photos do not show sexually suggestive material, Facebook use may serve as an effective intervention against risky sexual behaviors. Future research might examine whether our effects can be replicated in the domain of testing for sexually transmitted infections, where stigma reduces students' willingness to test for diseases such as HIV (e.g., Young, Nussbaum, & Monin, 2007), or in the domain of alcohol use, where students also tend to overestimate the peer-prevalence of risky behavior (e.g., Prentice & Miller, 1993; see also Schroeder & Prentice, 1998). In addition, research should examine whether

Facebook use might have detrimental effects on health behaviors in college settings where risky behavior is more commonly depicted in online photos.

More generally, we believe that researchers in psychology and other disciplines should investigate how Facebook affects students' perceptions of their peers' lives, and how these perceptions affect their expectations about their own lives. For example, recent research suggests that college students systematically overestimate the proportion of their peers who are out having fun at any given moment, whereas they underestimate the peer-prevalence of negative emotional experiences (Jordan, Monin, & Dweck, 2008). Such errors may detract from students' well-being. Does Facebook use—viewing photos of classmates at drunken parties, for instance—exaggerate or attenuate these errors in social perception? How does the answer to this question depend on cultural norms that dictate the content that students choose to present on their Facebook pages and depict in their photos? The study we presented in this chapter demonstrates the potential for such investigations to shed light on the social psychological complexity of online social networks and pave the way for interventions that improve student health behaviors and well-being.

References

Centers for Disease Control and Prevention (2003). *HIV/AIDS Surveillance Report 2002* (Vol. 14). Also available at: http://www.cdc.gov/hiv/stats/hasrlink.htm

DiClemente, R. J., Forrest, K. A., & Mickler, S. (1990). College students' knowledge and attitudes about AIDS and changes in HIV-preventive behaviors. *AIDS Education and Prevention, 2,* 201-212.

Eisenberg, M. (2001). Differences in sexual risk behaviors between college students with same-sex and opposite-sex experience: Results from a national survey. *Archives of Sexual Behavior, 30,* 575-89.

Freimuth, V. S., Hammond, S. L., Edgar, T., McDonald, D. A., & Fink, E. L. (1992). Factors explaining intent, discussion and use of condoms in first-time sexual encounters. *Health Education Research, 7,* 203-215.

Jordan, A. H., Monin, B., & Dweck, C. S. (2008). *Error and consequence in the social comparison of emotion.* Unpublished manuscript.

Lambert, T. A., Kahn, A. S., & Apple, K. J. (2003). Pluralistic ignorance and hooking up. *Journal of Sex Research, 40,* 129-134.

Page, R. M., Hammermeister, J. J., & Scanian, A. (2000). Everybody's not doing it: Misperceptions of college student's sexual activity. *American Journal of Health Behavior, 24,* 387-394.

Prentice, D. A. & Miller, D. T. (1993). Pluralistic ignorance and alcohol use on campus: Some consequences of misperceiving the social norm. *Journal of Personality and Social Psychology, 64,* 243-256

Roper, W. L., Peterson, H. B., & Curran, J. W. (1993). Commentary: Condoms and HIV/STD prevention—clarifying the message. *American Journal of Public Health, 83,* 501-503.

Schroeder, C.M., & Prentice, D.A. (1998). Exposing pluralistic ignorance to reduce alcohol use among college students. *Journal of Applied Social Psychology, 28,* 2150-2180.

Strader, J., & Beaman M. L. (1991). Comparison of college students' and sexually transmitted disease clinic patients' knowledge about AIDS, risk behaviours and beliefs about condom use. *Journal of Advanced Nursing, 16,* 584-590.

Young, S.D., Nussbaum, D., & Monin, B. (2007). Potential moral stigma and reactions to sexually-transmitted diseases: Evidence for a disjunction fallacy, *Personality and Social Psychology Bulletin,* 33(6), 789-799.

Selim Gunuc, Ozge Misirli, H. Ferhan Odabasi

15 Social Networks as a Communication Tool from Children's Perpective: A Twitter Experience

Abstract: Popularity and use of social networks among all ages for various purposes brings up the necessity for investigation of these networks on human psychology and interpersonal communication. As contrasted by different researchers, displacement and stimulation hypotheses arose on either side and resulted in the need for a wider examination of social networks. However, inferences neither theoretical nor practical descent alone will fail to enlighten every spot including effects of social networks on structure and wealth of the society. Thus, research is necessary to examine the influence of social networks all demographics within society, with the present chapter focusing on children.

This chapter discusses the effects of social networks on lifestyles and behaviors of people both psychologically and socially by linking theory and practice. The chapter itself is comprised of two sections; the first section presents an evaluation of role of social networks on children and its use as a communication tool, while the second section presents a sample case of from the social network Twitter.

The study was carried out in a private primary school in Turkey with 51 students. Use of Twitter was promoted by organizing a contest on Twitter. Communication through twitter was also promoted and experiences on use of Twitter as a communication tool are examined in detail. In terms of data collection, the study used a case study and a questionnaire, semi-structured interviews, document analysis, as well as open ended questions.. In this study, social networks were evaluated from children's perspectives and discussed in the light of theories.

15.1 Introduction

Technological advancements in interpersonal communication have made communication an even more important field of study. In particular, social networks like Facebook and Twitter are the most popular online communication tools within Turkey and worldwide (ICTA, 2011). In terms of children, Lenhart, Madden, Smith, Purcell, Zickuhr, and Rainie (2011) report that 88% use social networks for instant messaging and chatting with their friends. Besides chatting, children use social networks for publishing status updates, commenting on friends' status updates, sharing and commenting on photos and videos, as well as playing online social games. Another report claims that 51% of social network users are children aged 13-17, who visit social networks on a daily basis (Common Sense, 2012). Social network use habits of Turkish children between 9-16 ages were reported in a survey conducted by ICTA (ICTA, 2011). Participants' membership distribution varied as follows: Facebook (99%), Twitter (9%), MSN (8.6%), Netlog (4.6%), and MySpace (4%). Childrens' motives for using social networks were: communicating with friends (83.6%), exploring social media (32%), finding old friends (31%), and following friends' activities (28%). Results from this survey suggest that Turkish children within the 9-16 age range are mainly using social media for communication and Facebook the favored social media.

Social networks also have substantial importance in children's lives. Online communication is among the leading motives for children's social network use and it is an important part of their social lives. Indeed, children generally use internet for communicating their friends (Gross, 2004) by making use of communication oriented systems like blogs and social networks along with instant messaging, e-mail, and text messaging services (Subramanyan & Greenfield, 2009). However, while cyberspace may allow children to freely communicate with their peers; one should also note that strangers can take advantages of cyberspace to engage with children. The internet facilitates communication and learning, however children's benefits depend on its proper use.

15.2 Social Networks and Communication

Ever since technology became a part of our daily lives its effects have always been an issue of discussion. In several studies, it is reported that the Internet has both negative and positive effects on social interaction between individuals (Erwin, Turk, Heimbeerg, Fresco & Hantula, 2004; Hills & Angyle, 2003; Swickert, Hittner, Harris & Herring, 2002). Social networks could be said to be among the most important and common tools that aim at allowing individuals to establish communication with each other. Social networks are treated as important tools for social learning, communicating with new and old friends, peer support, and conducting school activities (Baruah, 2012; Greenhow & Robelia, 2009). Both displacement and stimulation hypotheses argue that online communication can affect individuals' relationships with their social environment (Valkenburg & Peter, 2011). Displacement hypothesis tries to explain the internet's side effects on children. Displacement hypothesis argues that, the internet harms existing friendships by reducing or replacing individual's effective/meaningful face to face social interaction with friends (Kraut, Kiesler, Boneva, Cummings, Helgeson, & Crawford, 2002; Kraut, Kiesler, Mukopadhyay, Scherlis, & Patterson, 1998; Mesch, 2003; Nie, 2001; Nie, Hillygus, & Erbring, 2002). Another assertion of this hypothesis is that the internet encourages children to communicate with strangers online (Valkenburg & Peter, 2007). This effect is exacerbated with individuals who have problems in making new friends. However, proper and effective use of online communication tools can reduce these risks. Conversely, stimulation hypothesis argues that online communication can foster friendships by supplying individuals with more communication time and facilities (Hampton, Sessions, Her, & Rainie, 2009; Valkenburg & Peter, 2011; Valkenburg & Peter, 2007; Wang & Wang, 2011 Wang & Wellman, 2010). As such, according to stimulation hypothesis online communication facilitates interaction with existing friends (Amichai-Hamburger & Hayat, 2011; Hamburger & Ben-Artzi, 2000; Hampton et al. 2009; Robinson, Kestnbaum, Neustadtl, & Alvarez, 2000).

15.3 The Role of Social Networks in Student Engagement

When social networks are used for the purpose of hybrid learning, or as a follow-up of face-to-face education, they strengthen communication and sharing not only between the teacher and students but also between the students themselves as well as helping achieve student engagement, especially out of class (Reynard, 2007, Coates, 2007). In this respect, it is pointed out that groups established or sharings made regarding courses on social networks such as Twitter and Facebook play an important role in increasing student engagement (Heiberger & Harper, 2008; HERI, 2007; Junco, 2012; Junco, Heiberger & Loken, 2011; Mix, 2010). Further, Cole (2009) stated that Wiki had influence, even a little, on student engagement. However, the fact that students use Wiki efficiently and that technology-related course designs are not interesting or effective leads to a further decrease in this influence. On the other hand, in their study Welch and Bonnan-White (2012) reported that the participants who enjoyed using Twitter had a higher level of engagement when compared to those who did not. In order for both social networks and other information and communication technologies to contribute substantially to student engagement, it is important to choose these technologies considering students' demands and to integrate them effectively in courses (Cole, 2009; Dietrich, 2012; Hancock & Betts, 2002; Hede, 2002; McGrath, 1998; Strom, Strom, Wing & Beckert, 2010).

If such environments and technologies such as social networks are not attractive for students or if technology is not effectively integrated, then benefiting from technology and increasing student engagement becomes problematic. In addition, while choosing the technological tool or the environment to be integrated into the course, considering the tools or environments favored by students could not only help them use social networks for the purposes of communication and sharing but also contribute to their interest and motivation in the course. Therefore, it is important that students, just like teachers, use these environments and keep communicating with other students out of class (Dietrich, 2012).

15.4 Twitter in Education

Twitter, one of widely-used social networks like Facebook, is a text-based social media application. Twitter differs from other social networks due to its restriction of the total number of characters to 140. Although this situation is considered to limit its usage, this restriction could, from a different point of view, be said to lead to creativity. The number of young individuals using Twitter, also favored by all other age groups, is gradually increasing. Depending on the examination of the youths' use of Twitter, it could be stated that Twitter, when compared to other social networks, has fewer young users. When children are considered, it could be quite difficult to say for what purposes children use Twitter because Twitter users cannot put photos as clear as they can using Facebook or Instagram; because instant messaging is not available in Twitter; and because Twitter is rather text-based. However, with its new features added, Twitter is seen to be increasingly popular among young people (Wasserman, 2013). Generally speaking, Twitter can be used by high school and higher education students for such purposes as providing them with feedback, allowing them to ask questions, share and make comments during in-class activities or conferences, share activities following courses, rehearse or revise what has been learnt in class, as well as to increase socialization and establish communication (Dhir, Buragga & Boreqqah, 2013; Elavsky, Mislan & Elavsky, 2011; Grosseck & Holotescu, 2008; Hsu & Ching, 2012; Reinhart, Ebner, Beham & Costa, 2009; Tyma, 2011; Wright, 2010).

Knowing that communication is one of the most important elements of educational environments, an educational use of Twitter has huge potential. Twitter can facilitate collaboration and comprehension, support personal and informal learning, facilitate distribution/sharing, support classroom activities, and establish personal learning networks (Anderson, 2011; Galagan, 2009; Greenhow, 2009). Users can utilize Twitter for communication, asking questions, requesting support, and participating in discussions (Grosseck & Hotescu, 2008; Tyma, 2011). Furthermore there are some users seeking popularity by increasing their follower counts (Utz, Tanis & Vermeulen, 2012). Considering the steep development curve of technology and learners' expectations for rapid information exchange, Twitter is expected to be a resourceful tool in educational environments. Twitter can be utilized for various purposes in educational environments. Teachers can use Twitter as a rapid feedback channel; for mediating communities within classroom activities; or as a communication channel for out-of-school activities (Galagan, 2009; Stieger & Burger, 2010). Besides, users have a second chance while writing, thus Twitter facilitates a healthier communication in comparison with simultaneous communication tools like the telephone (Gordhamer, 2010).

15.5 Twitter as a Communication Tool

Communication is one of the leading reasons for using microblogging systems (Morris, 2009). These microblogging systems are an extension of social networks, with Twitter being a well known example. Twitter itself is a social messaging and micro-blogging system that supplies users with blogging opportunity without establishing blogs. Personal of institutional Twitter users can swiftly reach masses and exchange information with interest groups (Brock, 2011; Ivey, 2009). Children frequently use twitter to update their statuses, keep updated with their favorite musicians/bands/celebrities, stay current with world phenomenons, and keep their friends up to date about themselves (Techcrunch, 2009). Twitter can prove beneficial for daily and educational use. Even though some students claim the 140 characters restriction to be a negative property, this can develop their critical thinking and creativity. Baruah (2012) recognizes that social media like Twitter can be used extensively for the purpose of communication in education, so effective integration of Twitter into educational context may result in better interaction and communication (Borau, Ullrich, Feng, & Shen, 2009; Dunlap & Lowenthal, 2009; Holotescu & Grosseck, 2009; Junco, Heiberger & Loken, 2011; Kop, Fournier & Mak, 2011; Lowe & Laffey, 2011; Rinaldo, Tapp & Laverie, 2011; Wright, 2010), formal and informal learning opportunities (Rinaldo, Tapp & Laverie, 2011), increased collaboration and motivation (McWilliams, Hickey, Hines, Conner & Bishop, 2011; Perifanou, 2009), increased discussion possibilities (Holotescu & Grosseck, 2009), and increased sharing (Dunlap & Lowenthal, 2009; Perifanou, 2009; Wright, 2010).

What makes Twitter special amongst other social networking tools is its ability to facilitate an actual communication channel with a massive receiver repertory. Twitter users can exchange information, organize events, ask for help, and publish up-to-date information (Joly, 2009). Twitter gained widespread use with its open access communication mechanism among its users (Smith, 2009). Albeit users have the option to protect their accounts, most of the users keep their accounts accessible. Thus, masses can read and participate in debates.

Most of the literature on using Twitter within educational environments focuses on higher education. However, contrary to its widespread use amongst children, there is little research concerning primary school children's Twitter use. In fact, use of Twitter within primary school children should be encouraged to understand whether they will also use Twitter for educational purposes. It is known that inclination to use technology is the predeterminer of the achievement brought with it. Ribble (2008) claims that use of different media by students also allows them to use the appropriate manner for that media. It is therefore that students should gain awareness and the necessary skills for new technologies. A review of international and especially Turkish literature reveals no studies focusing on the use of Twitter for communicative purposes among primary school children (Gao, Luo & Zhang, 2012).

The study presented below examines utilization of Twitter as a communication channel among primary school children. In this context this study will try to answer following questions:

Q1. To what extent do primary school children use twitter for communication?

Q2. What are primary school children's experiences of using Twitter for communication?

15.6 Method

15.6.1 Research Design

This research is a case study trying to describe Twitter's use as a communication tool among primary school children. A case study is a research model within naturalistic research. Yin (1994) explains a case study "as an empirical inquiry that investigates a contemporary phenomenon within its real-life context; when the boundaries between phenomenon and context are not clearly evident; and in which multiple sources of evidence are used". Since this study does not intend to generalize findings, as well as the procedures and context being authentic to this research, researchers selected case study as the research method. Exploratory design was chosen since the study has been considered as a prelude to further social research and the framework of the study was created ahead of time (Tellis, 1997). The means of data collection were questionnaire, document analysis, and interviews. The study was designed as a holistic single case design which allows a single unit to be analyzed holistically to investigate all the changes and the process (Creswell, 2007; Yin, 1989).

To answer the first research question of the study, a questionnaire and semi-structured interview were utilized. The questionnaire was given to all students, whereas only five students were interviewed. Document analysis was used to gather information about Twitter use during a 12 day period. Open ended questions were then utilized to answer the second research question. Table 15.1 presents research questions, data collection tools, and data analysismethods.

Table 15.1: Research questions, data collection tools, and data analysis methods

Research Questions	Data Collection Tools	Data Analysis Method
To what extent do primary school children use twitter for communication?	Questionnaire Semi-structured interview forms	Frequencies analysis Content analysis
What are primary school children's experiences on utilizing Twitter for communication?	Document Analysis Open ended questions	Content analysis Content analysis

15.6.2 Participants

The participants were 7th grade students studying in a private primary school in Turkey within the 2011 – 2012 academic year. 17 female and 34 male students aged 12-13 participated in this study. All 51 students had signed up for Twitter or organized existing Twitter accounts as requested before this study. However, only 32 students tweeted during the research. The students were all aged 12-13, a standard age for 7th grade students in Turkey. They all had a similar social background and thus they represented normal private primary school students in Turkey.

15.6.3 Data collection

Researchers tried to promote reliability and validity within the research by utilizing various data collection procedures. Data collection tools, reliability, and validity procedures are explained below.

Questionnaire: An edited questionnaire form was administrated to 51 students. Nine of the 51 students were Twitter users already. Two of these nine students were selected for semi-structured interview. In addition to this, 47 of 51 students were Facebook users currently. Three Facebook users were selected for semi-structured interviews.

Semi-Structured interviews: Semi-structured interviews were conducted with five students (two Twitter users and three Facebook users) prior to an informative seminar about Twitter. The aim of these interviews was to determine students' communicative Twitter use prior to study. In this context, recordings from the five students' interviews were analysed using content analysis to determine students' social network use for communication.

Document Analysis: Participant students tweeted for 12 days during the study. Content analysis was applied to these tweets. All 51 students had signed up for Twitter or organized existing Twitter accounts as requested before the study. However, only 32 students tweeted during the study.

Open Ended Questions Survey: Researchers prepared a survey with three open-ended questions. These questions were subjected to expert opinion prior to their use. The Open-Ended Questions Survey was then administrated to all participants seven days after the study. Students were required to be as detailed as possible when answering the survey questions. Three questions contained in the survey were:

- Have you had any difficulties while asking your questions for the competition on the Twitter?
- What do you think about Twitter as a communication tool?
- Considering this study, do you intend to use Twitter for communicating with your friends?

Table 15.2 summarizes data collection tools and their utilization in this study.

Table 15.2: Data collection procedures

Data collection tool	Time	Data type	Participants	Duration	Dates
Questionnaire	Before	Multiple choice	51	10 minutes	Dec 09, 2011
Semi-structured conversation	Before	Recordings	5	10 minutes x 5	Dec 09, 2011
Document analysis	At the end	Tweet	32	12 days	Dec 09, 2011 - Dec 21, 2011
Open ended questions survey	At the end	Text	32	15 minutes	Dec 23, 2011

Researchers requested family permission for data collection procedures and using collected data for research. Oral permission for voice recordings was also requested from students prior to interviews.

15.6.4 Data analysis

Two researchers analyzed all qualitative data separately. Inter-rater reliability of analysis was evaluated. Researchers compared their findings after completing all analyses. After establishing consensus between evaluations, findings were reported. Tweets were evaluated with the document analysis technique, in which tweets were categorized into groups according to their relationships. Researchers evaluated contents of these tweets in the context of communication. While analyzing the open-ended survey data researchers noticed that 19 students did not participate in the study (did not tweeted). Thus, data belonging to these students were left out of evaluation. Data from 32 students were transcribed and inputted before being evaluated with the content analysis techniques.
Procedures

15.7 Results

To what extent do primary school children use twitter for communication?
Pre-study data will be utilized to represent participants' social network use prior to this research. These data includes survey data administrated to 51 primary school students and semi-structured conversation data coming from interviews with five students.

Survey data suggest participants' social network use as follows; 47 of 51 students were Facebook users (92%), nine students were Twitter users (18%) and two students were MySpace users (1%). Participants who reported to be Twitter and MySpace users were also actively using Facebook. 31 of the students (60%) reported that they were primarily using social networks for communication. Participants were asked why they were not using Twitter. The majority of children (n=34; 67%) stated they did not find Twitter as an interesting platform. Furthermore 26 of these 34 children (76%) stated they had not any friends using Twitter.

Researchers conducted semi-structured interviews with two Twitter users and three Facebook users to gather detailed data about their use. A question in these interviews was: "What do you think about Twitter as a communication tool?" Student A's response was:

> *"I would rather use telephone even if my message reaches three minutes later. Since Twitter has no offline coverage, I never may know the time of my message's arrival or even my message reached. Thus, I do not consider Twitter for communication. Besides, since most of my friends don't use Twitter, I would rather use Facebook for messaging."*

Student H stated he was rarely using, and that he was not sharing much information via Twitter. Generally both Twitter users said they were not using Twitter for communication and they were not intending to use it in the future. The primary reason for this situation was their friends' absence on Twitter. Students argued that they should know if friends are online in order to communicate with them via Twitter. Nevertheless Facebook users also reported that they did not use Facebook primarily for communication, yet they reported occasionally using Facebook's messaging facilities. They also stated that they did not think about using Twitter and that they found Facebook more engaging.

Overall, the majority of these students were Facebook users. In comparison between the two social networks, students found Facebook more engaging and visual than Twitter. Furthermore, Facebook facilitates private messaging better than Twitter. It was due to these reasons that these students prefer Facebook to Twitter. These findings suggest that Twitter is not a popular social networking tool among primary school children.

What are primary school children's experiences on using Twitter for communication?

After collecting data concerning students' social network use, researchers conducted a seminar on effective Twitter use. Students were requested to direct their questions about the competition through Twitter. In this way students were supposed to gain tweeting experience. Students were observed tweeting about competition rules, competition period, editing user profiles, and the Twitter platform itself. A total of 105 tweets were transferred between researchers and participants. Of these 105 tweets, 51 came from students, whereas 54 of them came from researchers. Besides this participants also tweeted on their profiles or send tweets to other participants. However these tweets were left out of data analysis.

The analysis of student tweets revealed students' hesitations about tweets and their arrival. In particular, 11 novice Twitter users sent "trial" tweets to researchers. Furthermore, four participants asked whether the tweets had arrived. For example, Student C's tweet was: "*Do tweets appear on the page. I am in doubt if they arrive*". Student H wanted to make sure his name appear on the tweet and asked: "Hi, my name is _____. Did my tweet arrive?" These tweets can be considered rather strange for Twitter. However, this is due to their lack of experience with the Twitter platform.

Students' experiences concerning the use of Twitter for communication were collected via open-ended survey. Results from the analysis of these data are presented in Table 15.3.

Table 15.3: Themes, sub-themes and frequencies that emerged from content analysis of Tweets

	Theme	Sub-Theme	f
Positive views about their	Practicability	Twitter is a good/usable communication tool	28
		I did not have difficulties in communication	19
		I can follow celebrities via Twitter	5
		140 characters is long enough for communication	1
Negative views about their	Impracticability	Twitter is not a good/usable communication tool	12
		140 characters is not long enough for communication (I find Twitter restrictive)	6
		Everybody can read my Tweets	3
		I had difficulties in communication	2
	Refusing to use	I did not communicate with anybody	8
		I did not participated in the activity	2
	Preferring other media	I would rather use Facebook than Twitter (Facebook is better)	10
		All my friends are on Facebook. I would have used Twitter if my friends used it.	5
		I would rather use the telephone for communication than Twitter	1

As shown in Table 14.3, 16 themes emerged from analysis of students' responses to open ended questions. Of the students, 19 students stated they used Twitter for communication during the study. Furthermore, 28 of the students viewed Twitter as a good communication tool and stated their intention to use Twitter for communication. Some students' responses within this theme were:

"Twitter allows easier communication, it can help."

"When it comes to communication via Twitter, it is a good option. We can hear from friends and learn what they are doing."

Nevertheless, 12 of children reported they do not consider Twitter a good communication tool or that they have no intention to use Twitter for communication. The following are views of students within this theme:

"It is ridiculous to use twitter for communication."

"When it comes to communication I believe Twitter is behind other social networking tools. I don't find it much of a communication tool."

Students also stated that they are accustomed to Facebook's communication and chat facilities and had difficulties in using Twitter's messaging mechanisms. This theme also emerged in different tweets. A total of ten participants stated they found Facebook a better option for communication and that they preferred Facebook to Twitter for communication. Some comments within this theme are:

"Facebook is yet more qualified for communication."

"There must be a chat system like the on in Facebook. I believe Facebook is better."

Analysis of conversation and survey data revealed reasons for students' preference between Facebook and Twitter. According to their responses, students find Facebook more visual and user friendly for sharing media. Furthermore, Facebook's popularity over Twitter, Facebook's forerunner role as a social network, Facebook's higher user count, and having more friends on Facebook makes it more engaging for students. In interviews prior to this study three of the students reported that they use Facebook to communicate their friends, talk about schoolwork, and organize meetings. The other two students stated that they find communicating over social networks difficult since users are not constantly online. Within the same theme Student H reported his anxiety regarding the accessible nature of tweets. He wanted to chat with friends in private. A section from this student's statement is:

"Messaging is the sole option to communicate friends in private, that's why I love Facebook more than Twitter."

Six students reported they found Twitter's properties restrictive and stated their discomfort with 140 characters. Some views from students within this theme were:

"I don't like communicating with Twitter because of limited tools repertoire."

"I may use it, but message length restriction may cause problems."

It is clear that students are comparing Twitter's communication facilities with Facebook in their comments. In this way, the students' hesitation with message length restriction can be explained by their accustomance with other social networking tools.

The findings from this study can also be associated with group psychology. It is a known fact that children influence each other with their attitudes and this can also reflect upon their use of technology. In line with this, five students reported all their friends were Facebook users and they would only shift to Twitter if their friends did. The same theme was also expressed in pre-study interviews. Some students' comments regarding this theme were as follows:

"Everybody is on Facebook. Some of my friends outside the school said they did not find Twitter interesting. I may use Twitter if only my friends use it."

"I would like to communicate all my friends. It would be better if my friends have used Twitter."

Twitters unpopularity with adolescents can be exlained by the characteristics of adolescence. Children want to act with a group, and seek participation and reference. Despite these negative comments Twitter's characteristics gathered attention from students. Five students stated they could follow celebrities and communicate them via Twitter.

"Generally we can follow celebrities and learn about them."

"I can follow and learn about my favorite actors/actresses and musicians."

Despite social networks' proliferation and widespread use, students do not prefer these tools for ubiquitous communication. Student G stated that she prefers the telephone for private communication. Another student shared this idea within the pre-study conversation.

"I do not intend to use Twitter for communication. It is not as good as telephone for communication."

Children are not familiar with the notion of accessibility in Twitter. Tweets on Twitter are accessible to all users unless specified contrary. Therefore, three students stated they would not use twitter for communication because of the accessibility of tweets.

"I do not intend to use Twitter for communication at all, everybody can see what you write."

"I do not communicate friends through such an open channel."

This line of thought can be explained by the fact that these students are not familiar with Twitter and they are novice users. It is also known that children seek security and privacy. A review of participants' views and themes listed in Table 3 reveals that throughout this study students used Twitter for communication, learning about friends' updates, and following celebrities.

15.8 Discussion and Conclusion

The literature hosts a number of studies concerning social network use for communication. However, the majority of this research focuses on high school and college students (Gao, Luo & Zhang, 2012; McCool, 2011; Wright, 2010). In this way, studies conducted with primary school children should enhance the literature in this area. Communication is a crucial part of our lives. Thus, improving students' communication competences is sine qua non for their social development. Encouraging adequate and efficient technology utilization for communication in children willbe beneficial for society. Klien (2008) utilized social networks to overcome the communication barriers of the traditional educational environment, finding that children communicated better and established more efficient collaboration within social networking tools than traditional classroom settings. Furthermore, other research revealed that children use social networks for effectively communicating with peers outside the classroom (Holcomb, Brady & Smith, 2010; Pempek, Yermolayeva & Calvert, 2009). The present study aimed to examine Turkish children's experiences in using Twitter for communication and their views and expectations about this online communication tool. Furthermore, children's bias against using Twitter was also questioned. The children's views and experiences on using Twitter for educational and communicative purposes may help guide the improvement of educational environments through the incorporation of a microblogging systems.

Findings from this research demonstrated that participants use Facebook, Twitter, and MySpace (92%, 18%, and 1% respectively), with these findings being consistent with results from other studies (ICTA, 2011). The study also highlight that children pay more attention to visual social networking tools. Indeed, children stated that they preferred Facebook to Twitter both before and after taking part in the study. In this way, Facebook's communication and chat facilities are preferred by children. This may be attributed to children's unfamiliarity with Twitter, with better communication with online tools requiring a moderate body of literacy. Nicol, Minty and Sinclair (2002) differentiate face-to-face communication from online communication. Online socialization is learned through sufficient face-to-face communication experience in real life settings. Thus, one can conclude that children prefer visual mediums because they have not yet established adequate mental schemes for online communication.

Since the majority of children use internet regularly (Valkenburg & Peter, 2009), the effects of children's online communication is a common discussion topic among researchers. While some researchers support displacement hypothesis (Kraut et al., 2002; Kraut et al., 1998; Mesch, 2003; Nie, 2001; Nie, Hillygus, & Erbring, 2002) which suggests that online communication reduces social interaction and communication. Other researchers support the stimulation hypothesis which claims that online communication facilitates social interaction and communication (Amichai-Hamburger & Hayat, 2011; Hamburger & Ben-Artzi, 2000; Hampton et al., 2009; Robinson et al., 2000; Valkenburg & Peter, 2011; Valkenburg & Peter, 2007; Wang & Wang, 2011; Wang & Wellman, 2010). Overall, literature tends to support stimulation hypothesis rather than the displacement hypothesis (Valkenburg & Peter, 2007). In line with this, the current study found that participants tend to select the social networks preferred by their friends, a finding which supports the stimulation hypothesis (Techcrunch, 2009). The participants of this study did not prefer to use Twitter with respect to their ages and friendships. A report from Common Sense (2012) suggests that 49% of children prefer face to face communication, 33% of children prefer SMS (texting), 7% of children prefer social networks and 1% of children prefer Twitter for communicating with their friends. The findings of the current study suggest that, while children consider Twitter to be a communication tool, they do not prefer Twitter for communicating their friends.

Valkenburg and Peter (2007) argue that online communication has positive effects on children's relationships with existing friends. The findings of the current study suggest that children prefer to use online communication tools widely accepted by their peers. Therefore, students' and their peers' social network preferences must be taken into consideration while integrating these tools into educational contexts. In this way, while research suggests that Twitter is a good option for communication within educational environments, primary school children hold a rather different position. Children's preference for face-to-face communication over online communication (Bonetti, Campbell & Gilmore, 2010) challenges Twitter as a communication tool among children. Since texting is quick, private, easy to use, and allows children to consider their responses, it is the option of choice among children for communication (Common Sense, 2012). Children consider Twitter lame, uncommon among their age range, complicated, and hard to use for communication (Techcrunch, 2009). Similarly, participants from the current study claimed they do not use Twitter as a communication tool for following reasons, Twitter is uncommon among children, lacking a chat option, lacking privacy for communication, lacking audiovisual properties, restrictive for communication in terms for message length, and that it is considered to be a sharing platform rather than a communication tool. Since Twitter is a text oriented social network participants are reluctant to Tweet and read Tweets. They consider Twitter as time wasting, complicated, pointless for communication, and boring (Antenos-Conforti, 2009; Rinaldo, Tapp & Laverie, 2011; Techcrunch, 2009). These factors challenge Twitter's integration into education. Furthermore, Lowe and Laffey (2011) claim that over-tweeting and information overload caused by Tweets alienate students from Twitter. Participants of the current study reported that they do not prefer Twitter for communication because they find Twitter complicated and unreliable. Instead, they prefer to use the telephone or more common social networks among their friends.

While the majority of children expressed positive views about their Twitter experiences, most of them quit using Twitter after this study. They also stated they would not use Twitter for communication or any other purposes. However, recently there has been some research examining the use of Twitter for educational purposes. Grosseck and Hotescu (2008) reported that students used Twitter for communication after classes or activities. Furthermore, Twitter can be utilized for facilitating class communication within educational environments. Kroski (2008) reported that total strangers who were reading the same book communicated through Twitter. Schmucki and Meel (2010) indicated that Twitter utilization promotes staff and student communication in primary schools. Johnson (2011) found that Twitter creates opportunities for continued communication among college students after classes. Reinhart et al. (2009) reported participants used Twitter for communication before and during a conference. Furthermore, utilizing Twitter for communication within education settings facilitates student-student, student-teacher, and teacher-teacher communication and collaboration (Johnson, 2011; Junco, Heiberger & Loken, 2011; Leaver, 2011).

In this study primary school children were invited and encouraged to use Twitter for communication. While participants had some minor difficulties getting accustomed to Twitter, they managed to successfully use Twitter for communication. This conclusion was drawn from children's responses and tweets within the study. However, the majority of children did not consider Twitter as a communication tool and were observed to stop using Twitter after the study. They found Twitter unproductive and restrictive for communication. Furthermore, Twitter's low popularity among their peers was also a problem. If this was not a global trend among children (ICTA, 2011), this result may have been explained culturally due to the Turkish culture of sharing and communication. Since this is not the case, this study suggests that social networking tools favored by children should be integrated into educational cases in order to gain instructional benefits for primary school children.

Even though this research lasted only for a week, participants used Twitter for communication, keeping updated with their friends and favourite celebrities. Related literature suggests Twitter as a viable tool for communication, sharing, interaction, learning, education, and collaboration (Baruah, 2012; Borau et al., 2009; Dunlap & Lowenthal, 2009; Gao, Luo & Zhang, 2012; Holotescu & Grosseck, 2009; Junco, Heiberger & Loken, 2011; Kop, Fournier & Mak, 2011; Lowe & Laffey, 2011; McWilliams et al., 2011; Perifanou, 2009; Rinaldo, Tapp & Laverie, 2011; Techcrunch, 2009; Wright, 2010). While this body of research demonstrates the benefits of Twitter, it is hard to use Twitter as a learning tool. However, using Twitter as a complimentary/ supportive tool within educational contexts can be beneficial. Furthermore, since most of the research within this literature was conducted with adults and youngsters, the apparent benefits may not be applicable to to children.

Learners have social network preferences. Thus, one must consider learner preferences while integrating social networks within educational contexts. Twitter can support educational contexts with following dimensions.

- Increasing communication, social interaction, and collaboration among stakeholders of education
- Supporting lifelong learning by extending in-class communication to outside of the class
- Supporting learners with fast questioning and feedback opportunities
- Creating environmental and societal awareness
- Supporting mentoring processes among learners and experts
- Serving as a evaluation and monitoring tool for learners
- Developing students' self-expression skills
- Forming interest groups
- Developing participants' tolerance for counter ideas
- Creating a discussion environment
- Serving as a means to operate projects with collaborative sense
- Developing critical thinking skills
- Allowing hesitant students to participate and express themselves

Educational contexts need major arrangements in order to benefit from what Twitter has to offer. Among these arrangements are resolving infrastructure issues, as well as raising awareness and motivation among stakeholders, families, students, teachers, and policy makers. The present study suffered from limited numbers of participants, time limitations, and participants' prejudices and lack of motivation towards Twitter. The time limitation of the study originated from participants' lack of knowledge about Twitter. Furthermore, this study was limited to a state school and a class taking the Guidence and Counceling Lesson. These limitations are believed to reduce the generalizability of the research. However, findings from the study suggest Twitter to be a promising tool in educational contexts, although additional research is needed to rigorously examine its potential within different educational levels and contexts.

References

Amichai-Hamburger, Y., & Hayat, Z. (2011). The impact of the Internet on the social lives of users: A representative sample from 13 countries. *Computers in Human Behavior, 27*(1), 585-589.
Anderson, S. (2011). The Twitter toolbox for educators. *Teacher Librarian, 39*(1), 27-30.
Antenos-Conforti, E. (2009) Microblogging on Twitter: social networking in intermediate Italian classes. In: Lomicka L, Lord LG, (Eds.) *The next generation: social networking and online collaboration in foreign language learning.* (pp. 59–90). San Marcos, TX: CALICO Publications.
Baruah, T. D. (2012). Effectiveness of social media as a tool of communication and its potential for technology enabled connections: A micro-level study. *International Journal of Scientific and Research Publications, 2*(5).
Bonetti, L., Campbell, M.A. & Gilmore, L. (2010). The Relationship of Loneliness and Social Anxiety with Children's and Adolescents' Online Communication. *Cyberpsychology, Behavior, and Social Networking, 13*(3), 279-285.
Borau, K., Ullrich, C., Feng, J. & Shen, R. (2009) Microblogging for language learning: using twitter to train communicative and cultural competence. *In Proceedings of International Conference on Web Based Learning–ICWL.* (pp.78-87). Berlin: Springer-Verlag.
Brock, T. (2011) Twitter vs. Facebook. *Agency Sales, 41*(1), 53.
Coates, H. (2007). A model of online and general campus-based student engagement. *Assessment & Evaluation in Higher Education, 32*(2), 121-141.
Cole, M. (2009). Using Wiki technology to support student engagement: Lessons from the trenches. *Computers & Education, 52*, 141-146.
Common Sense (2012) 'Social media, social life: How teens view their digital lives'. Retrieved from http://www.commonsensemedia.org/sites/default/files/research/ socialmediasociallife -final-061812.pdf
Creswell, J. W. (2007) *Qualitative Inquiry & Research Design – Choosing Among Five Approaches* (2nd Ed.), SAGE Publications, Thousand Oaks, California
Dhir, A., Buragga, K. & Boreqqah, A. A. (2013). Tweeters on campus: Twitter a learning tool in classroom? *Journal of Universal Computer Science, 19*(5), 672-691
Dietrich, T.R. (2012). *Digital natives: A phenomenological study of authentic engagement among fifth-grade students.* (Yayınlanmamış doktora tezi). La Sierra Üniversitesi, California
Dunlap, J. C. & Lowenthal, P. R. (2009). Tweeting the night away: using Twitter to enhance social presence. *Journal of Information Systems Education, 20*(2), 129-155.
Elavsky, C. M., Mislan, C., & Elavsky, S. (2011). When talking less is more: Exploring outcomes of Twitter usage in the large-lecture hall. *Learning, Media and Technology, 36*(3), 215–233.
Erwin, B. A., Turk, C. L., Heimberg, R. G., Fresco, D. M., & Hantula, D. A. (2004). The Internet: home to a severe population of individuals with social anxiety disorder? *Journal of Anxiety Disorders, 18*(5), 629-646.
Galagan, P. (2009). Twitter as a learning tool. Really. *T+D, 63*(3), 28-31.
Greenhow, C. (2009). Tapping the wealth of social networks for professional development. *Learning & Leading with Technology, 36*(8), 10-11.
Greenhow, C. & Robelia, B. (2009). Old communication, new literacies: Social network sites as social learning resources. *Journal of Computer-Mediated Communication, 14*(4), 1130-1161.
Gao, F., Luo, T. & Zhang, K. (2012). Tweeting for learning: A critical analysis of research on microblogging in education published in 2008–2011. *British Journal of Educational Technology, 43*(5), 783-801
Gordhamer, S. (2010) '5 Levels of Effective Communication in the Social Media Age'. Retrieved from http://mashable.com/2010/02/08/communication-social-media/.

Gross, E. G. (2004). Adolescent internet use: What we expect, what teens report. *Applies Developmental Psychology, 25*, 633-649.

Grosseck, G. & Holotescu, C. (2008) 'Can we use Twitter for educational activities?', *The 4th International Scientific Conference: eLearning and software for Education*. Retrieved from http://www.morsmal.org/documents/members/admin/Can-we-use-Twitter-for-educational-activities.pdf.

Hamburger, Y. A., & Ben-Artzi, E. (2000). The relationship between extraversion and neuroticism and the different uses of the Internet. *Computers in Human Behavior, 16*(4), 441-449.

Hampton, K., Sessions, L., Her, E. J., & Rainie, L. (2009). *Social isolation and new technology: How the Internet and mobile phones impact Americans' social networks*. Washington, DC: Pew Internet & American Life Project.

Hancock, V. & Betts, F. (2002). Back to the future: Preparing learners for academic success in 2004. *Learning and Leading with Technology, 29*(7), 10-14.

Hede, A. (2002). An integrated model of multimedia effects on learning. *Journal of Educational Multimedia and Hypermedia, 11*(2), 177-191.

Heiberger, G. & Harper, R. (2008). Have you Facebooked Astin lately? Using technology to increase student involvement. In R. Junco, & D. M. Timm (Eds.), *Using emerging technologies to enhance student engagement. New Directions for Student Services*, (pp. 19– 35). San Francisco, CA: Jossey-Bass.

HERI-Higher Education Research Institute. (2007). College freshmen and online social networking sites. Retrieved from http://www.gseis.ucla.edu/heri/PDFs/pubs/briefs/brief-091107-Social-Networking.pdf.

Hills, P. & Argyle, M. (2003). Uses of the Internet and their relationships with individual differences in personality. Computers in Human Behavior, 19, 59-70.

Holcomb, L. B., Brady, K. P. & Smith, B. V. (2010). The emergence of "educational networking": Can non-commercial, education-based social networking sites really address the privacy and safety concerns of educators? *Journal of Online Learning and Teaching, 6*(2), 475-481.

Holotescu, C. & Grosseck, G. (2009) Using microblogging in education. Case study: Cirip.ro. In Proceedding of the 6th Conference on e-Learning Applications, Cairo, Egypt.

Hsu, Y. C. & Ching, Y. H. (2012). Mobile Microblogging: Using Twitter and Mobile Devices in an Online Course to Promote Learning in Authentic Contexts. *The International Review and Research in Open and Distance Education, 13*(4),211-227

ICTA. (2011) 'Çocukların Sosyal Paylaşım Sitelerini Kullanım Alışkanlıkları', *Information and Communication Technologies Authority*. Retrieved from http://www.btk.gov.tr/Etkinlikler/Ulusal_Etkinlikler/calistay/2011/dokumanlar/cspaar.pdf

Ivey, M. (2009). Communication these days is all a-Twitter. *Communication World, 26*(4), 8.

Johnson, K. A. (2011). The effect of Twitter posts on students' perceptions of instructor credibility. *Learning, Media and Technology, 36*(1), 21 – 38

Joly, K. (2009) 'Should you Twitter? Real and effective communication, 140 characters at a time'. Retrieved from http://www.universitybusiness.com/article/should-you-twitter .

Junco, R. (2012). The relationship between frequency of Facebook use, participation in Facebook activities, and student engagement. *Computers & Education, 58*, 162-171.

Junco, R., Heiberger, G. & Loken, E. (2011). The effect of Twitter on college student engagement and grades. *Journal of Computer Assisted Learning, 27*, 119-132.

Klien, J. (2008). Social networking fort he K-12 set. *Learning and Leading with Technology, 35*(5), 12-16.

Kop, R., Fournier, H. & Mak, J. (2011) 'A pedagogy of abundance or a pedagogy to support human beings? Participant support on massive open online courses', *International Review Of Research In Open And Distance Learning, 12*(7), 74–93.

Kraut, R., Kiesler,S., Boneva, B., Cummings, J., Helgeson, V. & Crawford, A. (2002). Internet paradox revisited. *Journal of Social Issues, 58*, 49-74.
Kraut, R., Kiesler, S., Mukopadhyay, T., Scherlis, W., & Patterson, M. (1998). Social Impact Of The Internet: What Does It Mean?. *Communications Of The ACM, 41*, 21–22.
Kroski, E. (2008). All a Twitter: Want to try microblogging?. *School Library Journal, 54*(7), 31-35.
Leaver, T. (2011) 'Twittering Informal Learning and Student Engagement in First-Year Units', in *Blended Learning*, ed. Anthony Herrington. Retrieved from http://www.tamaleaver.net/cv/LeaverT_TwitteringInformalLearning_preprint.pdf
Lenhart, A., Madden, M., Smith, A., Kristen Purcell, K., Zickuhr, K., & Rainie, L. (2011) 'Teens, kindness and cruelty on social network sites'. Retrieved from http://pewinternet.org/Reports/2011/Teens-and-social-media.aspx .
Lowe, B. & Laffey, D. (2011). Is Twitter for the birds?: Using Twitter to enhance student learning in a marketing course. *Journal of Marketing Education, 33*(2), 183-192.
McCool, L., B. (2011) *The pedagogical use of Twitter in the university classroom.* (Unpublished Master Thesis). Iowa State University, Iowa.
McGrath, B. (1998). Partners in learning: twelve ways technology changes the teacher-student relationship. *Technological Horizon in Education, 25*(9), 58-62.
McWilliams, J., Hickey, D. T., Hines, M. B., Conner, J. M. & Bishop, S. C. (2011). Using collaborative writing tools for literary analysis: Twitter, fan fiction and the crucible in the secondary English classroom. *Journal of Media Literacy Education, 2*(3), 238-245.
Mesch, G. (2003). The family and the Internet: The Israeli case. *Social Science Quarterly, 84*(4), 1038-1050.
Mix, K.K. (2010). *Online social networking: Exploring the relationship between use of web-based social technologies and community college student engagement.* (Yayınlanmamış doktora tezi). Texas Universitesi, Austin.
Morris, T. (2009). All a Twitter: A Personal and Professional Guide to Social Networking with Twitter. London: Que Publishing.
Nicol, D. J., Minty, I. & Sinclair, C. (2002). The Social Dimensions of Online Learning. *Innovations in Education and Teaching International, 40*(3), 270–80.
Nie, N. H. (2001). Sociability, interpersonal relations and the Internet: Reconciling conflicting findings. *American Behavioral Scientist, 45*(3), 420-435.
Nie, N. H., Hillygus, S. D., & Erbring, L. (2002). Internet use, interpersonal relations, and sociability: A time diary study. In B. Wellman & C. Haythornthwaite (Eds.), *The Internet in everyday life* (pp. 215–244). Oxford: Blackwell.
Pempek, T. A., Yermolayeva, Y. A. & Calvert, S. L. (2009). College students' social networking experiences on Facebook. *Journal of Applied Developmental Psychology, 30*, 227–238.
Perifanou, M. A. (2009). Language micro-gaming: fun and informal microblogging activities for language learning. *Communications in Computer and Information Science, 49*, 1-14.
Reinhardt, W., Ebner, M., Beham, G. & Costa, C. (2009) How People are using Twitter during Conferences. In: Hornung-Prähauser V, Luckmann M, (Ed.), Creativity and Innovation Competencies on the Web. (pp.145-156). In Proceedings of the 5th EduMedia Conference, St Virgil Conference Centre, Salzburg, Austria.
Reynard, R. (2007). Hybrid learning: Maximizing student engagement. Campus technology. Campus enterprise networking & infrastructure-Campus technology. Retrieved from http://campus-technology.com/articles/2007/05/hybrid-learning-maximizing-student-engagement.aspx
Ribble, M. (2008). Passport to digital citizenship: Journey toward appropriate technology use at school and at home. *Learning & Leading with Technology, 36*(4), 14-17.
Rinaldo, S. B., Tapp, S. & Laverie, D. A. (2011). Learning by tweeting: Using Twitter as a pedagogical tool. *Journal of Marketing Education, 33*(2), 193-203.

Robinson, J. P., Kestnbaum, M., Neustadtl, A., & Alvarez, A. (2000). Mass media use and social life among Internet users. *Social Science Computer Review, 18*(4), 490-501.

Smith, J. (2009) 'Will Facebook and Twitter Become Communication Tools or Identity Platforms?'. Retrieved from http://www.insidefacebook.com/2009/06/08/will-facebook-and-twitter-become-communication-tools-or-identity-platforms/

Stieger, S. & Burger, C. (2010). Let's go formative: Continuous student ratings with web 2.0 application Twitter. *Cyberpsychology, Behavior, and Social Networking, 13*(2), 163-167.

Strom, P., Strom, R., Wing, C. & Beckert, T. (2010). *Adolescent learning and the Internet. Education Digest, 75*(6), 10-16.

Schmucki, L. & Meel, S., K. (2010). Social Networking in Education: Practices, Policies, and Realitie. Retrieved from http://www.mmseducation.com/register2010/

Subramanyan, K. & Greenfield, P. (2009). Online communication and adolescent relationships. *The Future of Children, 18*(1), 119-146.

Swickert, R. J., Hittner, J. B., Harris, J. L., & Herring, J. A. (2002). Relationships among Internet use, personality, and social support. *Computers in Human Behavior, 18*(4), 437-451.

Techcrunch. (2009) 'Why don't teens Tweet? We asked over 10,000 of them'. Retrieved from http://techcrunch.com/2009/08/30/why-dont-teens-tweet-we-asked-over-10000-of-them/

Tellis, W. (1997). Introduction to Case Study. *The Qualitative Report, 3*(2), 1-5.

Tyma, A. (2011). Connecting with what is out there!: Using Twitter in the large lecture. *Communication Teacher, 25*(3), 175-181.

Utz, S., Tanis, M. & Vermeulen, I. (2012). It is all about being popular: The effects of need for popularity on social network site use. *Cyberpsychology, Behavior, and Social Networking, 15*(1), 37-42.

Valkenburg, P. M. & Peter, J. (2007). Online communication and adolescent well-being: Testing the stimulation versus the displacement hypothesis. *Journal of Computer-Mediated Communication, 12*, 1169-1182.

Valkenburg P.M. & Peter J. (2009). Social consequences of the internet for adolescents: A decade of research. *Current Directions in Psychological Science, 18*, 1–5.

Valkenburg, P. M. & Peter, J. (2011). Online communication among adolescent: An integratedmodel of its attraction, opportunities, and risks. *Journal of Adolescent Health, 48*, 121-127.

Wang, J. & Wang, H. (2011). The Predictive Effects of Online Communication on Well-Being among Chinese Adolescents. *Psychology, 2*(4), 359-362.

Wang, H., & Wellman, B. (2010). Social Connectivity in America: Changes in Adult Friendship Network Size From 2002 to 2007. *American Behavioral Scientist, 53*(8), 1148-1169.

Wasserman, T. (2013). Do teens really think Twitter is 'more important' than Facebook? Retrieved from http://mashable.com/2013/10/25/teen-twitter-facebook-study-debunk/

Welch, B.K. & Bonnan-White, J. (2012). Twittering to increase student engagement in the university classroom. *Knowledge Management & E-Learning: An International Journal, 4*(3), 325-345.

Wright, N. (2010). Twittering in teacher education: Reflecting on practicum experiences. Open learning: *The Journal of Open, Distance and e-Learning, 25*(3), 259–265.

Yin, R. K. (1989) *Case study research: Design and methods* (Rev. ed.). Newbury Park, CA: Sage Publications.

Yin, R.K. (1994) *Case study research: Design and methods* (2nd ed.). Beverly Hills, CA: Sage Publishing.

Shengli Deng

16 The Influence of Extraversion on Individuals' SNS Use

Abstract: In recent years, the fast proliferation of social networking sites (SNS) offers Internet users new possibilities for developing and maintaining their social networks, which has changed the way people interact with both information and their peers. With the interdisciplinary development of information behavior research, factors of cognitive, psychological and personal characteristics are gaining more attention. Different personality characteristics of the users interacted with the search task, the existing knowledge and experience, information sources and other environmental factors, which affected the user's cognition, emotions, and social behavior. Despite a growing interest in SNS, most previous research on SNS has been conducted from the perspectives of social network technology, social network user demographic information, social capital, and user behavior. Less research attention has been paid to SNS usage in terms of the trait of extraversion. This study develops a model to elucidate how extraversion, an important dimension of personality, affects the perceptions of Internet users and their continuance intention. A survey was conducted to collect data on SNS users' awareness, use, and personality influence. The research model was empirically tested and the results indicated extraversion positively affects perceived satisfaction, supplementary entertainment, and critical mass directly, as well as indirectly influencing both playfulness and SNS continuance intention. The practical implications of the findings to SNS are also discussed.

16.1 Introduction

In recent years, the increasing use of Social Networking Sites (SNS) has dramatically expanded peoples' life-styles. Internet-based social media allows users to interact easily with other individuals en masse and establish new social relationships or maintain existing relationships (Mangold &Faulds, 2009). According to Pew Internet trend data (Pew, 2013), in 2012 only 67% online U.S. adults used SNS, in May 2013, these figures rose with 72% online U.S. adults using SNS. In China, the most popular SNS operators are Qzone, which has 603 million active users (Ding, 2013), and Renren 136 million active users (Renren,2013).

While there is an ever-growing popularity for research on social media, most previous research on SNS has been conducted from the perspectives of SNS technological characteristics. However, there is only a limited understanding of how extraversion traits affect the use of SNS. Svendsen, Johnsen, Almås-

Sørensen,& Vittersø (2011)found extraversion has significant positive relations to behavior intention and this relation is fully mediated by the technology acceptance model (TAM) beliefs. The TAM engages in understanding the variety of factors that determine users' intentions to adopt a technology and their actual technology usage behaviors, such as perceived usefulness and perceived ease-of-use. In response to this research call, this study investigates SNS use by integrating extraversion from the Big Five personality model as a factor influencing SNS users' perception of an information system.

16.2 Literature Review

Personality is a stable set of characteristics and tendencies which determine commonalties and differences in people's psychological behavior, such as thoughts, feelings, and actions (Maddi, 1989). Personality is reflected in an individual's thoughts and actions (Chang, & Zhu, 2012), and describes the unique facets of each human being (Devaraj, Easley, & Crant, 2008). The Big Five personality model is one of the most widely used theories for investigating human personalities (John, Naumann, & Soto, 2008). It consists of five key factors: extraversion, openness, neuroticism, agreeableness, and conscientiousness.

16.2.1 The correlation between extraversion and user information behavior

User information behavior continues to change even as SNS and user expectations evolve. The changing needs and expectations of users create a new and developing environment where SNS operators are required to respond with flexibility. At present, social networks are usually used in order to maintain offline relationships or support the establishment of offline relationships (Amichai-Hamburger & Vinitzky, 2010). This raises the question of what types of people rely on these online social media tools in their interactions with others (Correa, Hinsley, & Zúñiga, 2010). Many studies conducted surveys and proved extraversion was related with user information behavior, such as students' information-seeking behavior (Heinström,2003), international students' information needs and information source preference (Sin, Kim, Yang, Park, & Laugheed, 2011), everyday life information seeking behavior in SNS(Sin&Kim,2013), Facebook use (Ross, Orr, Sisic, Arseneault, Simmering, & Orr,2009), Wikipedia use (Amichai-Hamburger, Lamdan, Madiel, & Hayat, 2008) and students' information competency (Kwon & Song, 2011).

Sin, Kim, Yang, Park, & Laugheed (2011) found that high extraversion respondents tended to report frequent usage of sources of information regarding people. Jani, Jang, & Hwang (2011) indicated that extraverted students have an enthusiastic, active and confident character, which was reflected in their information seeking. Users with different personalities may have different information needs and their satisfaction with seeking results will also be different. Extraverted people were found to be more purposeful in seeking information and their zeal in searching was found to be high. They were found to be actively using, sharing, and exchanging information to the maximum, a characteristic of high information seekers (Heinstrom, 2003). Information needs and source usage also vary with personality traits. Sin, Kim, Yang, Park, & Laugheed (2011)found that international student with high extraversion had challenges in finding information on the U.S culture Amichai-Hamburger, Lamdan, Madiel, & Hayat (2008) found that extroverts who surfed websites with nostalgia made greater use of social services than introverts who surfed websites that gave them similar feelings. Therefore, Individuals high in extraversion have the inclination to be sociable (Besser &Shackelford, 2007). Examining both users and non-users of Wikipedia, Amichai-Hamburger & Hayat (2011) found that women have a lower level of extroversion. Teh, Yong, Chong, & Yew (2011) found that university students with higher levels of extraversion have more favorable attitude towards online entertainment knowledge sharing.

Prior studies often found a strong relationship between extraversion and various aspects of SNS use. Extroverts tend to have a greater number of SNS friends (Amichai-Hamburger & Vinitzky, 2010; Moore & McElroy, 2012). However, findings are rather inconsistent on the relationship between extraversion and frequency of SNS use; some found a positive relationship (Correa, Hinsley, & Zúñiga, 2010), while others found a negative one (Moore & McElroy, 2012). Isbulan's (2011) findings indicated that individuals high in the trait of extraversion were found to belong to significantly more Facebook groups, as well as that extraverted people were more likely to use Facebook than introverted people. Also, extraversion has been shown to correlate with the use of instant messing and SNS (Correa, Hinsley & Zuniga, 2010). Ryan and Xenos (2011) found significantly higher levels of self-reported extraversion in Facebook users compared to non-users and also found extraversion to be correlated with the social use of Facebook. Ross, Orr, Sisic, Arseneault, Simmering, and Orr (2009) found that users high in the trait of extraversion participated in more Facebook groups. Amichai-Hamburger & Vinitzky's (2010) found that the extroverted personality has an effect on the use of Facebook groups, but not on the number of friends. Extraversion is thought to be an intrinsic quality of an individual exhibiting evident and strong effects on networking behavior. Accordingly, individuals with high scores on extraversion take more central positions in the friendship network (Wehrli, 2008), and post more photos for keeping social contacts on Facebook (Muscanell, 2012). Correa, Hinsley, & Zúñiga's (2010) study supported the hypothesis that extraversion was positively related with social media use. This finding, however, was affected by age in that the relationship between extraversion and social media use was particularly important among the young adult cohort.

Kalman, Scissors, & Darren (2010) found that extraverted individuals may be more likely to trust in virtual environments and may simply prefer virtual interaction with others over no interaction at all. Sin and Kim (2013) indicated that extraverted individuals like to exchange everyday information by SNS. Muscanell (2012) found that extraversion predicted likelihood of posting photographs, which was consistent with predictions since outgoing individuals should want to share pictures with others, and sharing photos is a social tool and not a replacement for actual social interaction.

16.2.2 The Influence of Extraversion on IS Use

Recently, several studies have highlighted the importance of including personality factors in IS adoption research. McElroy, Hendrickson, Townsend, & DeMarie (2007) argued that current IS adoption models are predominantly based on individual users' perceptions (i.e., perceived usefulness) rather than the more constant factors of an individual user's personality. In their study, McElroy et al. (2007) found that personality is a superior predictor of Internet use compared to cognitive variables, and they suggest that personality variables should be included in future IS adoption models. In this study, we integrate the "extraversion" personality variable in order to predict SNS continuance, since extraverts' SNS use should mirror their social life behavior.

Psychologists claim that extraversion represents an individual's ability to engage in the environment (Clark, & Watson, 1999). Extraverts show high levels of sociability, participation, and positive self-esteem. They are characterized as sociable, lively, active, assertive, carefree, dominant, venturesome, and sensation seeking (Amiel, & Sargent, 2004). Some prior research finds that extraverts behave differently in their use of IT innovations, such as in the context of web-based decision support systems (Gu, & Wang, 2009), monitoring systems (Zweig, & Webster, 2003), and Internet use (McElroy, Hendrickson, Townsend, & DeMarie, 2007). Extraverts are also found to be more likely to use the Internet for social interaction and have more friends compared to introverts (Ebeling-Witte, Frank, & Lester, 2007; Amichai-Hamburger, & Vinitzky, 2010). Krishnan, Lim, &Teo (2010) found that extraverts are likely to spend more time cyberloafing, and Ross, Orr, Sisic, Arseneault, Simmering, & Orr (2009) indicated that individuals with higher levels of extraversion join more Facebook groups. Extraverts tend to be more instrumental and goal-oriented in their use of the Internet, such as when searching for information or music sharing (Amichai-Hamburger, &Vinitzky, 2010). Furthermore, extraverts and introverts have different communication preferences, resulting in behavioral differences when using the Internet (Lu, & Hsiao, 2010). Cunningham, Thach, &Thompson (2008) suggest that extraverts have different preferences for website design compared to introverts; extraverts prefer pictures of people, whereas introverts prefer pictures of nature and solitude.

A handful of recent studies have tried to explain extraverts' behavioral differences by investigating how personality affects users' perceptions. Wang and Yang (2005) find individual extraversion positively relates to perceived performance expectancy, effort expectancy, facilitating conditions, and the social influence of online stocking services. Lu and Hsiao (2010) argue that social value has a stronger influence on perceived value for extraverts than for introverts. Interestingly, Rosen and Kluemper (2008) integrate the Big Five personality traits into the TAM to predict SNS acceptance. However, they only investigated the mediation effects of perceived usefulness and perceived ease of use on the Big Five personality traits regarding SNS use intention by using a correlation analysis—a basic statistic solution (Amichai-Hamburger, &Vinitzky, 2010). Their study offers limited insights into cause–effect relationships between personality and SNS use, and neglects the interaction effects between independent variables as well as model fit issues.

16.3 Hypotheses development

Extraversion indicates the tendency to be active, sociable, lively, and assertive. In addition to extraversion, our research model includes four additional variables for predicting SNS continuance intention: critical mass, satisfaction, playfulness, and supplementary entertainment. Critical mass refers to those who make major contributions to the collective action of later subscribers (Liu, & Li, 2011; Heijden, 2004). Critical mass represents an important segment of SNS users. A new network requires a group of subscribers if it is to start up, and the network starts to become mature after a critical mass has initially assembled (Heijden, 2004). The critical mass comprises the pioneers of an SNS who pay the start-up costs and set up a circle of acquaintances for newcomers; thereafter new subscribers to a mature SNS can join one after another rather than as a group (Heijden, 2004). According to the theory of reasoned action, Ajzen and Fishbein (1980) identified how extraversion—as one of the personality traits—affects beliefs about behavior. Prior research indicates that extraverts are preoccupied with external appearance and how others perceive their actions (Amiel, & Sargent, 2004). Extraverts like voicing their opinion and therefore become opinion leaders and have a stronger social influence over others' IS usage (Wang, & Yang, 2005; Thong, Hong, & Tam, 2006). Therefore, it is expected that extraverts are more likely to influence others and help form the critical mass. Hence, we hypothesize:

H1: Extraversion positively relates to critical mass.

Furthermore, a potential user may choose to subscribe to a specific SNS in order to join a circle of his/her acquaintances already using the SNS. In this sense, the acquaintances form the critical mass that has started a network, making it ready for her/him to join in. For an existing user, s/he may choose to continue using a SNS because the SNS maintains his/her critical mass, such as close friends and other acquaintances. Thus, we hypothesize:

H2: Critical mass positively relates to continuance intention.

It is self-evident that the use of SNS is related to the social connections it has for an extravert. Therefore, it is expected that it is more likely that extraverts will yield a feeling of satisfaction from their SNS use. Therefore, we hypothesize:

H3: Extraversion positively relates to satisfaction.

As proposed by Bhattacherjee (2001) the Post-Acceptance IS Continuance Model notes that satisfaction is a significant determinant of continuance intention. Based on the model and other prior studies (Hamburger, &Ben-Artzi,2000), it is expected that satisfaction will also drive SNS continuance intention. Hence, we hypothesize:

H4: Satisfaction positively relates to continuance intention.

Recent IS studies indicate the importance of investigating hedonic IS usage (Oliver, Marwell, &Teixeira, 1985; Allen, 1988). Hedonic use means that people use an IS in pursuit of a self-filling value, such as enjoyment, rather than utilitarian value (Oliver, Marwell, &Teixeira, 1985; Ajzen, &Fishbein, 1980). It is proposed that extraverts are more likely to feel enjoyment when using an SNS, as it is a social interaction oriented service and consistent with their propensity for sociability. Therefore, we hypothesize:

H5: Extraversion positively relates to playfulness.

Furthermore, playfulness or perceived enjoyment describes a sort of intrinsic motivation, and has been found to be a significant predictor of user satisfaction and continuance intention (Oliver, Marwell, &Teixeira, 1985; Rogers, 1983). Therefore, we hypothesize:

H6: Playfulness positively relates to satisfaction.

H7: Playfulness positively relates to continuance intention.

Supplementary entertainment refers to the entertainment services offered by a SNS. The entertainment services provided by a SNS aim to offer users the possibility to play entertaining games and compete with peers, but not for information sharing or communication purposes. Prior studies have indicated that extraverts enjoy exploring the functionalities of such IT innovations (Amiel, & Sargent, 2004; Hamburger, & Ben-Artzi, 2000). Hamburger and Ben-Artzi (2000) found that those with higher levels of extraversion tend to use more leisure services online. Indeed, extraverts are more likely to utilize instrumental and goal-oriented Internet services alike (Amiel,

& Sargent, 2004).Hence, it is expected that extraverts are more likely to explore the supplementary entertainment of SNS. Therefore, we hypothesize:

H8: Extraversion positively relates to supplementary entertainment.

Providing supplementary entertainment has been a widely adopted strategy for SNS operators. For example, the social game "Happy Farm" is one of the most popular social network games initiated by the SNS operator Qzone in China. There are about 23 million active users who log on to it every day. The provision of supplementary entertainment is expected to bring more pleasure to SNS users. Thus, we hypothesize:

H9: Supplementary entertainment positively relates to playfulness.

The research model is depicted as shown in Figure 16.1.

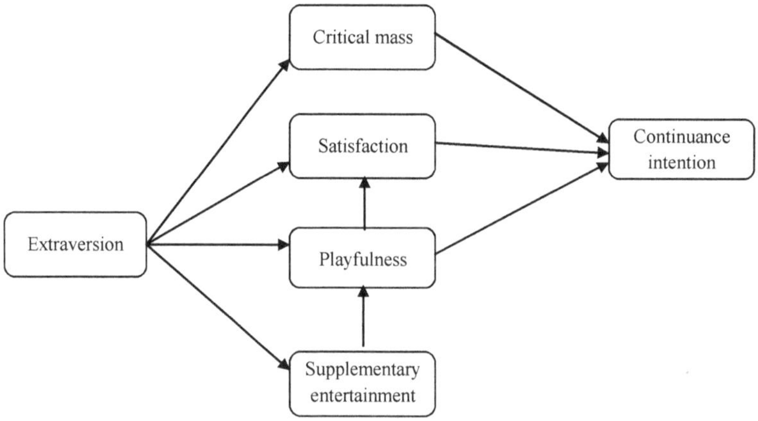

Figure 16.1: Research model

16.4 Research Methodology

The largest SNS provider in China, Qzone (http://www.qzone.com), was chosen as the research site for this study. It was created in 2005, by one of the largest web portals, Tencent, in China. A 5-point Likert scale ranging from 1 = "disagree" to 5 = "agree" was used to measure each indicator of the latent variables (see Appendix). The questionnaire was published on a professional online survey site to collect data between April 23, 2012 and April 30, 2012 –the survey site has more than 2.6 million registered subscribers. From this we collected 228 samples in one week. Seven of the respondents indicated that they had no prior Qzone use experience, and they were therefore discarded. The final valid sample base for this study was 221 respondents, consisting of 99 males (44.8%) and 122 females (55.2%). A total of 73.3% (n = 162) of the respondents had used Qzone for more than 3 years; and 44 respondents (19.9%) had 1–3 years' experience. Only 15 participants (6.8%) had used Qzone for less than 1 year. The demographic profile of the sample is given in Table 16.1.

Table 16.1: Sample characteristics

Characteristics		**Frequency(221)**	**Percentage**
Gender	Male	99	44.8%
	Female	122	55.2%
Age	Less than 20	51	23.08%
	21-30	152	68.78%
	31-35	13	5.88%
	Over 35	5	2.26%
Education	High school or lower	10	4.52%
	Undergraduate and academy	139	62.9%
	Postgraduate	52	23.53%
	Ph.D	20	9.05%
Time Using Qzone	Less than 1 year	15	6.79%
	More than 1-2 years	25	11.31%
	More than 2-3 years	19	8.6%
	Over 3 years	162	73,3%
Frequency of visiting Qzone every day	Less than 1 time	74	33.48%
	1-2 times	68	30.77%
	3-4 times	39	17.65%
	Over 4 times	40	18.1%

Table 16.2: Reliability and convergent validity statistics

Construct (no. of items)	**α**	**Composite reliability**	**Minimal factor loading**	**AVE**
Playfulness (4)	0.930	0.931	0.813	0.774
Supplementary entertainment (2)	0.819	0.822	0.802	0.698
Satisfaction (4)	0.941	0.941	0.868	0.801
Critical mass (2)	0.883	0.882	0.888	0.790
Extraversion (4)	0.865	0.866	0.716	0.619
Continuance intention (3)	0.967	0.967	0.934	0.909

Table 16.3: Discriminant validity

Construct	Pla	SE	Sat	CM	Ext	CI
Playfulness (Pla)	**0.88**					
Supplementary entertainment (SE)	0.75	**0.84**				
Satisfaction (Sat)	0.76	**0.56**	**0.89**			
Critical mass (CM)	0.43	0.37	0.45	**0.89**		
Extraversion (Ext)	0.21	0.20	0.24	0.25	**0.79**	
Continuance intention (CI)	0.65	0.40	0.67	0.51	0.19	**0.95**

The bold diagonals are the square roots of the AVEs of the individual constructs; off diagonal values are the correlations between constructs.

As shown in Table 16.2, the values of the factor loadings, Cronbach's alpha values, composite reliability, and the average extracted variance (AVE) of all the constructs satisfy the recommended level of 0.7, 0.8, 0.8, and 0.5 respectively, indicating good internal consistency. As shown in Table 16.3, the square roots of the AVE of all constructs are greater than the correlations estimate with the other constructs, supporting discriminant validity. The model fit indices are assessed and listed in Table 16.4, demonstrating a good fit between the model and the data. Further, Harmon's one-factor test was applied to test common method bias in the study. No factor was found to account for the majority of the covariance in the variables, suggesting that the data are unlikely to suffer from common method bias. Additionally, a single factor model test was conducted. The single factor model showed a poor fit (CMIN/DF:11.752; $p < 0.001$; GFI = 0.506; NFI = 0.545; TLI =0.511; CFI = 0.565; RMSEA= 0.221) against the existence of common method bias.

Table 16.4: Model fit indices

Model fit indices[33]	χ^2/df	AGFI	NFI	CFI	TLI	RMSEA
Recommended value	<3	>0.80	>0.90	>0.90	>0.90	<0.08
Measurement model	1.906	0.854	0.934	0.967	0.959	0.064
Structural model	2.135	0.838	0.922	0.957	0.948	0.072

χ^2/df, ratio between chi-square and degrees of freedom; AGFI, adjusted goodness of fit index; NFT, normed fit index; CFI, comparative fit index; TLI, Tucker–Lewis coefficient; RMSEA, root mean square error of approximation.

As shown in Figure 16.2, the significant level of the path coefficients is assessed based on a one-tailed t test. Eight of the nine hypotheses are supported. Against expectation, extraversion has no significant and direct influence on playfulness. Extraversion significantly affects supplementary entertainment (b = 0.210, p < 0.01), which in turn influences playfulness (b = 0.732, p < 0.001). Satisfaction is a product of both extraversion (b = 0.089, p < 0.05) and playfulness (b = 0.738, p < 0.001). Critical mass is significantly affected by extraversion (b = 0.264, p < 0.001). Playfulness (b = 0.311, p < 0.001) together with satisfaction (b = 0.365, p < 0.001) and critical mass (b = 0.250, p < 0.001) are direct determinants of continuance intention. The model interprets 48.5% of the variance of continuance intention, 4.4% of supplementary entertainment, 56.1% of playfulness, 58.2% of satisfaction, and 6.9% of critical mass. Furthermore, the results of the total effect analysis show extraversion has significant total effects on playfulness (b = 0.222, p < 0.01), satisfaction (b = 0.252, p < 0.01), and continuance intention (b = 0.227, p < 0.01).

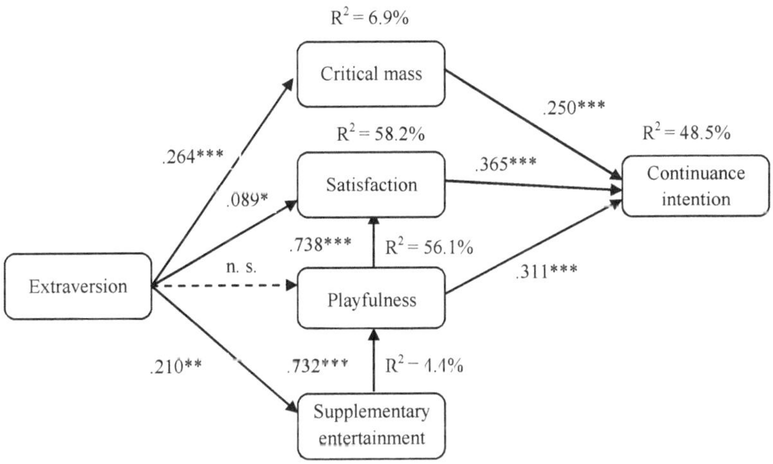

Figure 16.2: Results (n.s. : insignificant; *: p < 0.05; ** : p < 0.01; *** : P < 0.001)

16.5 Discussion and Implications

Previous studies suggest that personality is reflected in all of an individual's thoughts and actions (Devaraj, Easley, &Crant, 2008; Maddi,1989). The present study proved that human personalities, such as extraversion, also affect individuals' continuance intention regarding SNS. While most personality relevant IS studies gave an intuitive comparison of behavioral differences between extraverts and introverts, this study interprets extraverts' behavioral differences by modeling perceptions of an SNS. Consistent with our hypotheses, extraversion was found to have a significant influence on SNS perceptions and continuance intention(Correa, Hinsley, & Zúñiga, 2010;

Isbulan, 2011). This result is line with other investigations that have explored the link between extraversion and Facebook use (Ross et al., 2009; Hughes et al., 2012). Our findings are consistent with studies that concluded more extraverted people tend to take advantage of SNS for communication and socialization (Wilson et al., 2010; Correa, Bachmann, Hinsley, & Gil de Zúñiga, 2013). Supplementary entertainment mediates the effect of extraversion on playfulness. This may suggest that extraverts are more likely to utilize the supplementary entertainment services provided by an SNS. Also their use of supplementary entertainment brings them more happiness. In addition, extraverts are more likely to be satisfied with their SNS use—partly due to an enhanced perceived playfulness gained from using supplementary entertainment. Furthermore, a significant relationship between extraversion and critical mass indicates that extraverts are more likely to be accompanied by similar SNS users. Finally, all the five predictors were found to be significant motivators of SNS continuance intention. Specifically, extraversion and supplementary entertainment have significant indirect impacts on continuance intention, and playfulness, satisfaction, and critical mass have direct influences. Extraversion exerts an indirect influence on SNS continuance intention through the mediating effects of playfulness and satisfaction.

The study partly addressed the call to incorporate dispositional personality into cognitive perceptions of IS for modeling user behavior. Whereas most prior IS studies on the effects of the Big Five personality traits on IS use are based on the use of linear regression and correlation analysis, few of them employed structural equation modeling technologies. This study offers new insights by intensively investigating how extraversion influences perceptions of IS and motivates IS continuance intention. A number of new and significant relationships were reported, and the indices show a good model fit. Consistent with prior studies, the study shows that extraversion has important effects on users' IS behavior with regard to SNS.

The results contribute to several new insights for practitioners. First, SNS operators should pay more attention to consumer personalities when considering the importance of extraversion in shaping IS perceptions. Not only are extraverts more likely to continue using SNS services, but they also facilitate the extension of the critical mass. Hence, they appear to be a critical user group for retaining existing users and are vital to the profitability of SNS operators. In addition, extraverts are more likely to subscribe to supplementary entertainment services, which offer more revenue for SNS providers. Moreover, it is important to attract consumers with a provision of supplementary entertainment services, increasing user perceptions of both playfulness and satisfaction with SNS. Therefore, an investment in developing and providing supplementary entertainment services becomes necessary for SNS providers. Furthermore, maintaining a critical mass in a SNS is important for keeping users to continue using the SNS. If an individual's critical mass leaves an SNS and switches to other service providers, the user is very likely to follow his/her critical mass to the new SNS. In future research, users demographic and gender should be taken into account. Also, there are a lot research studying the personality impact on facebook, but other SNSs,such as Twitter, Social Q&A, need to be examined. Then, we need to take more research about personality impact on mobile applications. In addition, user experience is correlated with user personalities, highlighting the need to think more about user experience in future research.

This study has also has a number of limitations. First, other important personality traits, like openness or conscientiousness, were not included in the study, and they may have a significant influence on IS continuance. This provides avenues for future research. Second, the study is based on a sample of Chinese consumers. Special attention is therefore required when generalizing the research findings to users from different cultural backgrounds. Third, this study is the cross-sectional design, which provides us with a snapshot of a sample of a population at a single point in time. This raises the issue of measuring social characteristics over time in a single study –the objective of a longitudinal study.

Acknowledgments

This research is supported in part by Wuhan University Academic Development Plan for Scholars after 1970s for the project Research on Internet User Behavior and the National Funds of Social Science(No. 14BTQ044), PR China.

References

Allen, D. (1988). New telecommunications services: Network externalities and critical mass. Telecommunications Policy, 12(3), 257-271.

Amichai-Hamburger, Y., Lamdan, N., Madiel, R., & Hayat, T. (2008). Personality characteristics of Wikipedia members. CyberPsychology & Behavior, 11(6), 679-681.

Amichai-Hamburger, Y., & Vinitzky, G. (2010). Social network use and personality. Computers in Human Behavior, 26(6), 1289-1295.

Amichai-Hamburger, Y., & Hayat, Z. (2011). The impact of the Internet on the social lives of users: A representative sample from 13 countries. Computers in Human Behavior, 27(1), 585-589.

Amiel, T., & Sargent, S. L. (2004). Individual differences in Internet usage motives. Computers in Human Behavior, 20(6), 711-726.

Ajzen, I., & Fishbein, M. (1980). Understanding attitudes and predicting social behaviour. Englewood Cliffs, NJ: Prentice-Hall.

Besser, A., & Shackelford, T. K. (2007). Mediation of the effects of the big five personality dimensions on negative mood and confirmed affective expectations by perceived situational stress: A quasi-field study of vacationers. Personality and Individual Differences, 42(7), 1333-1346.

Bhattacherjee, A. (2001). Understanding information systems continuance: an expectation-confirmation model. MIS quarterly, 25(3), 351-370.

Chang, Y. P., & Zhu, D. H. (2012). The role of perceived social capital and flow experience in building users' continuance intention to social networking sites in China. Computers in Human Behavior, 28(3), 995-1001.

Clark, L. A., & Watson, D. (1999). Temperament: A new paradigm for trait psychology. Handbook of personality: Theory and research, 2, 399-423.
Correa, T., Hinsley, A. W., & De Zuniga, H. G. (2010). Who interacts on the Web?: The intersection of users' personality and social media use. Computers in Human Behavior, 26(2), 247-253.
Correa, T., Bachmann, I., Hinsley, A. W., & de Zúñiga, H. G. (2013). Personality and Social Media Use. In E. Li, S. Loh, C. Evans, & F. Lorenzi (Eds.) Organizations and Social Networking: Utilizing Social Media to Engage Consumers. Hershey, PA: Business Science Reference, pp. 41-61.
Cunningham, D., Thach, L., & Thompson, K. (2008). Innovative e-commerce site design: a conceptual model to match consumer MBTI dimensions to website design. Journal of Internet Commerce, 6(3), 1-27.
Devaraj, S., Easley, R. F., & Crant, J. M. (2008). Research note-how does personality matter? Relating the five-factor model to technology acceptance and use. Information Systems Research, 19(1), 93-105.
Ding, W.(2013). QQzone lives up to 600 million users. http://www.36kr.com/p/202706.html
Ebeling-Witte, S., Frank, M. L., & Lester, D. (2007). Shyness, Internet use, and personality. CyberPsychology & Behavior, 10(5), 713-716.
Gu, L., & Wang, J. (2009). A study of exploring the "big five" and task technology fit in web-based decision support systems. Issues in information systems, 10(2), 210-217.
Hamburger, Y. A., & Ben-Artzi, E. (2000). The relationship between extraversion and neuroticism and the different uses of the Internet. Computers in Human Behavior, 16(4), 441-449.
Heinström, J. (2003). Five personality dimensions and their influence on information behaviour. Information Research, 9(1), 9-1.
Hughes, D. J., Rowe, M., Batey, M., & Lee, A. (2012). A tale of two sites: Twitter vs. Facebook and the personality predictors of social media usage. *Computers in Human Behavior*, *28*(2), 561–569.
İşulan, O. (2011). Opinions of University Graduates about Social Networks According to Their Personal Characteristics. Turkish Online Journal of Educational Technology, 10(2).
Jani, D., Jang, J. H., & Hwang, Y. H. (2011). Personality and tourists' Internet behaviour. In Information and communication technologies in tourism 2011 (pp. 587-598). Springer Vienna.
John, O. P., Naumann, L. P., & Soto, C. J. (2008). Paradigm shift to the integrative big five trait taxonomy. Handbook of personality: Theory and research, 3, 114-158.
Kalman, Y. M., Scissors, L. E., & Gergle, D. (2010). Chronemic aspects of chat, and their relationship to trust in a virtual team. MCIS 2010 Proceedings. Paper 46.
Krishnan, S., Lim, V. K., & Teo, T. S. (2010). How does personality matter? Investigating the impact of big-five personality traits on cyberloafing. 31st International Conference on Information Systems, St. Louis, MO.
Kwon, N., & Song, H. (2011). Personality traits, gender, and information competency among college students. Malaysian Journal of Library & Information Science, 16(1).
Liu, Y., & Li, H. (2011). Exploring the impact of use context on mobile hedonic services adoption: An empirical study on mobile gaming in China. Computers in Human Behavior, 27(2), 890-898.
Lu, H. P., & Hsiao, K. L. (2010). The influence of extro/introversion on the intention to pay for social networking sites. Information & Management, 47(3), 150-157.
Maddi,S.R. (1989). Personality theories: a comparative analysis.CA: Dorsey Press.
Mangold, W. G., & Faulds, D. J. (2009). Social media: The new hybrid element of the promotion mix. Business horizons, 52(4), 357-365.
McElroy, J. C., Hendrickson, A. R., Townsend, A. M., & DeMarie, S. M. (2007). Dispositional factors in internet use: personality versus cognitive style. MIS quarterly, 809-820.
Moore, K., & McElroy, J.C. (2012).The influence of personality on Facebook usage, wall postings, and regret. Computers in Human Behavior, 28(1), 267-274.
Muscanell, N. L., & Guadagno, R. E. (2012). Make new friends or keep the old: Gender and personality differences in social networking use. Computers in Human Behavior, 28(1), 107-112.

Oliver, P., Marwell, G., & Teixeira, R. (1985). A theory of the critical mass. I. Interdependence, group heterogeneity, and the production of collective action.American journal of Sociology, 522-556.
Pew Internet (2013), " 72% of Online Adults are Social Networking Site Users ", available at: http://pewinternet.org/~/media//Files/Reports/2013/PIP_Social_networking_sites_update_PDF.pdf
RenRen. (2013).Data analysis of RenRen in 2013.http://www.199it.com/archives/108870.html
Rogers, E. M. (2010). Diffusion of innovations. Simon and Schuster.
Ross, C., Orr, E. S., Sisic, M., Arseneault, J. M., Simmering, M. G., & Orr, R. R.(2009).Personality and motivations associated with Facebook use. Computers in Human Behavior, 25(2), 578–586.
Ryan, T.,&Xenos, S. (2011).Who uses Facebook? An investigation into the relationship between the Big Five, shyness, narcissism, loneliness, and Facebook usage. Computers in Human Behavior, 27(5), 1658-1664.
Sin, S. C. J., & Kim, K. S. (2013). International students' everyday life information seeking: The informational value of social networking sites.Library & Information Science Research, 35(2), 107-116.
Sin, S. C. J., Kim, K. S., Yang, J., Park, J. A., & Laugheed, Z. T. (2011). International students' acculturation information seeking: Personality, information needs and uses. Proceedings of the American Society for Information Science and Technology, 48(1), 1-4.
Svendsen, G. B., Johnsen, J.-A. K. Almås-Sørenseen, L., & Vittersø, J. (2011). Personality and technology acceptance: The influence of personality factors on the core technology acceptance model constructs. Behaviour and Information Technology, 1-12.
Teh, P. L., Yong, C. C., Chong, C. W., & Yew, S. Y. (2011). Do the Big Five Personality Factors affect knowledge sharing behaviour? A study of Malaysian universities. Malaysian Journal of Library & Information Science,16(1).
Thong, J. Y., Hong, S. J., & Tam, K. Y. (2006). The effects of post-adoption beliefs on the expectation-confirmation model for information technology continuance. International Journal of Human-Computer Studies, 64(9), 799-810.
Van der Heijden, H. (2004). User acceptance of hedonic information systems. MIS quarterly, 695-704.
Wang, H. I., & Yang, H. L. (2005). The role of personality traits in UTAUT model under online stocking. Contemporary Management Research, 1(1), 69-82.
Wehrli, S. (2008). Personality on social network sites: An application of the five factor model. Zurich: ETH Sociology (Working Paper No. 7).
Wilson, K., Fornasier, S., & White, K. M. (2010). Psychological predictors of young adults' use of social networking sites. Cyberpsychology, Behavior, and Social Networking, 13(2), 173-177.
Zweig, D., & Webster, J. (2003). Personality as a moderator of monitoring acceptance. Computers in Human Behavior, 19(4), 479-493.

List of Figures

List of Tables

FSC
www.fsc.org
MIX
Papier | Fördert gute Waldnutzung
FSC® C083411

Kolibri 360 GmbH
Ferdinand-Jühlke-Straße 7
99095 Erfurt, Deutschland
produktsicherheit@kolibri360.de